THE INDIANIZATION OF ENGLISH

THE ENGLISH LANGUAGE IN INDIA

THE INDIANIZATION OF ENGLISH

THE ENGLISH LANGUAGE IN INDIA

BRAJ B. KACHRU

DELHI
OXFORD UNIVERSITY PRESS
OXFORD NEW YORK MELBOURNE
1983

Oxford University Press, Walton Street, Oxford OX2 6DP

LONDON GLASGOW NEW YORK TORONTO
DELHI BOMBAY CALCUTTA MADRAS KARACHI
KUALA LUMPUR SINGAPORE HONG KONG TOKYO
NAIROBI DAR ES SALAAM CAPE TOWN
MELBOURNE AUCKLAND
and associates in
BEIRUT BERLIN IBADAN MEXICO CITY

Filmset by All India Press, Sri Aurobindo Ashram, Pondicherry 605002
printed by Pramodh P. Kapur at Raj Bandhu Industrial Co.
C61, Mayapuri, Phase II, New Delhi 110064
and published by R. Dayal, Oxford University Press
2/11 Ansari Road, Daryaganj, New Delhi 110002

In Memory of
PHIROZE EDULJI DUSTOOR 1898–1979
and
JOHN RUPERT FIRTH 1890–1960

Truth, said a great Indian sage, is not the monopoly of the Sanskrit language. Truth can use any language, and the more universal, the better it is. If metaphysics is India's primary contribution to world civilization, as we believe it is, then must she use the most universal language for her to be universal. . . . And as long as the English language is universal, it will always remain Indian. . . .

It would then be correct to say as long as we are Indian—that is, not nationalists, but truly Indians of the Indian psyche—we shall have the English language with us and amongst us, and not as a guest or friend, but as one of our own, of our caste, our creed, our sect and of our tradition.

RAJA RAO, 'The Caste of English'
in *Awakened Conscience*

Foreword

India is estimated to have over eighteen million people using English as a necessary part of their daily working lives. This means that India vies with Canada as the country with the greatest number of English speakers after the USA and the UK. And although eighteen million is only a small fraction of India's vast population, it is of course a very important fraction, inevitably comprising the entire leadership of her economic, industrial, professional, political and social life. 'Indian English', a cover term for the varieties and range of English used in the sub-continent, is thus a vitally significant language, one that commands a great deal of interest, and one whose serious study is impeded by dauntingly severe complexities, both linguistic and sociological.

No one knows this better than Braj Kachru, long recognized as a world authority not only on English in India but on Indian linguistics (including his native Kashmiri), and indeed on linguistics in general. Not least, he has made an impressively persuasive contribution to the view that institutionalized language varieties can come into existence through 'interference' and that the Indianization of English is an outstanding example. The papers here brought together in a single convenient volume had a great impact upon the readership of the books and journals in which they originally appeared. I am confident that they will have an even greater impact through being revised and co-ordinated in their present attractive form.

RANDOLPH QUIRK

Vice-Chancellor
University of London
1 January 1983

Contents

Tables

Preface

This volume includes eight studies written over a period of almost two decades (1960–81). They are not presented in the order in which they were written: chronologically, chapters 3 and 4 would come first, since these embody the research initiated in 1959 at Edinburgh University.

In methodology and style, these studies are not uniform. They could not be, since the style, presentation, and focus of each chapter was determined by the particular readership, journal, or volume for which it was written. Therefore chapters 3 ('Contextualization') and 7 ('On "Mixing"') may be rather technical and somewhat polemical for a non-linguist, while chapter 8 ('The Pragmatics of Non-Native Englishes') may not be technical enough for a linguist. This is a compromise which I had to make for a specific readership. But all the studies have one thematic focus, that of the Indianization of the English language. The five sections according to which these studies have been arranged make the thematic unity clearer.

I have updated and revised all the studies, incorporating, where necessary, changes and additions. In a volume of this type it is not always possible to avoid repetitions. I have retained only those which I consider essential for cohesion, and for the understanding of particular studies.

One reason for the publication of this volume is that, by and large, these studies have appeared only in specialized publications and journals not easily accessible in South Asia and other places where English is used as a second language. I hope the present volume will make them easily available to scholars and students in South Asia and elsewhere. The timing of the publication in South Asia, while unintentional, seems most appropriate for several reasons. During the past decade, South Asian teachers and researchers, in the departments of both English and linguistics, have paid considerable attention to the linguistic and literary aspects of the steadily growing body of Indian English literature. This interest is evident in the large number of scholarly and popular works on this topic, in journals devoted to Indian English literature, and in the dissertations and theses written at various institutions in South Asia and other parts of the world. In the meetings of professional societies and at scholarly seminars, papers on Indian English are being presented more often ; they are received with great curiosity and are discussed with equanimity. That certainly was not the case in the 1960s, and I am saying this on the basis of my own experience. The credit for this changed attitude toward Indian English literature, research on English in India, and reorientation of the curriculum in English goes to, among others, P. E. Dustoor, V. K. Gokak, K. R. Srinivasa Iyengar, Ramesh Mohan, C. D. Narasimha-iah, and the young and energetic group of Indian English writers. In post-Independence India, we see Indian English as part of the linguistic repertoire of linguistically and culturally pluralistic India. At last, English in its Indian variety has become a part of our culture, as did Persian in the north of India and, much earlier, Sanskrit in many parts of the country. This volume, therefore, presents some aspects of that language contact and linguistic acculturation with the hope that this will encourage more extensive research and discussion on this facet of English in India.

It is difficult to acknowledge all the teachers, colleagues, and students who have influenced my ideas, provided insights, and thus shaped the thinking and writing of these studies; there have been so many of them in India, Britain and the United States. My major intellectual debt is to P. E. Dustoor, J. R. Firth, and M. A. K. Halliday, as I have discussed in the Introduction. Those of us who have been students of Halliday in Edinburgh know how unobtrusively he influenced us all. The impact of his thinking runs like a thread through almost all of these studies, whether formally acknowledged or not. The other members of the faculty who contributed to the linguistically challenging atmosphere of my 'Edinburgh days' (1958 to 1962) are David Abercrombie, J. C. Catford, R. W. M. Dixon, Angus McIntosh, Trevor Hill and Peter Strevens. All except Abercrombie and McIntosh have since left Edinburgh, and are now on various continents.

As a teacher one does not always know what one gives to one's students, but one is always conscious of what one receives from them. I have received much from my students, both in and outside classes, in the form of discussions and comments which helped me to clarify existing ideas and develop new ones. In addition to the students at the University of Illinois, and in several Indian institutions, I must also mention the students at the Linguistic Institutes of the Linguistic Society of America, where I used parts of these studies in my classes in 1969 and 1978, and the participants in the summer programme at Halifax, Nova Scotia, Canada.

My personal debt is owed to many individuals for their comments, suggestions, corrections, disagreements, and above all constructive criticisms. The following have performed one or more of the above roles, for which I am grateful: Yamuna Kachru, S. N. Sridhar, Ann Lowry Weir and Ladislav Zgusta. This volume is the better for their suggestions and advice; however, whatever blemishes and errors remain show my limitations and obstinacy. I must gratefully acknowledge the intellectual stimulation and encouragement for my research on the non-native varieties of English from Henry Kahane, Randolph Quirk and Peter Strevens. I owe special thanks to Randolph Quirk for his foreword to this volume.

The idea for this volume developed from an invitation of R. Parthasarathy, editor with the Oxford University Press, Delhi, and a distinguished poet and critic in English in India. His friendly guidance and gentle persistence facilitated the typescript's completion.

Over the past two decades, my research on South Asian English in particular, and on other language-related topics in general, has been possible due to the support and co-operation of the following agencies and institutions which I gratefully acknowledge: the American Institute of Indian Studies and the Director of its Delhi office, Pradeep R. Mehendiratta, who makes every visit to India intellectually meaningful; the Center for International Comparative Studies and the Research Board of the Graduate College, both of the University of Illinois at Urbana-Champaign; and the Central Institute of English and Foreign Languages, Hyderabad. I am also grateful to the Center for Advanced Study of the University of Illinois for my appointment as an Associate for the academic year 1971–72, and again for the academic year 1979–80. This recent opportunity provided a haven for much-needed recovery from the administrative duties which I performed at the University of Illinois from 1969 to 1979, and which delayed this volume by several years.

BRAJ B. KACHRU

University of Illinois
at Urbana-Champaign
1 December 1982

Abbreviations

The citations from Indian English writing used in this book are taken from the works listed below. They are identified by the following abbreviations.

ABP	*The Amrita Bazar Patrika*. Calcutta.
ABW	Anand, M. R. 1955. *Across the Black Waters*. London.
AD	Narayan, R. K. 1947. *The Astrologer's Day, and Other Stories*. London.
BA	Narayan, R. K. 1931. *The Bachelor of Arts*. London.
BH	Anand, M. R. 1947. *The Big Heart*. London.
BJ	*Bharat Jyoti*. Bombay.
C	Anand, M. R. 1936. *Coolie*. London.
CB	Rao, Raja. 1947. *The Cow of the Barricades and Other Stories*. Madras.
D	*Dharmayug* (Hindi). Bombay.
DC	*The Deccan Chronicle*. Hyderabad.
DD	Rajan, B. 1958. *The Dark Dancer*. London.
ET	Narayan, R. K. 1945. *The English Teacher*. London.
FE	Narayan, R. K. 1952. *The Financial Expert*. London.
FF	Ghosh, S. N. 1955. *The Flame of the Forest*. London.
FPJ	*The Free Press Journal*. Bombay.
H	*The Hindu* (Weekly Review). Madras.
HA	Lall, A. 1959. *The House in Adampur: A Study of Modern India*. London.
HE	Mukerji, S. N. 1959. *History of Education in India: Modern Period*. Baroda.
Hit	*Hitavada*. Nagpur.
HK	Ray, S. C. 1957. *Early History and Culture of Kashmir*. Calcutta.
HLSK	Lalla, Y. K. and Srikrishna, eds. 1975. *Hindī Lekhikāõ kī Śreṣṭh Kahāniyā̃*. ('Best Short Stories of Women Writers in Hindi') Delhi.
HS	*The Hindustan Standard*. Calcutta.
HT	*The Hindustan Times*. Delhi.
HW	Bhattacharya, B. 1960. *He Who Rides a Tiger*. London.
IE	*Indian Express*. Delhi.

IN	*Indian News*. London.
K	Rao, Raja. 1938. *Kanthapura*. London.
L	*Link*. New Delhi.
M	*The Mail*. Madras.
MI	*March of India*. Delhi.
MM	Bhattacharya, B. 1959. *Music for Mohini*. London.
MS	Narayan, R. K. 1952. *Mr Sampath*. London.
NS	Markandaya, K. 1954. *Nectar in a Sieve*. London.
OR	*Orissa Review*. Bhubaneshwar.
P	*The Pioneer*. Lucknow.
PD	Anand, M. R. 1958. *Power of Darkness*. Bombay.
RD	Shuklā, Srī Lāl. 1968. *Rāg Darbārī* (Hindi). Delhi.
RH	Rau, S. R. 1956. *Remember the House*. London.
S	*The Statesman*. New Delhi.
SD	Markandaya, K. 1960. *A Silence of Desire*. London.
SF	Markandaya, K. 1955. *Some Inner Fury*. London.
SH	*Sāptāhik Hindustān* (Hindi). Delhi.
SJ	Lall, Arthur. 1958. *Seasons of Jupiter*. London.
SL	*The Search Light*. Patna.
SMH	Bhattacharya, B. 1958. *So Many Hungers*. London.
SR	Rao, Raja. 1960. *The Serpent and the Rope*. London.
T	*The Tribune*. Chandigarh.
TI	*Times of India*. Bombay.
TN	Abbas, K. A. n.d. *One Thousand Nights on a Bed of Stone*. Bombay.
TP	Singh, K. 1956. *Train to Pakistan*. London.
U	Anand, M. R. 1935. *Untouchable*. London.
V	*Vakil*. Srinagar.
VG	Singh, K. n.d. *The Voice of God*. Bombay.
WM	Narayan, R. K. 1955. *Waiting for the Mahatma*. London.

Introduction

The studies collected here have a shared theme and focus concerning the twice-born[1] characteristic of English in India. The dominant theme is the study of the motivations and processes which resulted in what I have termed the Indianization of the English language. Since these studies were written over almost two decades in three linguistically and culturally distinct areas (Britain, the United States and India), each study has a history of its own and reflects the specific influence and background present at the time of its writing. The influences were of different types and included institutions and individuals (teachers, colleagues and students); in some ways, they determined my approach toward the study and analysis of Indian English. These influences on me and my linguistic thinking are therefore important for understanding these studies, and for understanding the framework adopted which, I believe, provides cohesion and unity to the volume.

As the title indicates, the main thrust of these studies is to examine the linguistic aspects of the Indianization of the English language in India. Because that cannot be done in a theoretical vacuum, these studies include a number of theoretical and methodological asides which, in my view, are crucial for the understanding of language in context.

The approach adopted here is both attitudinally and theoretically distinct from that displayed in the earlier studies on this variety of English by Whitworth (1907), Goffin (1934) and Smith-Pearse (1934), to name just three. I argue that in the earlier research one major point seems to have been ignored or missed: the *Indianness* in Indian English (or in a wider context, the *South Asianness* in South Asian English) is the result of the acculturation of a Western language in the linguistically and culturally pluralistic context of the subcontinent. These parameters of Indian culture and languages determine the language change and language adaptation. The Indianization of the English language is a consequence of what linguists have traditionally termed *interference* (or transfer). Indian English is thus an institutionalized example of what Quirk labels, in the foreword to this book and earlier

(1972:26), an 'interference variety' of English. The interference varieties are, as Quirk *et al.* rightly claim, 'so widespread in a community
and of such long standing that they may be thought stable and adequate enough to be institutionalized and regarded as varieties of English in their own right rather than stages on their way to more native-
like English'. In my use of the term interference there is no attitudinal
implication; it is merely indicative of linguistic changes in a culturally
and linguistically pluralistic language-contact situation. The aim is to
capture the processes and devices of the Indianness of this nativized
variety of English which has been used by Indians to serve the typically Indian needs in distinct Indian contexts for almost two hundred
years. As Raja Rao says (1978a:420), 'as long as we are Indian—that is
not nationalists, but truly Indians of the Indian psyche—we shall have
the English language with us and amongst us, and not as guest or
friend, but as one of our own, of our caste, our creed, our sect and of
our tradition'. The essays which follow aim to study those processes
which have been used in India to nativize the 'guest and friend' as one
of our own, of our caste and tradition.

   The Indianisms in Indian English cannot pragmatically be considered just 'linguistic flights ... which jar upon the ear of the native
Englishman' (Whitworth 1907:6), or necessarily interpreted as inade-
quacies in second-language acquisition. These 'linguistic flights' are
indeed culture-bound and language-bound. For the lack of a better
term, I call such Indianisms *deviations* (Kachru 1982a). Indianisms in
Indian English are, then, linguistic manifestations of pragmatic needs
for appropriate language use in a new linguistic and cultural context.

   An aside may be appropriate to make a distinction between a *deviation* and a *mistake*. The term 'deviation' serves a useful purpose
when it refers to the linguistic and cultural nativization of a variety of
English. Nativization is the result of the new 'unEnglish' linguistic and
cultural setting in which English is used as a tool of communication.
In the case of each variety of English, the cultural and linguistic context is different from that of London, New York, Toronto or Sydney;
therefore, the new setting determines the 'deviation' in language use.
The context-determined linguistic innovations are productive and
pragmatically essential. These may mark variety-specific features (e.g.,
Indian English, Caribbean English, Nigerian English), or they may
be shared with other non-native varieties of English. The productive
aspect of such formations and their functional relationship to new contexts makes them formally and pragmatically a part of a specific va-

riety. These formations are not idiosyncratic, and they have a role in what Firth terms 'the context of situation' (see Kachru 1981c).

On the other hand, a 'mistake' is unacceptable on several counts. This term may be restricted to those uses of English which show early stages in language acquisition. One might outright reject some uses of language as unacceptable since they are 'unEnglish'. The term 'un-English' is rather tricky. One way to explain the 'unEnglishness' of a 'mistake' is to say that in systemic terms it is not a result of the productive processes which characterize a particular non-native variety of English. One might also state that in sociolinguistic terms a 'mistake' is not functionally related to the cultural context of a non-native variety. But then dichotomies are not always clearcut and do not work in a neat way, and some gray areas cannot clearly be categorized: for example, how does one treat the Indian use of the English article? Or, what should one's reaction be to the Indian use of plural forms such as 'alphabets' or 'furnitures'? One has to be aware of such problems. However, it cannot be denied that, in the nativization of English in India, we find underlying linguistic and sociocultural motivations identical to those used earlier in South India to nativize Sanskrit, and, much later, in North India for nativizing Persian, which resulted in 'Indian Persian'. In the Indianization of English, then, the linguistic history of the subcontinent is merely being repeated.

What, then, are the influences which determine my approach to Indian English? The influences must be viewed in terms of the background against which these studies were written and which provided the insights and directions for the research. The following digression thus recognizes intellectual indebtedness, and traces the main influences underlying my research in Indian English.

In the 1950s when one talked of Indian English, one invariably thought of P.E. Dustoor, the stimulating teacher and scholar of the English language who spent most of his academic life at Allahabad University and then moved to head the English Department at Delhi University. In his own quiet way, Dustoor encouraged me to choose a research topic related to Indian English at a time when it was academically not well accepted and, as a research field, not well defined. In the 1950s, Dustoor was one of the few scholars active in the academic world who had developed a linguistically realistic attitude toward the Indian variety of English. Dustoor emphatically claimed that 'there will always be a more or less indigenous flavour about our English. In our imagery, in our choice of words, in the nuances of meaning we put

into our words, we must be expected to be different from Englishmen
and Americans alike' (reproduced in Dustoor 1968 : 126). He considered
the English of Rabindranath Tagore, Sarojini Naidu and Manmohan
Ghose 'the better, not the worse, for bearing the stamp of a national
temperament'. Dustoor saw ahead :

Our mental climate will always foster plants that do not flourish in England
or America; and such plants, just because they are somewhat exotic, add to
the charm of a garden. All lovers of English will, therefore, encourage them to
grow in the world-wide garden of English. It is only the weeds, which spring
up whenever ignorance, carelessness or pretentiousness infects the air, that
need to be pulled up by the roots.

In this metaphorical statement Dustoor has made a lucid distinction,
between 'indigenous flavour' or 'national temperament', between a
'deviation' and a 'mistake', and what may be termed acquisitional de-
ficiency.

It was again due to Dustoor's encouragement that in 1955 I was
indirectly thrown into the lap of what is known in linguistics as 'American Structuralism', when it was at its peak. My first encounter with
structuralism was at Pune, where the Linguistic Society of India and
the Deccan College Postgraduate and Research Institute, under the
inspiring leadership of S. M. Katre, had initiated Linguistic Institutes
with the support of the Rockefeller Foundation. At these Institutes the
enthusiasm of the Structuralists was contagious; the atmosphere was
full of attacks on the 'traditionalists', and challenges were thrown at
the traditional Indian pandits who had spent their lives with the study
and analysis of Sanskrit, Pali and other Indian languages. The impact
of these Institutes was substantial and certainly contributed toward
the development of modern linguistics in the subcontinent. For the
first time the Indian linguistic gurus and the 'modernists' became involved in controversies and polemic discussions very bewildering for
the uninitiated among us.

In 1958, I went from American Structuralism to what may loosely
be called 'British linguistics' at Edinburgh University. At Edinburgh,
at that time, the linguistics curriculum was being revitalized due to
the presence of M.A.K. Halliday and to the short-term visiting appointment of J. R. Firth during 1958, among others. It was a much
different linguistic scene from the one to which I had been exposed
at Pune.

The distinguished group of linguists at Edinburgh included Firth,
who had retired from the Chair of General Linguistics at London Uni-

versity in 1956. It was the first Chair of General Linguistics in Britain, established in 1944, and Firth was fond of reminding people that he had been its first occupant. Halliday had just moved from Cambridge University to a position at Edinburgh, in what was then the Department of English Language and General Linguistics. Firth had earlier been a Professor of English (1920-28) in Lahore (now in Pakistan); he had co-edited a textbook for Indian students.[2] After his return to Britain, Firth had again visited the subcontinent as a researcher, as a visitor and as a consultant. And equally important, he had been a teacher of several South Asian students in linguistics at the School of Oriental and African Studies in London. Firth died in 1960, and I was the last in that chain of students. Among the Indians my exposure to Firth's teaching was perhaps the shortest. But, as is well known, Firth always left a lasting impression on a person—the duration of the exposure was immaterial. Reaction to Firth as a teacher and as a man also varied from one person to another. In him one could see both the sahib and the pandit, as these terms are understood in their typical cultural connotations. One respect in which Firth reminded me of a pandit was his talent for *maukhik* ('oral') transmission of ideas, the Western tradition being essentially a written one. The Indian gurus inspire by *vāk* ('speech'); the written word is only secondary. Both in his lectures and in his writing, he developed a mystique. Consider, for example, the following, 'The voice of man is one component in a whole postural scheme, is part of a process in some sort of situation. And in this sense a man speaks with his whole body, and in particular with his breathing apparatus, his body, muscles and his head. . . . The brain gives us a grip on our world, and the world a grip on us' (Firth 1957c [Palmer 1968]:172). I am not surpised that, in the 1950s and 1960s, this style of linguistic writing was not well received by his fellow linguists on the other side of the Atlantic; it was considered 'obscure' and 'difficult'. After all, contrast this style with that of Leonard Bloomfield, Zellig Harris and Noam Chomsky. The difference is clear; so, I believe, are the underlying reasons for it. I have not found many who found Firth's lectures 'obscure', or who did not enjoy reading Firth *after* having listened to him in the class. The moral is that Firth could essentially inspire (and irritate) in person, like a guru. Perhaps in his writings he just whets the appetite but does not satisfy it; therefore he just irritates, and for that reason he is called 'obscure'. It was therefore a pleasure to watch Firth, the *whole man*,[3] in a lecture hall or to meet with him for individual consultation.

In his unique way, Firth would talk for hours on the personal, political and linguistic history of the members of what was then called the 'Firthian' or the 'London' group of linguists (see Kachru 1981c). I am told that this was Firth's way of initiating a *śiṣya* ('disciple', 'student'). I would sit in front of him, listening to his monologues (one rarely *discussed* things with Firth), to stories about his Indian experiences, and to his very insightful digressions on Indian English, Indianisms and the role and functions of English in India. It was precisely by listening to him that my earlier discussions on Indian English with Dustoor took a new form and shape. In many respects the views of these two were not different from one another. In 1956, Firth said that, 'in view of the almost universal use of English, an Englishman must de-anglicize himself as well' (Palmer 1968:96–7). This was a clear call for linguistic tolerance and anti-prescriptivism, especially with reference to English as an international language. Firth saw English as a tool of international communication, representing in each country a particular 'way of life',

international in the sense that English serves the American way of life and might be called American, it serves the Indian way of life and has recently been declared an Indian language within the framework of the federal constitution. In another sense, it is international not only in Europe but in Asia and Africa, and serves various African ways of life and is increasingly the all-Asian language of politics. Secondly, and I say 'secondly' advisedly, English is the key to what is described in a common cliché as 'the British way of life'.

Half a century ago, in 1930, Firth had given a realistic assessment of the future of English in India; his words are indeed prophetic and insightful. Firth was conscious of the fact that 'of all the civilized peoples of the world, the Indians are faced with the most difficult cultural and linguistic problems'. He adopted a rather uncharacteristically unEnglish position for that time when he further added that 'the superficiality characteristic of Indian education is an inheritance from the superficial Lord Macaulay. And so long as the English language is the instrument of power in the land, it will be difficult to get fathers ambitious for their sons to take their own languages seriously. But if India is to take any sort of equal place in our commonwealth they will have to be taken seriously; and the sooner the better' (Firth 1930:210-11). Firth must have been one of the very few Englishmen in the 1930s who would confess that 'it has often been said that Indian education was organized to turn out clerks. But by far the greater number of Indians "literate" in English are not even good clerks. The few bril-

liant men succeed in spite of the system.' Firth could foresee the future
direction of the Indian linguistic scene, and he predicted that 'the
great chemists and physicists of India will soon be able to do their
work in Urdu or Bengali or Tamil quite as well as in English' (1930
[1964]:210). This prediction has not as yet come true but, then, the
day may not be too far distant.

Firth was essentially a pragmatist and believed that 'to be linguistically solvent you must be able to exchange your terms somewhere and
somehow for gold of intrinsic social value' (1930[1964]:176). In the
1920s Firth's Indian experience had shown him that 'Babus, both
white and brown, in England and in India are often linguistically in-
solvent, though their creditors rarely force them into open bankruptcy.
Most Indian English is kept going by the government, and though it
has therefore, a certain local currency, it has no gold backing.'

In the twenties Firth was right: English acquired that 'gold backing'
in India after 1947, when the raj withdrew its all-powerful arms from
the subcontinent and India became free. Therefore, what was true
linguistically and attitudinally in 1930 is no longer true in 1982. However, Firth's observations are significant for their robust realism and
clear understanding of the linguistic tensions of India in the 1920s and
early 1930s. In the late 1950s, Firth was still uncertain about the future of English in India, but he was certainly observing (with a native
speaker's amusement) the Indianization and twice-born characteristics of Indian English.

It was through the various meetings and discussions with Dustoor,
Firth, and later Halliday that my approach to Indian English gained
a new perspective.

Halliday's views on Indian English (or other institutionalized varieties of English) were not much different from those of Dustoor and
Firth. In this sense, then, he provided more than mere continuity;
there was an attitudinal rapport about Indian English. What we saw
in print in 1964 (see Halliday, McIntosh and Strevens 1964) had
partly been discussed in preliminary versions in Edinburgh much
earlier. The book claims that 'the doctrine that there is an "Indian
English", to which Indian and Pakistani speakers should conform rather than aiming at a native model, whether British or American, is
one which commands sympathy...' (174). It accepts 'Educated Indian
English' (203) and recognizes varieties within the Indian variety of
English (295). There is a warning for those 'who favour the adoption
of "Indian English" as a model': they 'should realize that in doing so

they may be helping to prop up the fiction that English is the language of Indian culture, and thus be perpetuating the diminished status of the Indian languages' (1964). The warning was too late! By 1964, in many respects, English had already become an *Indian* language.

At Edinburgh, unlike the United States of the 1950s and 1960s, semantics and phonetics were relevant and exciting areas of linguistics; a phonetician did not have to use the backdoor. In fact, when sociolinguistics became popular in America, Halliday made an apt remark: 'What is now sociolinguistics in America has always been general linguistics for us in Britain.'

In 1961, a chance encounter with Robert B. Lees resulted in my joining his programme at the University of Illinois in 1963, after teaching for a year at Lucknow University. The process of learning and unlearning linguistics started again. It was like trying to move from one caste to another and being conscious of it all the time. The 1960s were a period of youth in linguistics; a generation of linguists was being retrained and reoriented in a fast-changing discipline. In this process some survived, some became a part of the new movement, some copped out, and many disintegrated and became bitter and cynical. Illinois was in the forefront of this new 'revolution', and it was at the University of Illinois that my third linguistic 'incarnation' began.

In the 1960s in the United States the attitude toward non-native Englishes was much different from what is emerging in the 1980s. The professionals saw English in the international context primarily as a pedagogical problem. The attitude reflected in Prator (1968) was typical of the period. I have responded to it in detail (Kachru 1976a); therefore I will not discuss it here.

The studies in this volume were written with such linguistic background and with reference to the context of these three 'incarnations'. It is, however, obvious to me that my second 'incarnation' has been the dominant one.

The studies have been arranged in three broad sections. Section I provides a historical and sociolinguistic overview of the English language in the *new* Indian context. The first chapter focuses on the South Asianness of English, recognizing the concept of South Asia as a linguistic area (see, e.g., Emeneau 1955 and 1956; Masica 1976), and showing that the term 'Indian English' may actually be misleading, since the *Indian* characteristics of English cut across regional, political and linguistic boundaries. The *Indianness* in Indian English is to a large extent shared with other South Asian countries, namely Bangladesh, Pakistan, Sri Lanka and Nepal. My use of the term 'South Asianness' therefore refers to pan-South Asian linguistic and cultural characteristics *transferred* to an adopted 'alien' language. The second chapter restricts these observations to data from Indian English. In section II, the impact of my second 'incarnation' is evident, especially the influence of Firth and Halliday, and Firth's concept of 'context of situation'. The chapter on 'Contextualization' outlines the development and the use of this concept by Firth, and illustrates it with examples from Indian English texts (also see Kachru 1981c), the aim being to give to the term 'Indianness' functional relevance and formal 'manifestation'. It is claimed here that the earlier approaches to the study of Indian English missed those cultural and linguistic generalizations which account for the underlying unity of Indian English (or South Asian English) and its formal and functional distinctiveness. Without insisting on such generalizations one might miss the productive processes of nativization in this variety of English. Section III includes two chapters on Indian English vocabulary. In the first, I discuss various types of lexical extensions and innovations, adding a brief survey of earlier research. The second chapter, 'Toward a Dictionary', develops a case for a new dictionary of Indian English, and summarizes the state of the art in lexicological research in some other institutionalized 'transplanted' varieties of English. Section IV turns to a little-researched aspect of the Indian language contact situation, summarizing, with illustrations, the development of new communicative codes by 'mixing' English and other Indian languages. This study makes a distinction between 'code-mixing' and 'code-switching', and further distinguishes 'code-mixing' from 'odd-mixing' and restricted lexical 'borrowing' and pidgins. The pragmatic or functional characteristics of such new codes of communication are discussed, showing that mixing is a *cline* with certain formal constraints. It makes formal and functional generalizations applicable to those bilingual or multilingual societies which have developed such codes of communication, and discusses the implications of code-mixed varieties for language change. Section V, the final section, is devoted to Indianization within the context of other institutionalized non-native varieties of English, drawing examples from each variety and showing similarities in such varieties. In terms of the functions of Indian English, a distinction has been made between the *international* and *intranational* uses of English (see Kachru and Quirk 1981): the concluding chapter, further attempts to show, with illustrations, that what is true of Indian English is also true of other non-native Englishes, and that the formal characteristics of these Englishes cannot be properly understood without considering the typical 'non-native' functions of these varieties in an 'unEnglish' pragmatic context. Obviously, in the study on the range and depth of the Indianization of English, several tasks crowd in on the writer: defining terms, making a decision about the inclusion or exclusion of an Indianism, determining the text and its relation to the context, and restraining attitudinal reactions. One question is invariably asked: What is 'Indian English' and who are its users? Sometimes it is asked innocently; at other times the questioners are displaying attitudinal reactions to the earlier use of the term by, among others, Goffin and Whitworth, in whose use 'Indian English' had acquired a disparaging meaning, conveying essentially acquisitional inadequacy. My use of the term has no attitudinal connotation: it refers to the body of material with typical linguistic and contextual characteristics which are the result of the Indianization of the English language. The reference is to 'educated' or 'standard' Indian English and to the sub-varieties within this variety. Therefore, in discussing the processes and manifestations of Indianization, the 'cline of bilingualism' has been found useful. (See chapter 4, pp. 128-30.)

A word of caution is in order concerning my use of illustrations of Indianization and Indianisms. As I have said earlier, the primary aim of these studies is to focus on the processes of Indianization, the motivations for such innovations, and the relationship of Indianisms to the Indian linguistic and sociocultural context. I have therefore avoided making claims about the frequency and spread of Indianisms. I have also not always indicated the restrictions on an Indianism, whether, for example, it is used in the spoken or the written form, or in both, though most of the Indianisms have been taken from written texts.

One cannot overemphasize the fact that certain Indianisms are only found in author-specific texts, and are never heard in the spoken form except for comic effect. For example, *sister-sleeper, dining-leaf, may the vessel of your life never float on the sea of existence*, are author-specific; one does not encounter them in the marketplace or among English-speaking groups in Delhi or Bombay. Such formations are essentially used to recreate a native speech event in a second language. On the other hand, the Indianism *welcome address* is very common, and is even used in the linguistically conservative *Statesman* and *Times of India*, which generally seem to resist certain types of Indianisms. Formations like

eve-teaser and *fly-catcher* are more common than,
for a non-vegetarian restaurant in South India
explained in chapter 6, 'minority forms' (Quir
or *mode-restricted* items are part of the process of Inc
in terms of frequency they remain in a class by
purposes of this study, among others, the following
have been treated as Indianisms:

1. Author-specific (e.g., *rape-sister, sister-sleepei*
   novels of Mulk Raj Anand);
2. Text-specific (e.g., *as honest as an elephant, as good as kitchen ashes,*
   in *Kanthapura* by Raja Rao);
3. Register-specific (e.g., *interdining, intermarriage*);
4. Area-specific (e.g., *coconut paysam, jibba pocket, military hotel, potato*
   bonda, religious diwan, yakka carriage).

There are other types of Indianisms (for example, pluralization as
in *alphabets, furnitures*) which are shared with some African varieties
of English (see Bokamba 1982), but are related to early stages in language acquisition.

Another aspect of English in India needs some comment. The story of
English in India (or in other non-native contexts) has, Janus-like, two
faces. One face is that of the Indianization of English: the other face, with
equal impact, involves the Englishization of South Asian languages.
The present volume is limited to the former aspect; the other aspect of
Englishization is only briefly mentioned in chapter 7. There are very
few linguistically oriented studies of the two major 'imposed' languages
in India, namely Persian in Islamic India, and English during and
after British rule (Kachru 1979). Such studies will no doubt provide
insightful data for our understanding of language contact, language
convergence (the *Sprachbund*) and language attitudes. I have merely
touched upon such topics related to English in India.[4]

I certainly do not mean to give the impression that the phenomenon
of Indianization is unique and, therefore, that Indian English has de-
viated considerably from other Englishes. That would be a rash conclusion. The Indian characteristics in Indian English at various linguistic levels provide the clues for the *identity* of this variety of English.
Labels such as American English, British English, West African English, or Caribbean English are merely for identification; they indicate
both the *shared* and *non-shared* characteristics of these varieties, which
constitute what may be termed 'world Englishes'. These identificational labels, in fact, provide clues for their distinctiveness. However,

...lity, the non-native varieties of English (e.g., South Asian and ...rican) share a number of processes marking their non-nativeness in grammar, vocabulary and the use of rhetorical devices in various functional styles. The reasons for their linguistic and contextual nativization are by and large identical, and references to such shared characteristics have been made in various chapters of this book. So far there has been no serious attempt toward developing a typology of nonnative Englishes. The following examples are given to illustrate the point.

The typical Indian use of function words, such as articles, is characteristic of several non-native varieties of English. Bokamba (1982) presents a brief discussion of this aspect with contrastive references to African languages. Another feature is that of reduplication of words. This feature is much more extensive in several varieties of non-native Englishes than in contemporary American or British English, except in the Black English of North America. It is however true that reduplication was much more frequent in the earlier historical stages of English. Examples from Indian English and Sri Lankan English are given in the relevant sections of this book. The same pattern is found in reduplications such as, *small small one, small small whiskey, long long one*, in Kenyan English, Malaysian or Singaporean English (see Kachru, ed. 1982).

In grammar, too, several identical tendencies are shared by South Asian English, African English and various Far Eastern varieties of English (see Bokamba 1982, Kachru 1969a and 1982e, and Platt and Weber 1980). A feature termed 'yes-no confusion' is common among Indian English speakers (see chapter 1). It implies a negative response from an Indian English speaker where a native speaker of English expects the affirmative response. Again, this feature of Indian English (or South Asian English in general) is shared by African English. Consider the following examples from Bokamba (1982).

1. Q. Hasn't the President left for Nairobi yet?
   A. Yes, the President hasn't left for Nairobi yet.
2. Q. Didn't you see anyone at the compound?
   A. Yes, I didn't see anyone at the compound.
3. Q. I hope you won't have any difficulty with your fees next term?
   A. I hope so (i.e., I hope what you have said will indeed be true).

And note parallel examples from Indian English:

1. Q. Didn't I see you yesterday in college?
   A. Yes, you didn't see me yesterday in college.

2. Q. You have no objection?
   A. Yes, I have no objection.

Here, as in many other languages (e.g., in Russian, Japanese, most Indo-Aryan and Dravidian languages, and many African languages), the choice of *yes* or *no* depends on the situation. If the situation is positive, the answer is *yes*; if the situation is negative the answer is *no* (see Bhatia 1974). Also as to lexical innovations, collocations and semantic extension and restriction, a number of processes seem to be identical, which I shall discuss in chapters 1 and 2.

Attention may be drawn to two more aspects of non-native institutionalized varieties of English which involve units larger than the sentence. The first is the shared concept of what constitutes a 'grand' (or 'good') style in written English; and second, the development of code-mixed varieties of English. These two aspects are briefly discussed in chapters 1 and 8. But a detailed typology of these features has yet to be undertaken and is overdue (see chapter 20 in Kachru, ed. 1982).

The shared features and shared processes in *new* Englishes should be reassuring to linguistic purists, who seem to have the rather depressing vision that the nativization of English might lead to the eventual loss of mutual intelligibility between various world varieties of the language. I have responded to this apprehension in detail (Kachru 1976a), and reference has been made to it in chapter 8. The native speakers of English seem to be hesitant to recognize that the linguistic innovations in the non-native varieties of English are the result of the international and intranational uses of English in various cultures and un-English contexts. Some such new formations ('non-nativisms') are amusing to native speakers of English; others are irritating. But these are linguistic facts and facts of language use worthy of cognizance and understanding. They were recognized for the first time by a group of native and non-native scholars in April 1978 at the two-week conference on English for international and intranational purposes (EIIP).[5] Another conference followed two months later, on English in non-native contexts; the latter was held at the University of Illinois in conjunction with the 1978 Linguistic Institute of the Linguistic Society of America (30 June–2 July 1978). The issues raised in some of the present studies almost two decades earlier formed the main focus of the Hawaii and Urbana conferences.[6]

This volume initiates the exploration of the intricate and complex issues involved in the Indianization of English. It seems that the processes for the nativization of other varieties of English are almost identical to those involved in the development of Indian English. The issues discussed go beyond the study of language contact, language convergence and language change. They touch upon topics such as prescriptivism v. descriptivism, intelligibility, the question of a 'model', variation within a variety, 'mixing', substratum influence, the expansion of the verbal repertoire and style range and the development of non-native English literatures. It is hoped that they will enhance our general understanding of second language acquisition, as well as provide another perspective for teaching English in intranational and international contexts.

NOTES

1. This is a translation of Sanskrit *dvija* (literally, 'twice-born'). The reference is to the three highest *varṇas*, i.e., *brāhmaṇa, kṣatriya*, and *vaiśya*. These three *varṇas* are entitled to wear the sacred thread at their initiation which marks a second birth. This initiation (or second birth) thus means admission to the study of the Vedas.

   The term *twice-born* was, as far as I know, first used in the context of Indian English literature by Meenakshi Mukherjee (see Mukherjee 1971).

2. The title of the book is *Pioneers: being selected prose for language study*, compiled and edited with notes, glossary and exercises by J. R. Firth and Madana Gopala Singh; London, Macmillan, ix, 259. I have seen this book first mentioned in Palmer (1968: vii). The only known library copy is claimed to be in the University of Calcutta.

3. See M. A. K. Halliday (1971), review of *Selected Papers of J. R. Firth, 1952-59*, ed. F. R. Palmer, in *Bulletin of the School of Oriental and African Studies*, **XXXIV**, 664-7.

4. For a detailed bibliography, see Aggarwal (1982).

5. For a brief discussion of this conference and its recommendations see Kachru and Quirk (1981).

6. See Kachru, ed. 1982.

I   HISTORICAL AND SOCIOLINGUISTIC CONTEXT

1
English in South Asia
An Overview

1.0. In recent years there has been a distinct change in attitude, both of South Asian and Western scholars, toward the *varieties*[1] of English which have developed primarily as second languages (hereafter abbreviated L_2) in South Asia and other parts of the world. This is essentially a post-World War II development which grew out of the new attitude of 'linguistic tolerance' after the rapid growth of the linguistic sciences in the West during that period. It was then that the demands of 'hands off pidgin' (see Hall 1955) or 'status for the colonial Englishes' were heard on both sides of the Atlantic and interest was shown in the *new Englishes*, namely West African English, Filipino English, South Asian English, etc. This tolerance became more marked when South Asian countries achieved freedom from direct political domination by Britain and the new independent governments in these areas decided to preserve English as a *link language* for national and international communication. There was a renewed enthusiasm for continuing English in three major countries in South Asia, i.e., Sri Lanka (Ceylon), India and Pakistan. Thus for the first time English had patronage from the local governments. Before 1947 English had a precarious position in South Asia. On the one hand, it was considered a symbol of British power and, what is worse, a politically superimposed language. On the other hand, the regional varieties of English were considered, by the English themselves, 'substandard' and were often characterized as *Babu English* or *Cheechee English*,[2] or simply labelled *Indian* or *Lankan* English in a derogatory sense.[3] The thirties and forties were times of acute pessimism about the South Asian varieties of English. It was during that period that J. R. Firth, who knew the Indian subcontinent so well, wrote in typical Firthian manner: 'Most Indian English is badly overdrawn. *But it is kept going by the government*, and though it has therefore a certain local currency, *it has no gold backing*' (my italics) (Firth 1930 [1964], 176). This was true in the thirties, and it took two more decades and the independence of the region from the British to create that 'gold backing' for English. The fact is that the British went to South Asia with the English language and, in due course, the natives took over the language and the Englishmen took over the land. It was later realized that English had much deeper roots in South Asia than the raj had. The raj crumbled and became a part of history; but the English language has been *South Asianized* and has become a part of the culture of that vast area.

The process of *South Asianization* of the English language manifests itself in three aspects. First, it supplies rich data for language contact study in a cross-cultural and multilinguistic context, thus being of interest from a sociolinguistic point of view. Second, it raises many typologically interesting theoretical and methodological problems about the descriptions of the *new Englishes* which have developed from the L₁ varieties of English (say, for example, American English, Australian English, British English, Canadian English) as *second* or *foreign languages*. Third, there is a large body of *South Asian English* (hereafter abbreviated SAE) literature in different forms (e.g., poetry, prose, fiction) which is interesting from a stylistic point of view. This rapidly increasing body of writing is now being recognized in the English-speaking world as a significant development of the English language in a subcontinent where English is spoken only by a small minority out of the total literate population.

I shall first briefly review the literature which gives a historical introduction to the spread of bilingualism in English in South Asia. This, I think, is directly connected with the three linguistically relevant aspects which will be discussed later.

2.0. THE SPREAD OF BILINGUALISM IN ENGLISH IN SOUTH ASIA

2.1. *The Beginnings of Bilingualism*

There is no detailed work on the early stages of bilingualism in English in South Asia. Whatever is published is found in the official reports or books, which deal mainly with the history of education, history, political science and histories of missionary work in the area. The following summary presents a review of selected literature on the sociopolitical and historical studies which deal with the development of bilingualism in English in South Asia.

The growth of bilingualism in English in this region is closely connected with the beginnings of colonization of the area by the British. The early serious efforts of contact with South Asia started in the sixteenth century and by the eighteenth and nineteenth centuries the area was under the political domination of the British. As the British were deepening their roots in the colonies, the English language also was taking root (earlier, perhaps, unconsciously); and eventually a large number of English L_2 speakers developed whose competence in English varied considerably (see section 3.1).

It is customary to trace the roots of English on the Indian subcontinent to 31 December 1600, when Queen Elizabeth I granted a Charter to a few merchants of the City of London giving them a monopoly of trade with India and the East.[4]

2.2. *Three Early Phases*

There are a large number of surveys which discuss the reasons given by three distinct groups for introducing bilingualism in English on the Indian subcontinent and Sri Lanka. The efforts of these three groups began as independent phases; eventually all three forces joined together. The first phase comprises the efforts of the missionaries who went to South Asia essentially for proselytizing purposes. The second includes the efforts of a small group of Lankans and Indians who were fascinated by the progress of the West and desired to use the English language as a vehicle for scientific and material progress. The third was a political phase which firmly established the English language in South Asia.

2.2.1. *First Phase: The Missionaries*

A detailed account of the impact of the missionaries is found in the publications of Duff (1837), Sherring (1884), Richter (1908) and Law (1915). The efforts started in 1614 and became more and more effective after 1659 once the missionaries were allowed to use the ships of the East India Company. In 1698, when the Charter of the Company was renewed, a 'missionary clause' was added to it (see Sharp, ed. 1920:3). This policy, however, changed again in 1765, when encouragement of missionaries was stopped. This created great resentment in missionary circles in England, and the Clapham sect started agitating for freedom for missionary work in India. The efforts of Charles Grant have been specially mentioned in this context.[5] Grant summarizes the main reasons for trouble on the Indian subcontinent in the following statement:

> The true curse of darkness is the introduction of light. The Hindoos err, because they are ignorant and their errors have never fairly been laid before them. The communication of our light and knowledge to them, would prove the best remedy for their disorders. (Grant 1831–32:60–61).

In 1813, with the efforts of Charles Grant, William Wilberforce, and the Foreign Secretary, Lord Castlereagh, the House of Commons in its 13th Resolution

> resolved that it is the opinion of this Committee that it is the duty of this Country to promote the interests and happiness of the native inhabitants of the British dominions in India, and that measures ought to be introduced as may tend to the introduction among them of useful knowledge, and of religious and moral improvement. That in furtherance of the above objects sufficient facilities shall be afforded by law to persons desirous of going to, or remaining in, India.6

This helped the missionary work in India, and thus the proselytizing and educational activities of the missionaries—which were very restricted and unplanned from 1600 to 1765—were revitalized. A brief account of the missionary activities in the three states of Bombay, Bengal and Madras is given in Kanungo (1962: 11–14) with useful bibliographical references.

In Sri Lanka the Reverend James Cordiner went as chaplain to the garrison in Colombo in 1799 and took over as principal of all schools in the settlement. There again, the efforts in teaching English were first made by missionaries, and it was not until 1831 that the government started imparting English education. By the time the government took over there were already 235 Protestant mission schools, out of which only ninety were under the direct control of the government.

The foundation of the 'Christian Institution' was laid in Sri Lanka in 1827 by Sir Edward Barnes, 'to give a superior education to a number of young persons who from their ability, piety and good conduct were likely to prove fit persons in communicating a knowledge of Christianity to their countrymen' (Barnes 1932:43; see also Ruberu 1962).

The Report of the Special Committee of Education in Sri Lanka makes it clear that in Sri Lanka up to 1886 a large number of schools were Christian (Report of the Special Committee 1943). It should be noted that during the earlier period the methodology of teaching and the language background of the teachers had great influence on SAE.

2.2.2. *Second Phase : The Demand from the South Asian Public*

A study of Adams's Reports (Basu, ed. 1941) shows that before Raja Rammohun Roy's plea for introducing English in India there was already a small group of Indians. especially in Bengal, who wanted to study English in addition to Persian and Bengali. Perhaps this was one way for Hindus to show their concern about the domination of Persian or Arabic; or perhaps this was done essentially for socio-economic and educational reasons. It is well known that, in aiding the passing of the crucial Minute of 1835, Macaulay's hand was considerably strengthened by a small group of Indians led by Raja Rammohun Roy, who preferred English to Indian languages for academic, scientific and other international reasons. Roy's often-quoted letter to Lord Amherst, dated 11 December 1823, is an important document which contributed to the introduction of bilingualism in English in the Indian subcontinent.[7]

2.2.3. *Third Phase : The Government Policy*

There is a considerable amount of literature on this phase of English in South Asia, but the main aim of the writers of these studies is not to present a systematic history of the English language in South Asia. These works are written either by political scientists or historians.

After 1765 the East India Company became a political power in India; its attention was, naturally, attracted by wider problems. The education of Anglo-Indian children became secondary, whereas it had earlier been one of the main objects of the schools. In 1787 the Court of Directors of the East India Company appreciated the efforts of the Reverend Mr Swartz to establish two schools in Tanjore and Marwar for the children of soldiers, encouraging him with a grant of 250 pagodas per year per school. It was an initial but crucial stage, for it might have left no mark had the later discussions not gone in favour of English.

The highly controversial and very significant Minute of 1835 was passed on 2 February. The Minute, however, was not passed without debate and controversy. At that time there were clearly two views about educating the people of South Asia in English. (This controversy, in different forms, has continued up to the present time.) One group which favoured English was led by Charles Grant, Lord Moira, and T. B. Macaulay. The other group, not very strong, was led by the Honourable H. T. Princep, who was against the use of English as a compulsory language and termed the Minute 'hasty and indiscreet.'[8] In his dissenting Minute he wrote: 'The next step will be to transfer the professors' allowance to teachers of English, and then will follow in due course the voting of Arabic and Persian to be dead and damned.'[9]

On the side of English there was Macaulay, a powerful person with very strong views, who looked at the problem differently and, as he says, aimed at forming 'a class who may be interpreters between us and the millions whom we govern—a class of persons, Indians in blood and colour, but English in taste, in opinion, in morals and in intellect'.[10] Referring to Sanskrit and Arabic, he says: 'I have no knowledge of either Sanskrit or Arabic. But I have done what I could to form a correct estimate of their value. . . . I am quite ready to take the oriental learning at the valuation of the orientalists themselves. I have never found one amongst them who could deny that a single shelf of a good European library was worth the whole native literature of India and Arabia.'[11]

The Minute received the seal of approval from Lord William Bentinck, and on 7 March 1835, an official resolution endorsing Macaulay's policy was passed. This firmly established the beginnings of the process of producing English-knowing bilinguals in India. In Sri Lanka however, the firm roots of English were established much later. Not until 1827 would merchants and planters settle in that part of South Asia.

2.3. *The Diffusion of Bilingualism in English*

After the initial stage, bilingualism in English spread wider on the Indian subcontinent and developed deeper roots in the educational system. On 9 July 1854, Sir Charles Wood sent the Court of Directors the Dispatch—which came later to Lord Dalhousie, the Governor-General of India. It was due to this Dispatch that in 1857 three universities were established in India, at Bombay, Calcutta and Madras.[12] By the end of the nineteenth century, the Punjab (Lahore) and Allahabad universities were established. With the spread of colleges and the increase of universities, the importance of English was rising, and in the early twentieth century English was formally established as the official and academic language of India. English thus became the 'prestige' language, completely replacing Persian and the Indian languages (or what were then called the *vernaculars*). In the second decade of the twentieth century, as the nationalist movement gained strength, an anti-English feeling emerged; but, strangely enough, the medium of the movement itself was English. By 1928 a reasonably influential English press and a taste for English publications had been created. After World War I, there was a significant increase in educational institutions and schools, and colleges spread to the interior of India. This naturally helped in spreading bilingualism in English further among the middle and lower classes of Indian society.

The comparative statement (cf. Edwards n.d.: 1) in Table 1.1 of the publications in Indian English and the Indian languages during this period should make it clearer that bilingualism in English was being rooted among the educated classes of India in the early decades of this century. (See also Chaudhuri 1976, McCully 1940 and Schuchardt 1891a [1980]; for further references, see Kachru 1982d.)

TABLE 1.1. *Statistics of publications*, 1928[13]

Language	Number of publications
English	240
French	1
Gujarati	506
Hindi	79
Kanarese	85
Marathi	677
Sindhi	346
Urdu	83
Classical languages	101
Other dialects	25

3.0. THE LINGUISTIC ASPECTS OF SOUTH ASIAN ENGLISH

In section 2, the desire for bilingualism in English was not viewed merely as a trend toward acquiring a new dominant language. There were sociopolitical pressure groups which were clearly divided; one favoured the spread of English, and another considered it dangerous for the indigenous languages and religions. Whatever the controversies, one thing was certain: slowly but definitely a South Asian variety of English was growing.

This variety is *transparently* South Asian, in the sense that the educated or 'standard' speakers of the area share a large number of features at different *formal* levels.[14] Thus it is possible to present an *overall* analysis (cf. Gleason 1961:324; 443; see also Hockett 1958:334ff.; 339ff.) of SAE roughly on the same principles as have been followed to describe 'educated' British English or 'standard' American English.[15] It is also possible to use the available research in this area to work out such an analysis.

3.1. *Standard South Asian English*

The use of a cover term SAE does not mean that I ignore the language diversity in the use of English in South Asia. The diversity in SAE is mainly of two types. The geographical diversity can be related to the differences in the languages of the area, and to some extent to the cultural differences. The second diversity is of class or ethnic groups; it is claimed that it cuts across the language boundaries. Spencer's (1966) analysis of Anglo-Indian[16] speech is perhaps the first attempt to describe the English of ethnic groups in South Asia. There are other groups, too, on which work may be done. Spencer, however, starts his statement with an erroneous presupposition that the Anglo-Indians are one 'distinct group of Indian citizens whose *native tongue* is English'. It is still true that this group's members have 'a characteristic way of pronouncing English, such that it has been possible in India to talk of an Anglo-Indian (or earlier Eurasian) accent'. (Spencer 1957: 66; see also Valentine 1978).

It may be said that a *standard* variety of SAE has evolved which has its regional subvarieties. The standard form has been termed an *educated* or *modified*[17]form of SAE. The literature shows that this identical educated standard has partly been achieved by the five main South Asian countries, i.e., Bangladesh (88.7m.; *The Statesman's Yearbook*, 1981–82:187); India (683m.;[18] *The Statesman's Yearbook*, 1981–82: 604); Nepal (13.42m.;[19] *The Statesman's Yearbook*, 1981–82:883); Pakistan (80.2m.;[20] *The Statesman's Yearbook*, 1981–82:954); and Sri Lanka (14.47m.; *The Statesman's Yearbook*, 1981–82:1114). There are mainly two language families in this area, namely Dravidian and Indo-Aryan. The speakers of other languages comprise a small proportion of the total population of the whole region.[21]

TABLE 1.2. *The main languages of South Asia* [22].

Bangla-desh	India				Nepal		Pakistan			Sri Lanka	
Indo-Aryan	Dravidian	Indo-Aryan		Dardic	Indo-Aryan	Tibeto-Burman	Dravidian	Indo-Aryan	Indo-Iranian	Dravidian	Indo-Aryan
Bengali	Tamil	Assamese	Kashmiri		Nepali	Newari	Brahui	Gujarati	Baluchi	Tamil	Sinhalese
	Tulu	Bengali						Punjabi	Pushto		
	Telugu	Gujarati						Sindhi			
	Malayalam	Hindi						Urdu			
	Kannada	Marathi									
		Oriya									
		Punjabi									
		Sindhi									
		Urdu									

The features of an overall analysis of standard SAE would include those phonological features which cut across the political and/or geographical boundaries of the area. It is crucial to emphasize the notion 'standard' or 'educated' because the competence of the speakers of English varies so much that one is prone to find a kind of confusion. It has been suggested that the English speaking bilinguals of this area should be ranked on a *scale*—even an arbitrary one—so that one can separate them on the basis of their competence in different modes of English. I have used the term *cline of bilingualism* to refer to such a scale (see chapter 4, pp.129-30). The cline comprises three 'measuring points', i.e., the *zero point*, the *central point*, and the *ambilingual point*. These three points present a gradation towards an educated form of SAE. The zero point is the bottom point on the axis, but it is not the end point at the bottom. In South Asia it is very common to come across users of English who have acquired some control of restricted items of English but who cannot use the language in any serious sense. Some such varieties have been labelled *Babu English, Butler English, Bearer English, Kitchen English* (Yule and Burnell 1903).

There are already some collections of South Asian writing in English from different points on the cline of bilingualism. Hunt, Gokak,[23] and others have published some such examples from Indian English as written by bilinguals who rank around the zero point. The following observation by Kindersley is interesting.

In that well-known example of Indian English *Onoocool Chunder Mookerjee : A Memoir* (1873), such sentences as the following occur : *The house became a second*

Babel, or a pretty kettle of fish. His elevation created a catholic ravishment throughout the domain under the benign and fostering sceptre of great Albion.

This adventurous kind of English is still used, especially by professional petition-writers and in the writing of young Indians who have lately left school or college. The extent of its use has, however, in the opinion of the writer and of the above observers consulted by him, been much over-estimated (Kindersley 1938).

Referring to 'educated' Indian English he continues:

The English commonly spoken and written by professional men and clerks in most provinces is a more cautious and restricted type of language. Great use is made of a limited number of clichés, such as 'do the needful in the matter' and 'better imagined than described'. More metaphorical expressions are used on occasion; but they come from a very limited and stereotype repertory. Pleonastic clichés such as 'each and every' are substituted for simple forms. In general, the language has little variety or range; but the caution observed in its selection does not secure the complete exclusion of malapropisms (Kindersley 1938:26).

The educated variety of SAE is mainly used by those bilinguals who rank around the central point. This includes the large number of civil servants or educators in Bangladesh, India, Nepal, Pakistan and Sri Lanka who make use of typically South Asian *registers*[24] of English in their respective areas of operation.

3.2. *The South Asianness at Different Levels*

3.2.1. *Phonetics and Phonology*

There have been more studies on phonetics and phonology of SAE than on any other area. There may be two reasons for this: First, during approximately the last thirty years South Asia has been exposed to the structuralist linguists; their undue emphasis on phonetics and phonology manifests itself in the research. Second, pedagogically this level has always been treated as primary, and since these studies were done essentially from a pedagogical point of view, the pedagogical presentation naturally attracted more attention.

These studies are mainly about the *regional* varieties of SAE, treating the L_1 of the speaker as a demarcation point; or, in some cases, about the larger areas such as *Dravidian English*, *North Indian English* or *Lankan English*. It seems that so far not much research has been done on the major varieties of Dravidian English (i.e., Kannada, Malayalam, Tamil, Telugu). Gopalkrishnan (1960) presented a very sketchy analysis of the South Indian pronunciation of English. The following studies, for example, refer to the general phonetic characteristics of SAE speakers of a large area cutting across the language boundaries: Barron (1961a and 1961b), Lahiri (1956), Pandit (1964), Passé (1947), Plechko (1971), Rao (1961), S. Varma (1957).

3.2.2.
The phonetic and phonological deviations in SAE are essentially determined by the phonetic and phonological structures of the L_1.[25] These deviations are of two types, (a) those of segmental phonemes, and (b) those of non-segmental phonemes. In most analyses of SAE it is mainly the segmental differences which have been worked out except in Prabhakar Babu (1971), DeLanerolle (1953), Hai and Ball (1961) and Passé (1947). The discussions on the nonsegmental features are either very sketchy or have been completely ignored.

3.2.3. *The Segmental Phonemes*
On the basis of available analyses (both contrastive and noncontrastive), it is possible to present certain generalizations about SAE. The basis of such generalizations can be the underlying features of the languages of the region. These generalizations are of two types, i.e., *structural* and *systemic*.

3.2.4.
By structural and systemic differences, in the case of SAE, I mean the following. The term *structure* is used in a syntagmatic sense, and the term *system* in a paradigmatic sense. Thus in many cases the structure of L_1 may be absent in L_2 (in this case, English) or the structure may be 'identical', yet there may be systemic differences. Consider, for example, the following three languages of South Asia: Hindi-Urdu, Kashmiri and Sinhalese. We find that in these three languages (as in English) *CVC* morpheme structure is possible. Thus in this restricted sense these languages may be considered 'identical' with English at the phonetic level. Note, however, that these vary in the *elements* which operate in the systems (cf. Barron 1961a and 1961b; Pandit 1964). For example, /f, θ, ð/ do not occur in the above languages as members of any system; this results in *transfer* or *substitution* of L_2 elements by L_1 elements. In phonetic terms this transfer is of two types. First, it may involve a substitution of one or more phonetic elements in a full series of sounds, e.g., the fricative series, which is not absent in South Asian

languages (hereafter abbreviated SAL) but which shows 'gaps' when compared with the same series in English. Second, there may be complete transfer of a series, e.g., the whole alveolar series is replaced by a retroflex series in SAE. The degree of retroflexion in SAE varies from the south to the north of India. Note also that systemic differences may occur in terms of *distribution*. A SAL and English may have 'identical' phonetic elements, but these *shared* sounds may operate in different systems. For example, both in Hindi and in English the following clusters are present: *sk, st, sp*. The differences, however, are distributional, i.e., structurally these elements are shared but systemically they differ. In many varieties of Hindi *sk, st, sp* do not occur in word initial position. The result is that in Indian English (as spoken in the Hindi region) we get the following forms:

station	[ɪsṭeɪʃn]	speak	[ɪspiːk]
school	[ɪskuːl]	stall	[ɪsṭɑːl]

What happens, usually unconsciously, is that the most approximate sound is substituted from the phonological inventory of L_1 wherever there is a 'gap' in the system. This substitution and 'overhauling' of the phonological systems (both segmental and non-segmental) results in the deviations and, ultimately, in the phonological characteristics termed *South Asianness*.

A detailed typological analysis of the systems should give us the *subvarieties* of SAE. These subvarieties, as discussed earlier, apply to the regional varieties, and also to the ethnic varieties of SAE. We may then start with the broad classification of *Dravidian English*, and *Indo-Aryan English*[26] and work towards the subsystems of these on the basis of individual languages, for instance, Tamil, Malayalam, Hindi, Sinhalese. The features of Dravidian English or Indo-Aryan English may thus be abstracted on the basis of the typological features of these languages.

An overall analysis of SAE is an abstraction of the same nature as *Standard American* or *Educated British English*. There has not been any attempt to work out an analysis of this type for SAE. The aim of the aforementioned analyses has been essentially pedagogical, resulting in contrastive descriptions of a very superficial type. It is important that an overall analysis be ultimately related to the phonetic level, where deviations may be shown in terms of the phonetic substance in the different language regions of South Asia.

In a general typological statement of SAE, two things are to be taken into consideration: first, the subsystem of the loan phonology of different South Asian languages; second, the subsystems of *nonshared* items in different SALs. A good example of the first is provided by Hindi-Urdu, Punjabi, Kashmiri and Sinhalese. In the spoken English of the L_1 speakers of the above languages, the /ph, f/ distinction is maintained by a large number of people who are exposed to the loan phonology (say, acquired from Arabic, Persian, or other languages) in their respective L_1s. Note that the /ph, f/ distinction is not found in the non-loan phonology of these languages.[27] In Sinhalese /ʃ/ is found only in Sanskrit loanwards. A number of such examples may be added from other languages, too. Thus it is on the basis of two phonological systems, the main system and the subsystems, that the analysis of SAE is to be worked out. By nonshared items in SALs I mean, e.g., the implosive in Sindhi or lateral flap in Marathi, which are not shared by all South Asian languages.

It is possible to abstract from the aforementioned analyses[28] the influence of (a) nonshared items, (b) ethnic-group differences (Spencer 1957), (c) caste dialects[29] and (d) religious dialects[30] of the SALs on SAE. In many North Indian or Pakistani varieties of English we find that certain distinctions found in one language merge into one distinction in another language. Consider, for example, the phonemes /s/ and /ʃ/. In Bengali, English *same to you* becomes *shame to you*. On the other hand, on the borders of Bengal and Orissa the situation is quite the opposite; there /ʃ/ changes to /s/, thus *she* and *see* are homophonous.

There has been a controversy in linguistic literature to determine the undelying reasons for 'readjustments' in the consonant system of English in SAE (cf. Rao 1961; Pandit 1964), especially the initial /p, t, k/. Rao does not consider that the L_1s and the process of transfer can be the main reason. 'The *real* explanation lies elsewhere. It is in the way that English is taught in India, and in the way English is spelt.' (Rao 1961). Pandit suggests that 'the non-realization of aspirated voiceless allophones of the phonemes /p, t, k/ by Indian speakers should be interpreted in the larger framework of the consonant systems of English and Indian languages. Most of the Indian languages (except Assamese and perhaps Tamil - Malayalam) have a five-way position contrast from bilabial to velar and a four-way manner contrast of voiceless *v.* voiced, and unaspirated *v.* aspirated in the stop consonant series' (Pandit 1964). We might then say that certain features, such as series substitution (e.g., retroflex series for alveolar series), are typically South Asian; other features may depend both on the *competence* of speakers in English and on their L₁ backgrounds.

3.3. *Nonsegmental Phonemes*

The main phonological features of SAE which separate it from the L₁ varieties of English are not necessarily the deviations in the segmental phonemes but the deviations in stress, rhythm, intonation, etc. It is obvious that the intelligibility between an L₁ speaker of English and an SAE speaker suffers much because of the second type of deviation. There still is a lack of indepth studies of this extremely interesting feature of SAE. Passé (1947), DeLanerolle (1953), Gopalkrishnan (1960), Hai and Ball (1961) and Sisson (1971), for example, have discussed certain nonsegmental features of some varieties of SAE. Usmani (1965) has given an analysis of Urdu and English. The main points of Passé are:

1. All stressing in Lankan English is comparatively weak, as 'stress (or force accent)' is comparatively weak in Sinhalese and Tamil.
2. There is no vowel reduction.
3. There is no distinction between strong and weak forms.
4. The English words are 'incorrectly' stressed.

The observations of Usmani on the role of stress in Urdu and English are naive and misleading. He gives the following rules for the stress pattern of Urdu:

1. Single-syllable words with short vowels are slightly less loud than those with long vowels:
   /mɪl/ 'mix'   /miːl/ 'mile'
2. Polysyllabic words have an 'even scale of stress' if all syllables have short vowels:
   /'bʌr'tʌn/ 'pot'
3. Polysyllabic words have louder stress on the long vowels if they have short and long vowels:
   /zə'maːnaː/ 'period'

Usmani concludes, 'Urdu stress depends in some cases upon the length of the vowels. In general the stress pattern is very simple and kept to an even scale of loudness.' His analysis of the intonation of Urdu is equally superficial and misleading (e.g., 'A comparative study... shows that Urdu and English follow the same pitch patterns.')[31]

Gopalkrishnan's observations on the English spoken by South Indians also apply to the Tamil-speaking Lankans.[32] His main points are summarized below:

1. A general unawareness of the patterns of primary as well as secondary stress, e.g.,
   /'mækbeθ/ for /mek'beθ/ ; /'tju:ʃʌn/ for /tju:'ɪʃn/

2. A tendency to ignore differentiating the stress patterns of nouns and adjectives on the one hand and verbs on the other hand.

3. An unawareness of the shift in stress found in different parts of speech derived from the 'same Latin or Greek root'.

Taylor's study, 'The Indian English Stress System', is based on a widely spoken North Indian language (Hindi). The North Indian English stress features, however, are not different from what Gopalkrishnan has written about Dravidian English. Taylor's tentative conclusion, subject to the findings of much wider speech samplings, may be summed up as follows:

The Hindi L_1 speakers of English tend to give generally stronger and more nearly equal stress to the unstressed and weak syllables of English. Their stress distribution and points of juncture tend to be unpredictable. Within the overall framework of relatively stronger stress for unstressed and weak forms, the observed speech samples indicate the following deviations:

1. A tendency in some instances to place stress on the suffix itself and in other instances randomly rather than where predictable on the penultimate syllable.
2. A tendency to accord weak-strong stress to nouns as well as verbs in the group of two-syllable words showing grammatical contrast through stress.
3. A general lack of recognition of the primary/tertiary pattern of stress for compound nouns as opposed to the secondary/primary pattern used with free noun/noun combinations; a tendency to use the secondary/primary pattern of both.
4. *A strong* tendency to give full value to auxiliary verb forms written as contractions, and to accord them a relatively strong stress as well.
5. A strong tendency to break up grammatical units arbitrarily within sentences, thus violating the confines of 'sense groups' and placing a strong stress on words other than those normally found to have 'sense stress'.[33]

It may be mentioned here that the underlying reasons for the deviations in stress are the following: all the main SALs are syllable-timed languages, as opposed to English, which is a stress-timed language. This

results in a distinct South Asian rhythm in SAE which is based on arranging long and short syllables, and not stressed and unstressed syllables. This may be the main reason for labelling SAE as 'sing-song'
English, and for stating that it hampers intelligibility with the L_1 speakers of English (see also, e.g., Nelson 1982).[34]

The above fragmentary studies on the three major areas of SAE
speakers (i.e. Sri Lanka, South India and North India) show that on
the whole the characteristics of this phonological feature are shared
by all. It may then be said that these typical features of South Asian
stress (if a system can eventually be worked out) and rhythm, rather
than the segmental phonemes, mark a typical SAE speaker.

3.4. *Grammar*

3.4.1. The grammatical characteristics of SAE should prove a very
interesting area of investigation. In order to obtain clearer clues about
the role of L_1s in standard SAE grammar, detailed contrastive analyses may provide a helpful background. In recent years the grammatical aspect has attracted the attention of some scholars.[35]

There have also been studies on restricted topics concerned with certain grammatical points. A very obvious characteristic of SAEs is the
absence of a *parallel* category of the article in their deictic system as opposed to that of English. The manifestation of this feature has been
worked out in detail by Dustoor (1954; 1955), using Indian English
writing as the basis. Dustoor's analysis, however, is of restricted value,
for two reasons. First, there is no mention of the specific sources which
were used for his analysis. Second, he does not provide any clues as to
the competence of his writers in English. This naturally makes it difficult to rank them on the cline of bilingualism.

There is also a comparative grammatical statement of 'identical' restricted languages in British English and Indian English.[36] Its aim is
to present a comparative statement about (1) the deviations in structures and systems in the verbal groups and nominal groups; (2) the
frequency of grammatical patterns in the two varieties, with their statistical significance. This attempt has failed to show any revealing
differences. The reasons for this failure are both methodological and
theoretical. It is, however, interesting to note that the two registers
of Indian English under discussion do not show statistically very significant deviations from British English, which was treated as the norm.

The following are the results of the study. In the verbal group, at the primary degree of *delicacy*, the differences are not very significant. (The term *delicacy* is used here in a technical sense referring to a dimension of analysis which recognizes increasing 'depth of detail' [see Halliday 1961]). Perhaps the differences are not significant for the reason that a conscious attempt was made to choose the Indian text from the upper point on the cline of bilingualism. There are, however, marked differences in the elements which operate in the structures. (1) The differences in the use of finite and non-finite verbs do not show a marked deviation. The Indian English text has a high percentage (1.96%) of finite verb forms. The British English text has 1.96% more non-finite verb forms than the Indian English text. (2) In the extension of finite verbs Indian English has the highest frequency (i.e., 1.35%). The difference between the two texts is 1.49%. The X^2 test (Chi-squared test) shows that, in the following three categories the differences are significant: *interrogative*, *negative*, and *modalized* verbs. In the case of *passive*, *preterite*, *continuous* and *perfect*, the differences are not significant.

In the nominal group, again, the texts under discussion do not show any marked differences at the primary degree of delicacy. The differences become marked only in the elements which function in the nominal group. Consider, for example, the following: (1) In relation to total words, the nominal group shows a higher percentage of 1.49 in Indian English texts. (2) In the two texts, the grading of nominal modifiers shows that the maximum number of items has been modified by one item. The modifiers are used on a 'descending' scale up to the maximum of five. Note the differences shown in Table 1.3. The analysis was based on a very restricted corpus, and the results cannot be generalized.

TABLE 1.3. *Grading of modifiers*

Number of modifiers	Indian English	British English
One modifier		2.36
Two modifiers		0.09
Three modifiers	2.29	
Four modifiers		0.02
Five modifiers	0.04	(no occurrence)

Note also that, in a comparative study of this type another distinction was needed between (1) those deviations which are *contextually* significant, and (2) those deviations which are *stylistically* significant. In the verbal group, for example, the frequency differences in *negation*, *interrogation* and *person* are included in (1), and *aspect*, *mood* and the *time* categories are included in (2).

3.4.2.

An earlier paper by Kindersley (1938:25) has some interesting observations. These, he makes clear,

> are concerned not with the broken sort of English spoken by servants or other Indians of little or no 'English' education, but with the English of those who have learnt the language in schools. They apply, generally speaking, to the English of clerks and of the less well educated among the professional Indians who use English daily, such as pleaders and magistrates. That is, they apply to a form of speech intermediate between the almost completely normal English of many Indian writers on the one hand, and the dog English of the school-boy on the other. Many of the usages herein contained, however, occur only from time to time in the English of the highly educated. Of this fact ample evidence could be produced in the shape of notes taken from books and speeches by well-known Indians.

Kindersley comments on the following grammatical features of Indian English, tries to give reasons for them and identifies the area (s) of their usage, if applicable.[37]

1. In the reflexive verbs (e.g., *enjoy, exert*) the reflexive pronoun is omitted. 'This is usually due to inaccurate observation in the first instance, followed by the spreading and stereotyping of the mistake.'

2. In place of transitive verbs, intransitive verbs are used (e.g., *reach, waive*), or the other way round (e.g., *preside, dissent*).

3. In constructions such as verb + particle (e.g., *dispose of*), the particle is added to such verbs as normally do not take the particle (e.g., *rear off, eat off*). The reasons, says Kindersley, are that 'These are derived to some extent by extension of English usage. But a strong influence has been the extremely common use of ancillary verbs, both in Indo-Aryan and Dravidian, as Hindustani *mar-gayā*, Tamil *irandu-vittār*' (1938:27-28). His observations on 'the syntax of the verb' are useful and open up an area of potential research. He has also attempted to give the underlying reasons for these deviations. The complete list of deviations mentioned by Kindersley is given below.

> A number of Indicisms is found in the syntax of the verb. In detailing the principal of these, the verb *to do* (transitive) or *to run* or *come* (intransitive), will be used as examples.
> 1. *I am doing* for *I (constantly) do*. P, B, D.
>   Similarly *I was doing* for I *(constantly) did*. P, B, D.

2. *I am doing it* (for *I have been doing it*) *since six months.*
   Similarly with the past tense. P, B, D. Dr. as well as IA usage.
3. *I did* for *I have (just or hitherto) done.* P, B, D.
4. *I had run* for *I ran,* following the use of the IA pluperfect form, H *maĩ daurā thā,* which carries the implication that something of greater interest, or some change has occurred since, but not the reference back from one point of time to an anterior point which is borne by the European pluperfect. P, B, D.
5. *It is done* for *It has been done ;* and *It was done* for *It had been done.* P, D.
6. *If I did* for *If I do.*
7. *When I will come* and *If I will come* for *When I come* and *If I come.* P, B, D.
8. *You will do* for *I beg you will do* or *Will you please do ?* P, B, D. Dr. as well as IA usage.
9. *Would* to express a vague future or indefinite present. P, B, D. Dr. as well as IA usage.
10. *May* in jussive sense. Cf. *You may kindly come,* I *may* (for *let me*) *go.*
11. Favouring of the passive voice rather than the active. P, B, D. Due partly to the passive form, with agential case, of the IA preterite. But also found in other tenses of the verb, especially in the jussive form of the present. Cf. *This may be done* for *Please do this.* B, D.
12. *For doing* for *to do,* expressing purpose or object. Cf. *Award imprisonment for improving his character.*
13. Idiomatic use of the perfect participle active : *I did this after taking thought* for *I took thought after doing this,* or *I did not do this without taking ~~due thought~~ beforehand.* (Kindersley 1938:28)

Kindersley gives the following reasons for these deviations :

In the IA area the above are all due to vernacular usage, except for 11, which has no foundation in Bengali so far as the preterite is concerned. 11 may be inferred to have spread from neighboring IA regions into Bengal. Similarly a number of the above, originating in purely IA usage, may be inferred to have spread from the IA into the Dr. area (Kindersley 1938:29).

In 'A Transformational Treatment of Indian English Syntax', Robert P. Fox 'attempts to show that language learners who have passed the beginning stages of language learning make errors only on the transformational level of grammar'. Fox's analysis is based on the written papers of Hindi L_1 speakers who are at least graduates of Indian universities. The study is divided into the following sections :

Chapter I is devoted to a discussion of the role of the English language in India from its introduction up to the present time, and to the method and corpus used for the study.

Chapter II is the main chapter of the dissertation. It is the analysis of selected, syntactically deviant sentences from the corpus to illustrate the level on which the deviancy occurs. The system of analysis is that presented by Noam Chomsky

in his *Aspects of the Theory of Syntax*. The analysis concentrates on nominaliza-
tion, pronominalization, adjectivalization and various aspects of the verb
phrase. The comparative, passive, questions, expletive 'there', adverbs and
deletions are also discussed.

In Chapter III, questions, relatives, nominal modifiers, subject-verb agreement, the comparative and passive in Hindi and English are contrasted. The
contrastive analysis is included in an attempt to show that despite differences
in the base component, it will be the transformational component that will
be the source of difficulty for the language learner. (Also see M. Verma 1974).

3.5. *Lexis*

In lexis I shall include two characteristic types of SAE vocabulary.
The first is concerned with that part of lexis which is, by and large,
nonshared with those varieties of English which are used as the L_1. The
other comprises those items which are transferred from the SALs
to the L_1 variety of English and have become part of the borrowed
lexicon of English.

It was mainly the first aspect of SAE vocabulary that captured the
attention of earlier scholars. The reasons for this attention were mainly
pragmatic; most of the lexical items in this category are *register-restricted* and *culture-bound*.[38] The administrators of the raj, who worked
in the interior of South Asia, needed such lexical items for communication with the natives. This type then is represented by those South
Asian lexical items which are used, for example, in the registers of administration, agriculture, law, etc. Such studies are no contribution to
lexicography in any serious sense.

Note the following observation of Yule and Burnell (1903:xv):[39]

> The most notable examples are (of brief and occasional character), the
> Glossary appended to the famous *Fifth Report* of the Select Committee of 1812,
> which was compiled by Sir Charles Wilkins; and (of a far more vast and com-
> prehensive sort), the late Professor Horace Hayman Wilson's *Glossary of
> Judicial and Revenue Terms* (40, 1855) which leaves far behind every other
> attempt in that kind.

A collection of such items for Sri Lanka was published in 1869 under
the title *Ceylonese Vocabulary*.

The second type of lexical work is of interest to us. In 1886, Yule and
Burnell published a glossary of what they termed 'Anglo-Indian Words'
with a hybridized title *Hobson-Jobson*. This soon became a classic for
its wealth of information and its style. The main title was chosen 'to
have an alternative title at least a little more characteristic'. The preface says,

If the reader will turn to *Hobson-Jobson* in the Glossary itself, he will find that phrase, though now rare and moribund, to be a typical and delightful example of that class of Anglo-Indian *argot* which consists of Oriental words highly assimilated, perhaps by vulgar lips, to the English vernacular; whilst it is the more fitted to our book, conveying, as it may, a veiled intimation of dual authorship (Yule and Burnell 1903 :ix).

The second edition, edited by William Crook, was published in 1903.

During this period English had already started borrowing (and often assimilating) words of South Asian origin. In 1892 Fennell listed the following numbers of South Asian words: Hindoo, 336; Sanskrit, 32; Dravidian, 31 (Fennell 1892). It should be noted that

Words of Indian origin have been insinuating themselves into English ever since the end of the reign of Elizabeth and the beginning of that of James, when such terms as *calico, chintz* and *gingham* had already effected a lodgment in English warehouses and shops, and were lying in wait for entrance into English literature. Such outlandish guests grew more frequent 120 years ago, when, soon after the middle of the last century, the numbers of Englishmen in the Indian services, civil and military, expanded with the great acquisition of dominion then made by the Company; and we meet them in vastly greater abundance now (Yule and Burnell 1903 :xv).

Before the publication of *Hobson-Jobson*, Wilson (1855) and Whitworth (1885) had published their works, and Yule and Burnell drew intensively upon their materials. Lentzner (1891) also included some 'Anglo-Indian' words in his glossary of 'Colonial English'.

It was much later that many specialized studies on the South Asian elements in English appeared. Lexicographers and linguists had earlier been conscious of the South Asian element in English. Serjeantson gave a short and useful account of loanwords from 'Indian dialects' and the Dravidian languages in her book, *A History of Foreign Words in English* (1961). In 1954 Subba Rao's study, *Indian Words in English*, appeared posthumously.

It brings together the history of the British in India and the result of this in enriching their own language during a period of three centuries and a half. It gives in detail the extent to which the words thus made familiar have played their part in English literature from the seventeenth century down to the present time (see Craigie 1954 :v).

3.5.1.
There is another aspect of SAE which may be discussed in the section on lexis, i.e., *collocational deviation*.[40] There are references to it in Goffin (1934) and Passe[41]; and in two recent papers (Kachru 1965, 1966)

this aspect of Indian English has also been discussed. It is argued there that collocational deviation is one crucial feature that marks what may be termed the *South Asianness* of SAE.

In chapters 3 and 4 I have shown that the collocational deviations may be of three types. First, there may be grammatical deviations from the varieties of English which are used as the first language. This would account for a large number of examples of Lankan English listed under 'ignorant-English' by Passé (1947), or some examples of Indian English given by Smith-Pearse.[42] Second, there may be *loan shifts* or *lexis-bound translations* from SALs; thus in English these naturally appear deviant (Kachru, 1965, 1966 and 1975a). Consider the following examples from Lankan English (Passé 1947) : *to break rest ; bull work ; to give a person bellyfull*. These examples show the transfer of *fixed collocations* of Sinhalese into English. The following are 'literal translations' of Sinhalese expressions: *to buy and give ; to jump and run ; to run and come* (home) *; to take and come*. Third, the deviation may be contextual and not formal. This involves a *semantic shift* of English lexical items (see section 4.0).

Examples of such deviations may be given from Standard Indian English writing. The following possibilities of deviation from L_1 varieties of English have been shown.

1. The members of a collocation may be usual in the sense that in L_2 varieties of English that collocation is possible, but the contextual use of the collocation may be typically Indian (e.g., *flower-bed* [MM[43]105]).

2. The lexical items of a collocation may be collocated in non-native collocations. Thus we get lexically and contextually Indian collocations (e.g., *sister-sleeper* [VG 130], *dining-leaf* [WM 84]).

3. The contextual use of a collocation may present no difficulties to L_1 users of English, only the collocability of an item with the *node* of a collocation may be unusual, e.g., *dining-leaf*. This, then, may be explained as violation of a selection rule of the language (see also chapters 3 and 4).

3.5.2.

Another interesting lexical feature of SAE is the use of *hybridization*. A hybrid (or *mixed* formation) is described as one which comprises two or more elements and in which at least one element is from a SAL and one from English (e.g., *kumkum mark* [K 159], *tiffin-carrier* [DD 78]). It is possible to make a further distinction between (a) *open-set* hybrid items (e.g., *lathi-charge* [HS 15 June 1959], and (b) *closed-system* hybrid items (e.g., *policewala* [SMH 61]). (Cf. Kachru 1965; 1966 and 1975a).

This aspect of SAE should provide fascinating material for sociolinguistic studies of different areas of South Asia.[44]

3.6. *Style-features and Tone*

By *style-features* and *tone*[45] I mean those formal features which are attributed to the different varieties of SAE. These may overlap with some of the features discussed earlier under grammar (see section 3.4.) and lexis (see section 3.5.). They may be summed up as follows:

1. *Latinity:* There is a tendency toward a kind of Latinity in SAE. An Indian, says Goffin (1934), would prefer *demise* to *death*, or *pain in one's bosom* to *pain in one's chest*.

2. *Polite diction:* An excess of polite forms (Goffin 1934) is immediately discovered by native speakers of English when they visit South Asia. The main reason for this is that originally the registers of English introduced in India were of administration and law; both these registers are full of polite forms, and these became part of South Asian conversational English.

3. *Phrase-mongering:* A tendency toward phrase-mongering (Goffin 1934:31; see also section 3.5.1.), as mentioned earlier, is determined by the structure of L_1 and also by various types of collocational deviations. The underlying reasons for it have not been given. Goffin (1934) gives the following examples of what he terms 'phrase-mongering': *Himalayan blunder; nation-building; change of heart; dumb millions*.

4. *Initialisms:* In this area SAE seems to surpass the official registers of American English. Note the following:

H.E.'s P.A. has written D.O. to the A.S.P. about the question of T.A.'s. The D.C. himself will visit the S.D.O.P.W.D. today at 10. A.M.S.T.

This letter should read as follows:

His Excellency's Personal Assistant has written a demi-official letter to the Assistant Superintendent of Police about the question of Travelling Allowances. The Deputy Commissioner himself will visit the Sub-Divisional Officer of the Public Works Department today at 10 a.m. Standard Time. (Goffin 1934)

5. *Moralistic tone:* Goffin makes a specific reference to the English of the Indian subcontinent and considers it moralistic, in the sense that Indians cannot keep God out of it (Goffin 1934).

6. *Clichés:* Kindersley gives the following examples to illustrate the excessive use of clichés in Indian English: *better imagined than described*

(easily imagined); *do the needful; each and every* (pleonastic for 'each');
leave severely alone (for 'leave alone') (Kindersley 1938:26).

7. *Deletion:* In a large number of South Asianisms in English (e.g.,
Indianisms, Lankanisms) a syntactic unit belonging to a higher rank
in the L₁ variety of English is reduced to a lower rank in SAE. In certain cases where an L₁ speaker of English tends to use a group or a clause,
an SAE user might use a unit of a lower rank. In SAE many nominal
formations of modifier + head + qualifier (MHQ) structure are reduced to MH structure (Kachru 1965).

A large number of Indianisms are thus produced by *rank reduction*,
i.e., they involve first the process of deletion and then permutation of
the lexical items. Consider, for example, the following nominal groups
of English: (1) *an address of welcome*, (2) *a bunch of keys*, and (3) *love of
God*. In Indian English these are reduced to (1) *welcome address* (*IE*
14 August 1959), (2) *key bunch* (*AD* 178), and (3) *God-love* (*U* 205).
It is argued 'that the tendency towards deletion in IE [Indian English]
results in many such Indianisms which vary not necessarily grammatically, but only in the "acceptability" by a native speaker of English;
the reasons for "non-acceptability" are varied.... The acceptability
of IE collocations forms a scale, and the native speaker's reaction toward such Indianisms may be *acceptable, unacceptable,* or *more-or-less acceptable*' (Kachru 1965:405). The rank reduced formations have been
labelled by Whitworth 'wrong compounds', and Goffin finds in these
formations a tendency toward 'phrase-mongering'. Whitworth thinks
that Indians are following the process of analogy of Sanskrit *tatpuruṣa*
compounds, like *deva-putra* ('son of God') and transfer such formations
into Indian English (e.g., *deva-putra* as 'God-son').

8. *Yes-no 'confusion':* Goffin also makes observations about the spoken
form of the Indian variety of English. The first observation is with regard to the 'curious over-use of the opening "well. . . ."'; the second
deals with the use of 'no' where an Englishman would say 'yes'. Goffin
holds the English textbook readers responsible for the first point, where
the 'dialogue' is amply treated, and he also thinks it may be a device
used to gain time in replying. Perhaps the use of 'well' as a hesitation
marker in SAE needs further investigation. The second point seems to
be the result of wide confusion not only in Goffin but also in other
scholars. The explanation for the 'yes-no' confusion (if this is confusion)
is purely formal. What happens is that in many languages (e.g., Russian, Japanese, South Asian languages) the choice of *yes* or *no* in a question depends on (a) the form of the question and (b) the facts of the

situation. If the above (a) and (b) have the same polarity (both positive or both negative) the answer is positive. If, on the other hand, the polarity is not the same (say, the question is in the positive and the situation is negative, or the converse) the answer is negative. The selection of *yes* or *no* in English mainly depends on the facts of the situation. If the situation is positive, the answer is *yes*; if it is negative, the answer is *no*. Kindersley also mentions this point. (Cf. ' "Yes" is answer to a negative question, for English "no", i.e., *You have no objection? Yes, I have no objection* [following IA and Dr. usage]' [Kindersley 1938; see also French 1949:6]; cf. also Bokamba 1982 for African English).

9. *Reduplication:* The high frequency of reduplication of items (often in the spoken medium) is usually noticed as an SAE marker by the L_1 speaker of English. The reason for the reduplication of the verbs and nouns (and other items, too) is again the underlying structure of the SALs. This is a typological feature which all SALs share. Passé gives the following examples from Lankan English showing the transfer from Sinhalese: *punci punci keeli* '(to cut into) small, small pieces'; *unu unu* '(to eat something) hot, hot'; *hemin hemin* '(to proceed) slowly, slowly'; *andaa andaa yanavaa* 'to go crying crying'; *monava monava* 'What and what (did he say)?'; *kavuda kavuda* 'Who and who (came to the party)?' (Passé 1947:384–85). It is not rare to find, for example, that Hindi, Telugu or Kashmiri speakers transfer this feature into their English.

10. *Bookishness:* There are two possible reasons for what is referred to as bookishness of SAE users. The first is that in both spoken and written mediums SAE users tend to use certain lexical items and grammatical constructions which either have been dropped or are less frequent in modern English. Mathai, commenting on this aspect of Indian English, writes:

Although there were 'English' teachers of English in many of the schools and colleges of India, inevitably the Indian learned a great part of his English from books. Indian English was therefore always inclined to be bookish, and not adequately in touch with the living English of the day; and when we remember that the books which we re-read as models of good English were the works of Shakespeare and Milton and the other great English poets and dramatists and prosewriters, it is not surprising that the more eloquent utterances of Indians (whether spoken or written) were often freely garnished with phrases and turns of expression taken from the great writers. Sometimes these phrases were used without proper recognition of their archaic or obsolescent or purely poetic character (Mathai 1951:97–8).

The second reason in a way stems from the first. Spoken SAE does not sound *conversational*, as the spoken medium has been seldom taught as an academic discipline in the South Asian educational system. Thus the SAE speakers are not made conscious of the characteristics of spoken English; for example, the contracted forms (see also Kachru 1982a).

4.0. LINGUISTIC ASPECTS OF SOUTH ASIAN ENGLISH LITERATURES

In the last three decades a considerable body of creative writing in English has grown in South Asia.[46] It is not only South Asian in a geographical sense, but also in content and form. The largest contribution has been made by the Indian writers. The Indian part of South Asian writing is generally termed *Indian English* writing, though for a long time there has been a controversy regarding a proper label for it. The discussion in this section will be mainly concerned with the Indian part of SAE writing, and especially with its linguistic aspects.

In Indian English writing a distinction is made between the following types: 1. Anglo-Indian; 2. Indo-Anglian; 3. Indo-Anglican; 4. Indo-English; and 5. Indian English.

The term *Anglo-Indian* writing has been restricted to that body of creative writing which treats the Indian subcontinent as the central theme. But the main point to note is that Anglo-Indian writers are those non-Indian writers of English who use English as their L_1. These writers have two points of linguistic interest for those working on SAE. First, they create many formations for the Indian contexts; second, they borrow profusely from the SALs. These include, for example, Rudyard Kipling, E. M. Forster and John Masters. A detailed treatment of these authors is given in Oaten (1908; 1907–27) and Singh (1934), to name two.

Indo-Anglian writing essentially includes the work of those Indians who use English as an L_2 and write mainly about India. The confusing term *Indo-Anglican* gained currency for a short time during World War II and now is slowly being withdrawn (Iyengar 1945; 1962). *Indo-English* seems to have been alternately used with Indo-Anglian until recently, when Gokak attempted to redefine it in the following terms: 'What I would call "Indo-English" literature consists of translations by Indians from Indian literature into English' (see Gokak 1964). I am not sure if such a separate category is needed at all, or what it accomplishes. The term *Indian English* sounds perhaps less elegant but is linguistically significant and contextually self-explanatory. This term is gaining more currency and replacing other terms, certainly in linguistic literature. The first group of Indian scholars who used this term were Anand, Bhushan, Dustoor and Jha.[47]

Since World War II serious work has been done in the writing and critical evaluation of the Indian part of SAE writing. In the 1930s this new development was viewed with considerable pessimism, which slowly disappeared after World War II. Consider the following statements. Bhupal Singh, discussing 'some Indian writers of Indian fiction' in a 'note' as an Appendix to his 1934 study commented:

An interesting feature of twentieth century Anglo-Indian fiction is the emergence of Indians as writers of fiction in English. This is a natural result of the spread of education in India and the increasing familiarity of Indians with English literature (1934:306).

Concluding, he says:

Indian writers and story-tellers, on the whole, do not compare favourably with Anglo-Indian writers. That they write in a foreign tongue is a serious handicap in itself. Then few of them possess any knowledge of the art of fiction; they do not seem to realize that prose fiction, in spite of its freedom, is subject to definite laws. In plot construction they are weak, and in characterization weaker still (1934:309–10).

Gokak, himself a noted Indian English writer, presents a recent attitude toward Indian English writing:

Indo-Anglian writing is direct and spontaneous—like creative writing in any other language. It is conditioned in many ways by the peculiar circumstances of its birth and growth . . . . Gordon Bottomley is said to have described typical Indo-Anglian poetry as 'Matthew Arnold in a *sari*.' He should rather have referred to it as Shakuntala in skirts. (1964:162).

In South Asia now, SAE writing is being considered a part of the literary heritage of the area in the same sense in which the regional literatures are part of the culture of South Asia. Iyengar's following statement is significant. He asks: 'How shall we describe Indian creative writing in English?' And answers: 'Of course, it is Indian literature, even as the works of Thoreau or Hemingway are American literature. But Indian literature comprises several literatures . . . and Indian writing in English is but one of the voices in which India speaks. It is a new voice, no doubt, but it is as much Indian as others' (1962:3).

Rao has succintly summarized the position of a South Asian writer in English.

The telling has not been easy. One has to convey in a language that is not one's own the spirit that is one's own. One has to convey various shades and omissions of a certain thought-movement that looks maltreated in an alien language. I use the word 'alien,' yet English is not really an alien language to us. It is the language of our intellectual make-up—like Sanskrit or Persian was before—but not of our emotional make-up. We are instinctively bilingual, many of us writing in our own language and in English. *We cannot write like the English. We should not. We cannot write only as Indians. We have grown to look at the large world as part of us. Our method of expression therefore has to be a dialect which will some day prove to be as distinctive and colourful as the Irish or the American.* Time alone will justify it (see Raja Rao 1938, 1963 ed.:vii; my italics).

Referring to the Indian 'style' of English, he continues:

After language the next problem is that of style. The tempo of Indian life must be infused into our English expression, even as the tempo of American or Irish life has gone into the making of theirs. We, in India, think quickly, we talk quickly, and when we move we move quickly. There must be something in the sun of India that makes us rush and tumble and run on (Rao 1938, 1963 ed.).

The question now is: Why is SAE writing of interest to a linguist? A partial answer has been given in the Introduction (see section 1) and other chapters of this study (see also Kachru 1982b and 1982e; S. Sridhar 1982). This body of writing has rightly been termed 'contact literature' for its stylistic and sociolinguistic significance. This aspect of SAE has not so far attracted the attention which it deserves from linguists or literary critics.

The linguistic study of the following features of SAE has proved useful not only in understanding the formal features of the texts, but also in relating these to typically Indian contexts:

1. Register variation
2. Style variation
3. Collocational deviation
4. Semantic shifts
5. Lexical range

There is no detailed work on any of these features. I will attempt to elaborate upon what I mean by these terms.

1. *Register variation.* The term *register* is used here in the British sense, meaning a restricted language which is contextually delimited on the basis of formal features. In South Asia, non-British or non-American registers of the caste system, newspaper writing, social roles, etc., have developed and have been discussed in chapters 3 and 4. The notion of register and its interplay in culture is perhaps specially relevant in under-

standing creative writing in English. It is claimed that a register is South Asian in the sense that, both contextually and formally, it has certain features which are absent in L_1 varieties of English (Kachru 1966: 268ff.). A large number of *register-determined* formal terms can be found in the newspapers published in English in South Asia or in other SAE writing.

2. *Style variation.* I have used the term *style* broadly in the sense in which it is used now in linguistic literature. It refers to those formal features of a text which enable us to distinguish not only the participants but also the *situationally determined choices* which are made by a writer out of the total closed-system or open-set choices possible in a language.

By *style variation* is meant the variation in formal exponents in SAE writing for the participant relationships in typically South Asian contexts. These contexts may either be nonexistent in the cultures of L_1 speakers of English, or one may have to redefine a context in a South Asian situation. The following examples from Indian English fiction will illustrate what is meant by these two types of variation:

1. *'Welcome! My eyes have gone blind looking at the way along which you were to come to grace my house.' (C).*
2. *' "Since you have blessed my hovel with the good dust of your feet, will you not sit down a moment and drink the cold water of a coconut?" Girish hurried to fetch a floor mat.'* (*SMH*)
3. *'Why did you sit down on my foot step? . . . You have defiled my religion ! . . . now I will have to sprinkle holy water all over this house.' (U)*
4. *'He caught the jelebis which the confectioner threw at him like a cricket ball, placed four nickle coins on the shoe-board for the confectioner's assistant who stood ready to splash some water on them.' (U)*

1 and 2 above are *speech functions* used in greetings and are determined by the relationship of the participants; 3 and 4 cannot be appreciated unless the register of the caste system and the *contextual units* (Kachru 1966:259–60, 268ff.) are first understood in the typically Indian sense. Note that in the register of the caste system certain formal items acquire a distinct meaning in terms of the participants; if this distinct characteristic of the register is ignored, the formal deviations are obscured. Thus the intelligibility of such items (for English L_1 speakers) depends on the understanding of the appropriate (Indian) contexts. Those items which operate in specific contextual units have been termed *contextual items* (see chapter 3). A *contextual item* has been defined as an item of any grammatical rank which has normal collocation, but at the contextual

level the item needs specific semantic markers. A good example of extremely Indianized use of style variation may be found in Raja Rao's *Kanthapura*, both in the character types and in the *style range* which is given to the characters. This work may provide an interesting study for stylistic analysis. Consider, for example, the following nominal groups (modifier + head structure) labeled *identificational* and formally deviant from the L₁ varieties of English: *cardamom-field Ramachandra* (p. 19); *corner-house Moorthy* (p.5); *four-beamed house Chandrasekharayya* (p.22); *front-house Akkamma* (p.4); *gap-tooth Siddayya* (p.10); *iron-shop Imam Khan* (p. 133); *that-house people* (p.21).

3. *Collocational deviation.* Collocational deviations have already been defined in section 3.5.1. On the basis of comparative stylistic analyses at the collocational level, one might find that stylistically collocations provide a crucial clue for marking the South Asian features of SAE.

4. *Semantic shifts.* There is no detailed investigation of *semantic shifts* of English lexical items in SAE. The following three types of shifts may be mentioned with illustrations from Indian English fiction. First, an item of English may be assigned additional semantic markers in SAE which are not necessarily assigned to it in the L₁ varieties of English. This may also lead to *register shift* (or *extension*) and thus, for an L₁ speaker of English, it results in what is termed *register confusion*. Consider, for example, the use of *flower-bed* (*MM* 90) in the sense of *nuptial bed*, or the terms *government* (*TP* 40) or *master* (*VG* 19) as *modes of address*. Second, an item of English may be assigned an extra feature in SAE literature. In English *brother*, *sister*, or *brother-in-law* all belong to the lexical set of kinship terms. In SAE (in this case Indian English) extra semantic features are assigned and their range of functions in other lexical sets widened, e.g., [+ affection], [+ regard], [+ abuse], [+ mode of address]. Kindersley (1938:30), for example, mentions the item *co-son-in-law* used for wife's sister's husband (cf. Tamil *cakalan*). A list of other items with such semantic shifts in Indian English is given by Kindersley.[48] Note, among others, the following: *bawl, beat, charm, respectable, senseless, thrice.*

The result of these shifts is that ambiguities are caused which can be resolved only when the texts are understood in terms of South Asian semantic features. Thus these lexical items are to be *redefined* in terms of South Asian contextual units.

5. *Lexical range.* The question of lexical range (or lexical 'openness') of SAE has been discussed in section 3.5 of this chapter and in chapters

5 and 6. This aspect becomes very obvious not only in SAE creative writing but also in SAE journalism. A large-scale borrowing from a large number of SALs is thus responsible for widening the distance between SAE and other varieties of English. Lexical borrowing manifests itself in two ways. First, it is a simple transfer of lexical items; and second, it results in hybridized formations (see section 3.5.2; also see Kachru 1975a, and 1980a).

TABLE 1.4. *South Asian languages in hybridization*

Language	Percentage
Bengali	3.8
Dravidian (other than Tamil)	4.1
Gujarati	0.4
Hindustani	38.6
(High) Hindi	38.6
Marathi	0.8
Punjabi	0.8
Tamil	2.0
(High) Urdu	8.9
Doubtful language-source	2.0

Note that, in Table 1.4, the distinction between Hindi, Hindustani, and Urdu is not very clear. By 'doubtful items' I mean lexical items such as *tiffin-carrier*.

5.0. SOCIOLINGUISTICS AND SOUTH ASIAN ENGLISH

In South Asia the fact that the English language has become part of the sociocultural setting has significant formal implications. The interrelation of formal and contextual categories from a sociolinguistic standpoint has not been discussed in any single work in detail. Sociolinguistically relevant questions have, however, been raised in chapters 3 and 4 (see also Kachru 1966 and later).

In Kachru (1966:255) 'The categories have been set within the framework of linguistic science, the aim being "to make statements of meaning so that we can see how we *use* language to *live*"[my italics]. This approach has contributed towards bringing out the *Indianness* of the Indian idiom of English as opposed to the *Englishness* of British English and the *Americanness* of American English.'

In chapter 4 the collocational deviations have been discussed in detail in relation to the contextual units of South Asia. Though in this study the illustrative material has been drawn from Indian English, the process is not typically Indian and applies to the whole of South Asia.

It has also been suggested that a sociolinguistically relevant distinction is needed between a *formally determined collocation* and a *contextually determined* (or *culture bound*) *collocation* (Kachru 1965). It is further argued that *America-returned* (*FF* 105) is formally deviant, while *bangled-widow* (*K* 233), *forehead-marking* (*MS* 206), and *carfestival* (*OR* 15 July 1959) are contextually deviant.

5.1.

Sociolinguistically significant aspects of SAE are, for example, the following:

(1) South Asian registers of English; (2) South Asian speech functions.

The term *register* has already been discussed (see section 4); under it I shall also include *social roles*. The social roles are, however, to be separated from what have been termed *speech functions*. In demarcating language according to social roles, one must first find the relevant contextual units and then establish parallel exponents at one or more formal levels (See chapter 3).

The formal exponents may or may not deviate from the L_1 varieties of English. The dividing points for the contextual units referring to the social roles are arbitrary, since the *roles* overlap and clear demarcation lines may not be established.

In order to illustrate this important aspect of SAE I shall consider the registers of *ceremonies*, *rituals* and *politics* essentially at the lexical level in Indian English. Note the following items, which have been used in Indian English writing for individual or social ceremonies or rituals by Raja Rao and others.

1. *Individual: hair cutting ceremony* (*K* 56); *hair ceremony* (*K* 28); *invitation-rice* (*K* 173); *naming ceremony* (*NS* 160); *rice-eating ceremony* (*K* 171); *rice-invitation ceremony* (*SMH* 30); *seventh-month ceremony* (*K* 37); *turmeric-ceremony* (*MM* 70).

2. *Social: ashirvad ceremony* (*MM* 115); *bath-milk* (*HW* 130); *brother-anointing ceremony* (*HW* 160); *ploughing ceremony* (*FF* 88) (see also chapter 3).

In the South Asian political register the problem is not one of 'redefining' items (such as the use of *democracy* or *dictatorship* in the USA and the USSR) but of finding typically South Asian meanings of lexical items. Consider, for example, the lexical items used in the political writing of the Indian subcontinent. (A linguistically interesting study of this register of SAE can be made from the speeches delivered at Indian National Congress sessions and from the political writings of Indian leaders.) The three lexical items *ahimsa, satyagraha* and *khadi* or *khaddar*, used in Gandhian context, illustrate the point. These are now included in most lexicons of English. These, then, give us the following *lexical sets: ahimsa camp; -leader; -soldier (WM* 78); *ashram disciple (MM* 82); *-sweeper (U* 218); *khadiboard (SL* 8 June 1959); *-camp (WM* 82); *-competition (WM* 97); *-clad (SL* 6 June 1959); *-coat (K* 148); *-shop (K* 135); *khaddarclad (TN* 14); *-jibba (WM* 44); *-sari (WM* 48); *satyagraha campaign (BJ* 7 June 1959); *field satyagraha (K* 240). Note also *salt-march (RH* 36); *salt-laws (HA* 55); *salt-making (HA* 35) which are related to Gandhi's campaign for removing the salt-tax in India. *Swadeshi-movement, swadeshi-cloth* are used with Gandhi's campaign for *khaddar*.

The above examples illustrate a very restricted aspect of the political register. An earlier study[49] examines a large number of lexical items which function in the context of inter-religious conflicts.

5.2.
The acculturation of SAE has crucial linguistic implications; the more *culture-bound* it becomes, the more *distance* is created between SAE and the L$_1$ varieties of English. An interesting example of this has been presented earlier, in the extended semantic domain of kinship terms of English in one variety of SAE (see section 4).

6.0. THE IMPACT OF ENGLISH ON SOUTH ASIAN LANGUAGES

In previous sections I have reviewed those studies which discuss essentially the process of transfer from SALs to SAE. This accounts for only a part of the linguistic situation and gives one side of the picture. There is another linguistically and stylistically interesting aspect to it, i.e., the influence of the English language on SALs. This influence has been of two types. First, English has affected SALs at all the formal levels. Second, it has introduced new literary genres in many SALs (see chapter 7, also Kachru 1978a, 1978b and 1979).

The vocabulary of practically all SALs shows transfer from English.

Rao claims, for example, that spoken Telugu contains 'at least 3000 English words' (Rao 1954:2). Mishra (1963) has shown how various literary forms of Hindi have been influenced by English.

A limited number of studies on this aspect of English in South Asia are already available. But they include very meagre information on the formal impact of English on SALs. I will refer here only to some of the more important studies. Latif (1920) has discussed the influence of English on Urdu. Sen (1932), Das Gupta (1935) and Bhattacharyya (1964) have taken three separate aspects of Bengali. Mishra's (1963) work shows deeper insights than Chandola's (1963) sketchy paper on Hindi. Walatara (1963) discussing the impact of English on Sinhalese, writes:

In Ceylon [Sri Lanka] the contact with English has revitalized Sinhalese literature. New genres have appeared in Sinhalese—the novel and the short story. . . . not only have Sinhalese writers imitated these foreign models, but they have even absorbed their influence and produced something on their own . . . Sinhalese drama has thriven on English and Western models.

And Gokak (1964) observes: 'It is no exaggeration to say that it was in the English classroom that the Indian literary renaissance was born.'

I will discuss some aspects of the formal transfer from English into Hindi to illustrate the influence of English on SALs.[50] The process has been roughly identical in other SALs, though the extent of influence and its manifestation in each language varies.

Bhatia (1967) and Dhar (1963) have shown the scope of lexical borrowing of English into Hindi and have also shown how the borrowed items have been assimilated into the phonological system of the language. It should be noted that, in all the languages, the borrowing has been *register-determined*. Mishra (1963:163) has given short lexical lists showing the 'translation equivalence' of English and Hindi lexical items in a large variety of registers. In addition to lexical borrowing, there has also been borrowing of idioms and sayings. A large number of adverbial phrases have been transferred into Hindi. Note, for example, *after sometime*, 'kālāntar'; *according (to orders)* 'ājñā anukūl'; *according to rule*, 'niyamānusār'; *on the other hand*, 'dūsrī or'.

It is claimed that the grammatical influence of English on SALs has been of two types. First, the categories of grammatical description were directly borrowed from the grammatical theories of English, which were based on Latin and Greek. Second, some syntactic features of English have been transferred to SALs (see, e.g., Mishra 1963:177; Kachru 1979).

In support of the first assumption some evidence is available, but in support of the second we have only superficial fragmentary analyses. Consider, for example, the following features which Mishra presents as evidence of the influence of English syntax on Hindi (Mishra 1963 : 171ff.).

1. *Change in word order*. Hindi sentences have subject-object-verb construction, and in certain texts this order is changed. Instead we find object-subject-verb or subject-verb-object construction.

2. *Use of parenthetical clause*. Kamta Prasad Guru claims that this structure was not found in Hindi before the influence of English. It was first found in Lalluj̄ Lāl (1763–1835).

3. *Use of amorphous sentences*.[51] This evidently is a very superficial analysis, and ignores the fact that the above syntactic deviations may have been used as a stylistic device. Such permutation does not always need a foreign influence. In fact there are scholars who doubt that the parenthetical clause is owing to the influence of English. It is claimed that this stylistic device was also used in early Brajbhāshā prose.

The other syntactic feature of Hindi that shows English influence is the impersonal construction (e.g., *kahā jātā hai, dekhā gayā hai, sunā gayā hai*), which may be traced back to English structures such as *it is said, it has been seen, it has been learnt*. In Hindi the active forms (e.g., *kahte hai, dekhte hai, sunte hai*) would normally be used. This feature is essentially lexical. It has been termed *Anglicized Hindi* by Chandola (1963 : 12–13). This, however, applies to other SALs too (e.g., Punjabi, Kashmiri). For further discussion see Kachru, 1978a, 1978b and 1979).

7.0. THE PLACE OF ENGLISH IN CURRENT LANGUAGE PLANNING IN SOUTH ASIA

In recent publications on language problems and language planning in South Asia, the reaction toward English shows five distinct attitudes demonstrated by five groups. The motivations for these attitudes—or the change of attitudes—is not always determined by educational or administrative factors; instead, the sociopolitical pressure groups play a very distinct role. Thus the present attitudes toward English are determined on the one hand by *language loyalty* and on the other hand by pragmatic considerations: these two are not always in conflict.

In language planning the South Asian countries face two types of questions. First, what should be the place of English *vis-à-vis* the regional languages? Second, which is linguistically more pertinent, what L₁ variety of English should be accepted as the model for the teaching of English in South Asia?[52] Or, should 'educated' SAE be treated as the model? The first question has been debated in recent literature and official reports. The second question, though crucial, has not been discussed in any serious sense.

A brief discussion of publications showing the attitudes of various groups toward English may not be out of place here. The groups are: (1) South Asian governments, (2) South Asian English writers, (3) South Asian anti-English groups, (4) South Asian pro-English groups. Perhaps a fifth, the non-South Asian group, should be included here, i.e., those scholars who belong to that part of the English-speaking world which uses English as L₁. Their attitude towards SAE has shown marked changes. The attitude of this fifth group may be shown in two ways: first, how they react to SAE creative writing[53]; second, what future they visualize for SAE. This group, however, does not directly affect the language planning in the area, although by many indirect means it has been in a position to influence the decisions of educators or politicians in South Asia.

7.1.
The attitudinal trend of South Asian governments toward English has had three phases: the first before independence; the second immediately after independence; and the third, after the period of reassurance which resulted once the post-independence nationalistic upsurge had subsided. In a way the process has been identical in the three main South Asian countries, i.e., India, Pakistan and Sri Lanka, though the magnitude of language problems and reactions toward English have been varied. It is difficult to sum up the current policy of the South Asian governments towards English.[54] On the whole, English continues as an important *link language* for national and international purposes. And one or more of the regional languages is given the status of a national language. In Sri Lanka, Sinhalese and Tamil have that status. The Constitution of India (Articles 343–51) decrees that 'Hindi in Devanagari script' is the 'official language of the Union'. In addition to Hindi the Indian Constitution also recognizes sixteen other languages, including English and Sanskrit. In Pakistan, Urdu is recognized as the national language; while, in Bangladesh, the official language is Bengali.

In language planning, religious and political considerations determine policies.[55] Consider, for example, the following statement of Hamid Ahmad Khan, Vice-Chancellor, University of Punjab:

It is difficult to express yourself in a language in which you do not think, and it is therefore desirable to develop Urdu so that it becomes rooted in West Pakistan. *Urdu, like Bengali, is an India-based language. Ultimately, we do not want in this country to have India-based languages* (Khan 1964:279; my italics).

The new role assigned to the SALs has created new problems in *language planning*. Pietrzyk (1964; see also Kachru 1971) has discussed these problems in relation to Hindi in India. In South Asia English is now to be viewed essentially as a *link* or *complementary* language.[56] The recent position is presented in chapter 2, especially section 6.0.

The *three-language formula* has been proposed by the present Indian government. It involves learning three languages, namely the regional language, Hindi and English. The so-called Hindi-speaking area, according to this formula, is expected to encourage the study of a Dravidian language from the south. This formula has not been accepted by all states. Kachru (1971) sums up the present position of English in India as follows:

In India English is the widely taught second language at practically all levels of education. All the Indian universities, graduate colleges, and junior colleges have separate departments for the teaching of English. But unfortunately in these departments a majority of students get no serious exposure to English as a living language. Their appreciation of the classics of English—often taught to a dazed class—is very superficial. The teachers are not trained at all in the basic methodology of teaching languages or in teaching the structure of English. This has created a serious pedagogical and educational problem.

The English departments and professors of English continue to believe that teaching literature is 'prestigious'. The result is that there is a large number of teachers of literature with no enthusiasm for language teaching. The textbooks and teaching techniques are outdated and often not relevant to the Indian context or appropriate to the future needs of a student.

A small group of scholars and educators has realized the problem. After serious deliberation, a Central Institute of English was set up in Hyderabad in 1958 (see Kachru 1975b): It was later renamed the Central Institute of English and Foreign Languages. The announcement of the Institute reads as follows:

Whereas, considering the falling standards of English in India, especially at the secondary stage of education, it is deemed necessary to take steps to improve the teaching of English, both through organization of research in the teaching of this subject and the training of teachers in the most suitable techniques. . . .

Some of the education ministries of various states have also started regional institutes of English which function in close co-operation with the Central Institute of English and Foreign Languages.

The approach to the teaching of English is becoming increasingly realistic. Professors of English and academic administrators are slowly realizing that there is a pressing need (1) to develop 'register-oriented' teaching materials in English suitable to the Indian educational system; (2) to train teachers of English at all levels in contemporary methods of language teaching and in the different branches of the linguistic sciences; (3) to reorganize graduate and undergraduate programme in English both in literature and in language; (4) to reduce the dichotomy between literature-oriented and language-oriented faculties; (5) to develop a realistic attitude toward teaching English literature in India; and above all, (6) to initiate debate and co-operation among literary scholars and language specialists in Indian universities, so the Indian scholars themselves can give some theoretical foundations to the teaching of English and also make it goal-oriented and significant to Indian linguistic, cultural and educational settings.

The new Indian approach to the teaching of English has to be relevant to the needs of students at different levels in the Indian educational system. It is also being realized that the training centres for the teaching of English as a foreign (or second) language in the English-speaking countries (America or Britain) are unable and ill equipped to understand the problems of the non-English speaking areas of Asia. Their current programmes, therefore, have no serious relevance to these countries. There is also cynicism about the academic content and theoretical foundations of such Western programmes. (See Kachru 1971: 5–6.)

7.2.

The term *South Asian English writers* includes not only creative writers but also SAE journalists. The importance of the SAE press can be seen from the part English newspapers play among overall daily publications in South Asia (See Tables 1.5-1.6).

The statistics for book production in South Asia further demonstrates that the functions of English in the linguistically pluralistic subcontinent are very significant. According to various statistical surveys, partially presented below, we are able to get some idea about the importance of English in book publication (see, *UNESCO Statistical Yearbook*, 1972

TABLE 1.5. *Number of newspapers and periodicals published in India according to language and periodicity, 1978*

Language	Dailies	Weeklies	Others	Total
Assamese	3	16	34	53
Bengali	31	321	786	1,138
English	95	352	2,638	3,085
Gujarati	36	157	441	634
Hindi	294	1,961	1,941	4,196
Kannada	59	137	277	473
Malayalam	96	90	423	609
Marathi	102	296	515	913
Oriya	10	23	135	168
Punjabi	21	140	188	349
Sanskrit	2	3	22	27
Sindhi	4	12	46	62
Tamil	50	105	548	703
Telugu	24	130	329	483
Urdu	103	569	458	1,130
Bilingual	23	312	943	1,278
Multilingual	5	63	236	304
Others	24	38	146	208
Total	982	4,725	10,106	15,813

Source: Press in India, Part 1, 1979. Ministry of Information and Broadcasting, Government of India.

TABLE 1.6. *Daily newspapers in different languages in Bangladesh, Nepal, Pakistan and Sri Lanka, 1981*

Countries	Languages Bengali	English	Nepali	Newari	Sindhi	Sinhalese	Tamil	Urdu	Total
Bangladesh	35	5							40
Nepal		5	4	1					10
Pakistan		12			12			88	112
Sri Lanka		4				4	2		10

[pp. 700–701] and 1980 [p. 1070], and *The Statistical Yearbook*, United Nations, New York, 1979 [pp. 943–45]).

Let us consider first the case of India. In 1970, out of the total books published, 33% were in English, followed by Hindi (18.6%), Marathi (8.1%), Bengali (7.4%), and Tamil (6.7%). The other languages ranged between 5.2% (Gujarati) and 0.4% (Sanskrit). In 1975 and 1976, to choose two years from the 1970s, the figures for English were the highest, again followed by Hindi. It is interesting that this trend compares favourably with earlier years, too, for example, 1957 and 1964. In 1957, out of the total publications, 40.8% were in English and 17.5% in Hindi. In 1964, English publications accounted for 51.2% and Hindi publications for 12.8%. As Ray (1969:121) shows, the comparative figures between English and Hindi for 1957 and 1964, show an increase of 25% for English in 1964, and a decrease of 37% for Hindi in that same year.

The statistics for book production in various languages in Pakistan and Sri Lanka present a somewhat different profile from India. But even in that profile, the role of English in these countries is significant, though considerably less than that of India. In Pakistan, for example, in 1977, a total of 1331 books were published. Out of these, 357 were in English, 835 in Urdu, and the rest in other languages. For the same year, a total of 533 books were published in Sri Lanka. The highest figure was in Sinhala (267). The difference between Tamil and English was that of one book, 108 and 107 publications, respectively. There are no figures available for Bangladesh and Nepal. The above figures, and the figures for other years not given here, provide an important insight into the domains in which English is used. I have made no attempt here to break down these figures into books in each area of specialization.

A large number of these figures, certainly for India, account for books in various genres (e.g., fiction, poetry, criticism) written by SAE creative writers. I will not discuss the position of an SAE creative writer here. I have, however, briefly referred to it in this chapter and other chapters. In a way, in terms of the attitude toward such writers, their position continues to be ambivalent. At home they are still suspect and, on the whole, in the wider international context they do not, even now, feel very secure. They are suspect in the sense that the writers of regional languages suspect their loyalties and motivations as writers.[57] They are insecure because they really do not know what their position is in the vast world of the English-using creative writers. They look at English as the medium which raises their creative capabilities before the international reading public. This is both an advantage and a challenge. Iyengar has discussed the creative writer's problem in detail (1962:17). Gokak sums up the attitude of SAE writers as follows:

The English language has linked India with the world. It has conducted sparks of inspiration from the world outside to India and from India to the world. We are blessed with the two-way traffic that English has afforded us. We have paid a heavy price in the past for this privilege. But in our indignation over the price that has been paid, let us not throw away the privilege that is already ours. We may then have to condemn ourselves like Othello:

> of one whose hand,
> Like the base Indian, threw a pearl away
> Richer than all his tribe.

English is certainly not richer than our tribe. But it is a pearl all the same, and it would be foolish to throw it away. (Gokak 1964:178–79).

In this section I have very briefly shown the conflicting atttudes in South Asia toward English, and the influence of these attitudes on language planning. The situation is not finally settled. In the present context, it is difficult to visualize what the role of the English language will be in South Asia after two decades.[58] The following remarks, written by J. R. Firth in 1930, remain very meaningful: they were meant for India (then undivided), but they apply to the whole of South Asia.

Of all the civilized peoples of the world, the Indians are faced with the most difficult cultural and linguistic problems. It is becoming increasingly clear that the 'higher' but psittacistic, alien culture will have to be sacrificed to popular enlightenment in the popular languages. And the great chemists and physicists of India will soon be able to do their work in Urdu or Bengali or Tamil quite as well as in English. The superficiality characteristic of Indian education is an inheritance from the superficial Lord Macaulay. And so long as the English language is the instrument of power in the land, it will be difficult to get fathers ambitious for their sons to take their own languages seriously. But if India is to take any sort of equal place in our Commonwealth they will have to be taken seriously, and the sooner the better. It has often been said that Indian education was organized to turn out clerks. But by far the greater number of Indians 'literate' in English are not even good clerks. The few brilliant men succeed in spite of the system. The increasing Indianization of the Services will make the abandonment of English as the official language of the more or less autonomous provinces easier of accomplishment. The few Englishmen who go to provincial services can do their work in the official language of the province.

English will still be necessary at Imperial Headquarters and perhaps in the
central Assemblies for many years, though the mutually intelligible Hindi-
Urdu-Hindustani might eventually be more satisfactory, as they are spoken by
over ninety million people. That English, even in an Indian form, can ever be
more than a second language to the future educated classes of India, it is quite
impossible to believe. (Firth 1930:210–11)

In 1930 it took a Firth to say this. To a large extent his words have
been prophetic and are still true.

8.0. CONCLUSION

In this review SAE has been seen in a wider context by including the
process of bilingualism in English in this region, and also by including
attitudes toward English. The discussion on the spread of bilingualism
was considered essential in order to put the development of SAE in the
right perspective. I have throughout emphasized the formal aspects of
the South Asian variety of English but, at the same time, the formal
and non-formal aspects have been viewed in the whole linguistic and
cultural setting of South Asia. One might say with justification that a
South Asian variety of 'educated' English has developed, both in the
spoken and written modes. The large body of South Asian writing in
English (e.g., fiction, poetry, prose) has by now established itself as an
important part of the Commonwealth literatures in English.

It has also been argued that the English language has not only been
South Asianized by the South Asian linguistic and sociological contexts,
but, what is more important, on its part the English language has left
a definite mark on the major SALs and literatures. Thus the process
of influence has been two way.

It is difficult to assess the future of the English language in South
Asia. One can, however, definitely say that, both from linguistic and
literary points of view, the English language has contributed substantially to the languages of the area and has also been influenced by the
sociolinguistic setting. This impact has added a new dimension to both
the English language and literature and the languages and literatures
of South Asia. In many respects this is a unique example of the growth
of an international language with different varieties (and sub-varieties)
on different continents.

NOTES

This chapter is a revised version of 'English in South Asia' in Thomas A. Sebeok, ed., *Current Trends in Linguistics, Vol.5, Linguistics in South Asia* (The Hague: Mouton, 1969), pp. 477–551. An updated version was published in Joshua A. Fishman, ed., *Advances in the Study of Social Multilingualism* (The Hague: Mouton, 1978), p. 627–78. In this version there are several additions and modifications.

1. I shall use the term *variety* to mean two or more varieties of a language 'developed' in different *contextual* settings. These may either be those varieties which are used as *first* or *primary* languages (e.g., American English, British English, Canadian English), or those varieties which are used as *second* or *foreign* languages, (e.g., Indian English, Filipino English, West African English or Japanese English). Note also that following J. C. Catford's convention I shall use the abbreviations L$_1$ for a *first* or *primary* language, and L$_2$ for a *second* or *foreign* language. See Catford 1959.

2. In Yule and Burnell 1903, there is the following note: 'A disparaging term applied to half-casters or *Eurasians* (q.v.) (corresponding to the Lip-Lap of the Dutch in Java) and also to their manner of speech. The word is said to be taken from *chi* (Fie!), a common native (S. Indian) interjection of remonstrance or reproof, supposed to be much used by the class in question . . .' p. 186. See also p. 133 for *butler-English*.

3. Cf., e.g., the use of the term in Whitworth 1932. An earlier edition was published in England (Letchworth, Herts in 1907). See also Passé, 1947. Cf. also Mathai 1951:96–100. 'Indian English has sometimes been the subject of amusement and has been made fun of under names like "Babu English". It is true that some Indian users of English made amusing mistakes . . . in unwarranted coinages and "portmanteau" expressions. As examples of unEnglish expressions that may be met with in the speech and writing of even well-educated Indians we may cite "to marry with", "to make friendship with", "make one's both ends meet", "England-returned", "a pindrop silence", "a failed B.A.", "a welcome address". . . . Expressions such as these are recognized as wrong or clumsy by the more careful writers and speakers in India, but certain neologisms of Indian origin are frequently used even by the most careful.' (p. 98–9).

4. For a brief discussion and excellent bibliography on the historical aspects of Indian education and the role of English in it, see Nurullah and Naik 1951. For a discussion on this and related topics see also Chatterjee 1976; Desai 1964; Hennessey 1969; John 1969; Kachru 1982d; McCully 1940; Rajagopalachari 1962; Sinha 1978 and M. Verma 1974.

5. See Morris 1904; see also 'Observations on the State of Society among the Asiatic-Subjects of Great Britian, particularly with respect to morals, and the means of improving it' by Charles Grant (1831–2:8.734).

6. *Parliament Debate*, 26:562–3 (1813).

7. The following excerpts from his letter are illuminating:
   'Humbly reluctant as the natives of India are to obtrude upon the notice of Government the sentiments they entertain on any public measure, there are circumstances when silence would be carrying this respectful feeling to culpable excess. The present Rulers of India, coming from a distance of many thousand miles to govern a

people whose language, literature, manners, customs and ideas are almost entirely new and strange to them, cannot easily become so intimately acquainted with their real circumstances as the natives of the country are themselves. We should therefore be guilty of ourselves, and afford our Rulers just ground of complaint at our apathy, did we omit on occasions of importance like the present to supply them with such accurate information as might enable them to devise and adopt measures calculated to be beneficial to the country, and thus second by our local knowledge and experience, their declared benevolent intentions for its improvement.'

'... When this Seminary of learning (Sanskrit School in Calcutta) was proposed, we understand that the Government in England had ordered a considerable sum of money to be annually devoted to the instruction of its Indian subjects. We were filled with sanguine hopes that this sum would be laid out in employing European gentlemen of talents and education to instruct the natives of India in mathematics, natural philosophy, chemistry, anatomy, and other useful sciences, which the natives of Europe have carried to a degree of perfection that has raised them above the inhabitants of other parts of the world....'

'... We now find that the Government are establishing a Sanskrit school under Hindoo Pundits to impart such knowledge as is clearly current in India....'

Roy then gives some arguments against spending money on Sanskrit studies and continues:

'If it had been intended to keep the British nation in ignorance of real knowledge the Baconian philosophy would not have been allowed to displace the system of the schoolmen, which was the best calculated to keep the country in darkness, if such had been the policy of the British legislature...' Cf. Roy 1823:99–101. See also Wadia 1954:1–13. Note also the following remarks of Deb 1965:8:

'It has been a misfortune that no discussion of the beginnings of English studies in India has brought to the fore the sociocultural as opposed to the political facts. I have heard not merely polemists and hot-headed revivalists but sincere educationists telling me that English was forced on the Indian public by the English conquerors of India. The facts are very much otherwise. English was not taught because the English desired it; in the beginning they were actively opposed to such a measure, but because Indians wanted it for their advancement. Specially the Hindo [*sic*] majority and the growing urban Hindo middle class whether in Calcutta or in Madras anxiously demanded it, not merely to get out of the hands of the narrow-minded and corrupt Mughal Government of the day, but also to find a way to the light of the clear and unsullied world of Western science and thought, away from the close and oppressive air of the Sanskritic learning of the day.' (p. 6). '... it would be a prejudiced version of the history of India which said that English was forced upon the Indian, it was welcomed by the Indian, specially between 1815 and 1890, if not as late as 1905. No more distinguished thinkers could be chosen from among the eminent men of the years 1800–50 than Raja Ram Mohan Roy and Dwarka Nath Tagore. Both were opposed to the teaching of Sanskrit, if it was to continue in the old pattern; they felt that the mind of India's youth was being shut off from the light of the modern world. The leaders who followed these two great men were equally anxious to keep up the study of English. They felt that, in spite of the humiliation of political subjugation, so complete after 1857, India and England should not be opposed to one another in the field of education and intellectual enquiry.'

(p. 8). For a discussion on Macaulay see also Banerji 1878; Chatterjee 1976; Clive 1973; Singh 1964 and Sinha 1978.

8. Cf. *Selections from Educational Records* 1781–1839:103–5 (see Sharp, ed.)
9. *Selections from Educational Records* 1781–1839:103–5.
10. *Selections from Educational Records* 1781–1839:116.
11. *Selections from Educational Records* 1781–1839:109.
12. Historically this Dispatch is significant in two ways: First, it emphasizes the use of *vernaculars* instead of Sanskrit and Arabic. Second, it says, 'The English language should be taught where there is a demand for it.' See *Selections from Educational Records*, 1800–1900:367–8.
13. This statement does not include Bengali, Tamil, Telugu, etc.
14. Cf. Halliday 1961:3. Most of the technical terms in this chapter have been used roughly in the Hallidayan sense.
15. The term 'educated' is used here in the sense in which J. R. Firth uses 'educated English' (Firth 1930:198–9): 'Educated English, then, shows wide range of permissible variation in pronunciation and usage. It is controlled partly by a literary norm and partly by social sanctions, though the half educated often abandon good local speech for something which is difficult to refer to a norm.... On account of the wide range of permissible variation, educated English is difficult to describe. Many speakers of educated English have an accent, traceable to familiar or local speech habits. They are apt to use words which among the "best" people would sound "bookish". They do not exactly talk like books, but they sometimes give common social currency to words and phrases which in other circles are meant to be seen and not heard.'
16. Yule and Burnell, 1903:344. The term *Anglo-Indian* was originally used for persons of mixed European and Indian blood. Also see Bayer 1979; Spencer 1966 and Valentine 1978.
17. See, for example, Passé 1947:34. He suggested 'modified English' as a possible standard for Sri Lanka. 'For practical and other reasons the almost certain course will be the teaching of the Sinhalese variety of "Modified Standard" English.'
18. *The Statesman's Yearbook* 1979:603. These figures include Sikkim and exclude the Pakistan-occupied areas of Jammu and Kashmir.
19. *The Statesman's Yearbook* 1979:873.
20. *The Statesman's Yearbook* 1979:949. Note that in this chapter the term Indian subcontinent refers to political entities, such as India, Pakistan and Bangladesh.
21. For a detailed discussion on the languages of South Asia and South Asia as a *linguistic area* see *Census of India, 1961*, 1964:1:2c(ii). CLIX-CCXXVI. Language Tables: Brown, ed., 1960; Dil 1966; Emeneau 1955, 1956 and Masica 1976.
22. Cf. Perren and Halloway 1965. See also *Census of India, 1961*, op. cit. Note that this is not an exhaustive list and includes only the major languages. The Tibeto-Burman group and the tribal languages have not been included here.
23. See Hunt 1931; 1935. See also Gokak 1964:6. He has given a large number of examples to illustrate that 'There seem to be as many kinds of English as there are candidates appearing for an examination.' This helps in showing how SAE writers greatly vary in their competence in the language. See especially pp. 6–9.
24. This is used as a technical term. Cf. Kachru 1966:26 ff; also cf. Halliday *et al*. 1964:87–98.

25. The language-wise distribution of some of the selected studies which consider L_1 transfer into L_2 is as follows:

   1.   Dravidian:
   (a) *Kannada :* Sreekantaiya 1940 ; Viswanath 1964.
   (b) *Tamil :* Theivananthampillai 1968, 1970.
   (c) *Telugu :* Anantham 1959.
   2.   Indo-Aryan:
   (a) *Bengali :* Hai and Ball 1961 ; Jalil 1963 ; Datta 1972–3.
   (b) *Gujarati :* Harry 1962.
   (c) *Hindi :* Bansal 1962 ; Hill 1959 ; Kachru 1959 ; Spencer 1957.
   (d) *Marathi :* Kelkar 1957 ; Limaye 1965.
   (e) *Oriya :* Dhall 1965.
        (f) *Sinhalese :* Passé 1947 ; DeLanerolle 1953 ; Samarajiva and Abeysekera 1964 ; Samarajiva, 1967.

26. For the phonetic analysis of these two varieties see Gopalkrishnan 1960 ; Passé 1947 ; S. Varma 1957.

27. This does not necessarily apply to Sinhalese.

28. Cf. studies listed in note 25.

29. Since some of the caste dialects vary in their phonological systems, this naturally reflects on the speakers' L_2. See, e.g., Bright 1960a.

30. For a discussion of religious dialects with special reference to Kashmiri see Kachru 1969b, 1973b.

31. Usmani 1965: 120. Note also that his phonemicization of Urdu vowels is as misleading as are his statements on the stress system and intonation in Urdu.

32. Gopalkrishnan 1960. The transcription of the segmental phonemes in the examples is the same as given by the author. I doubt that differences are only of stress.

33. Cf. Taylor 1969. Also note the following observations of Spencer 1957: 66–7, about the stress pattern of the Anglo-Indian speakers of English in India : 'It is, however, in certain prosodic features that the most distinctive deviation from R.P. [Received Pronunciation] is to be observed ; in particular the relationship between stress, pitch and syllable length. The tendency in Anglo-Indian is for stressed syllables to be accompanied by a fall in pitch ; indeed for a fall or low-rise to replace stress, since Anglo-Indian pronunciation does not show such marked variations in syllable intensity as R. P. The fall in pitch on the "stressed" syllable is normally followed by a rise on the succeeding syllable, even on final unstressed syllables in statements. The tonic "accent" is accompanied by a lengthening of the syllable in question ; but this lengthening usually takes the form of a doubling of the final consonant(s) before the transition to the following "unstressed" syllable.'

34. See Abercrombie 1964 for a discussion on stress-timed languages and syllable-timed languages. Note also that in the South Asian languages, by and large, there is no distinction between contracted forms and noncontracted forms in verbs ; that may be one of the reasons why SAE sounds more *bookish* than *conversational* (cf. section 3.6 Style Features and 'Tone'). For a detailed discussion on this topic see Nelson 1982.

35. E.g., Shivendra K. Verma using the scale and category model of Halliday, has worked out a comparative description of Hindi and English verbal groups (see Verma 1964) ; see also Manindra K. Varma 1971. See Aggarwal 1982 for other references.

36. Kachru 1961. The two restricted texts were taken from the debates on 'fisheries', i.e., (i) *Lok Sabha Debates* 4:5, 7 April 1953 and (ii) *Parliament Debates* (Commons), 25 July 1955.
37. Kindersley 1938:25. Note the following abbreviations which Kindersley uses: B, Bengal; Bo., Bombay and Sind; D, Dravidian linguistic area of South India; Dr., Modern Dravidian languages of South India; E, English; Guj., Gujarati; H, Hindustani; IA, Modern Indo-Aryan languages of India; Ind E, Indian English; P, Punjab; Tam., Tamil; Tel., Telegu [*sic*]. He adds: 'The initials P, B, and D signify, unless the word "only" is affixed, that, in addition to being common in the Bombay Presidency and Sind, the usage in question is found in common use in the province or area indicated' (fn. p.25).
38. Wilson 1855. '*Ryot* and *Ryotwar*, for instance, suggest more precise and positive notions in connection with the subject of the land revenue in the South of India, than would be conveyed by cultivator, or peasant, or agriculturalist, or by an agreement for rent or revenue with the individual members of the agricultural classes.' p.i. (Cf. also K.S.N. Rao 1961: 3, footnote 1).
39. Yule and Burnell 1903. An Indian edition (reprint) of it has been published by Munshiram Manoharlal, Delhi in 1968.
40. For a detailed discussion of the term 'collocation' see Halliday 1961 and 1966; Kachru 1966: 265 ff.
41. Passé 1947, footnote 4. Note that Goffin 1934 has termed such deviations 'phrase-mongering' and Passé 1947 'errors of expression that have become more or less fixed in Ceylon [Sri Lankan] English and which the user would be startled and shocked to hear stigmatized as "unEnglish".' It is obvious that Passé has taken a stand from a pedagogical point of view and ignores the underlying linguistic reasons. Another view on Lankan English is presented in Kandiah 1981.
42. Smith-Pearse 1934. Note that this is essentially a pedagogical manual for the guidance of school teachers.
43. For the meaning of this and the following abbreviations see the List of Abbreviations on pp. xv-xvi.
44. A detailed treatment of this aspect is given in Kachru 1975a. Also cf. Kachru 1965.
45. The term 'tone' is used in a non-technical sense, as used by Goffin 1934.
46. For a detailed account of it see Iyengar 1945, 1962; Kandiah 1971; Lal 1969; Mukherjee 1971; Naik *et al.* 1968; Narasimhaiah 1976; Parthasarathy 1976 and Sarma 1978.
47. Cf. Anand 1948 and Bhushan 1945a and 1945b. Bhushan uses the term 'Indo-English'. These two works of Bhushan are representative anthologies of Indian English poetry and Indian English prose. See also Dustoor 1954, 1955; Jha 1940.
48. Also Passé 1947 has given a large number of such items from Sri Lankan English, for example, consider the following: *place, junction, fronthouse.*
49. Kachru 1966: 278–80. Notice also the use of such items as *fissiparous tendencies* (*Leader* 23 November 1965).
50. There is a large number of published and unpublished works on this aspect of South Asian languages. In this study I shall restrict it to some selected features of Hindi. Note also the following remarks of Priyaranjan Sen (1932:382–3). 'We have found that the literature has been affected by its contact with an alien culture, a foreign literature, and that the changes extend both to the thoughts which constitute the

matter or contents, and also to the forms of expression both in prose and verse. The language itself shows signs of the new influences; there has been remarkable con-tribution to the vocabulary; the prose style has been formed and the poetic improved in quality.... Bengali drama has been practically a new form; such has been the case with Bengali novels; and the epic has grown into something new, quite distinct from the *mangal gans* that has been the vogue in the centuries that had preceded. The lyric also shows abundant signs of the richness of the new influence, and its technique at the present day, the prosody and the phrasing owes much to the model of English literature. The greatest change, however, is noticeable in Bengali prose. Whether the essay or the periodical literature, the prose biography or history through prose, theological dissertations or philosophical discourse—everything is a departure from the established ways of the previous centuries. If this is so with regard to the mere form, how much remains to be said as regards the spirit of the literature, its new moods and tendencies, its matter and contents!'

51.   Mishra 1963:179. Mishra uses Jespersen's definition of an amorphous sentence. See O. Jespersen 1933: 105: 'While the sentences of complete predicational nexuses are (often, at any rate) intellectual and formed so as to satisfy the strict requirements of logicians, amorphous sentences are more suitable for the emotional side of human nature. When anyone wants to give vent to stong feeling, he does not stop to consi-der the logical analysis of his ideas, but language furnishes him with a great many adequate means of bringing the state of his mind to the consciousness of his hearer or hearers.'

52.   See Tickoo 1963. Note also the following interesting observation of Passe 1947:33. 'It is worth noting, too, that Ceylonese [Sri Lankans] who speak "standard Eng-lish" are generally unpopular. There are several reasons for this: those who now speak standard English either belong to a favoured social class, with long purses which can take them to the English public schools and universities, and so are dis-liked too much to be imitated, or have rather painfully acquired this kind of speech for social reasons and so are regarded as the apes of their betters; they are singular in speaking English as the majority of their countrymen cannot or will not speak it ... standard English has thus rather unpleasant associations when it is spoken by Ceylonese [Sri Lankans].' See also Kachru 1976a, 1977 and 1982a.

53.   The reaction of L1 speakers of English has varied during the last two decades. Ear-lier it was more patronizing than critical. Only recently SAE writing has been cri-tically evaluated. Note also Balachandra Rajan's following observation on Indian English writers in Rajan 1965. 'The difficulties are compounded for the writer in English. There is a sense in which English has never had it so good. The obituary notices for the language, written and postponed over the last seventeen years, have now been reluctantly withdrawn. English is described in officialese as a "link lan-guage" which means that an instrument of imperialist exploitation has now been ironically transformed into an important force in bringing about national unity.... The *bonafides* of the writer in English are continually being impugned. Using what is allegedly a foreign language, he is said to be incapable of expressing the inward-ness of Indianness. He is accused of selling his artistic conscience for financial re-wards, though one glance at his royalty statements will usually show that he earns considerably less than the writer in Bengali or Malayalam. His mixed sensibility is not only cosmopolitan but rootless. He has no nationality and therefore no iden-tity. The critical assumptions behind these attacks (which, characteristically, are

usually made in English) do not deserve serious scrutiny. . . . A further rite of extenuation is the pursuit of chimeras such as Indian English. This is not to deny the possibility of an English specific to India, rooted in both the contemporary and the metaphysical landscape. Such an English, however, can only emerge as the creative product of writers determined to be writers. It cannot spring from gestures of cultural appeasement; and it must at all times be clear that if a man writes in English which enables his vision to proclaim its deeper life, it cannot be held against him that his language is not "Indian". Nationality is only a blueprint unless authenticity makes it a creative act.'

54. For a detailed treatment of the language question in India see *Report of the Official Language Commission, 1956* (1957); Asrani 1964; Narasimhaiah 1964; Pande 1964; Shah, ed., 1968. See also Brass 1974, Das Gupta 1970 and Kachru 1982d.

55. A summary of these problems about South Asia is given in the following among others, Dil 1966; Kandiah 1964; Le Page 1964; Perren and Holloway 1965.

56. Cf. Mathai 1951:101, 'When we remember that after nearly a century of English education only something like 3 per cent of the population know English, it seems obvious that English cannot be the language in which the millions of India will be educated. In 1900 the urban population of India received English as the language of the future, a knowledge of which was essential for their advancement. Today, though English is still the only language that serves as a *lingua franca*, and a knowledge of it is still necessary for participation in national and international affairs, it seems certain that the future in India does not lie with English. What will actually happen in the future it is difficult to say, but it seems clear that for many years to come it will be in India's interest to retain English at least as an important second language and thus keep open her only door to the knowledge and culture of the larger world.'

57. Iyengar 1962:17, discussing the position of Indian English creative writers in India, says: '. . . the interest in Indo-Anglian literature is pitifully fitful, and the impression still is that the Indo-Anglians are India's literary cranks if not worse, that their work lacks both vitality and any intrinsic worth, and that it is best to leave them alone'. Cf. also Rajan 1965 and fn 53 above. See also S. N. Sridhar 1982.

58. The arguments of the anti- and pro-English groups have been discussed, among others, in the following works: Kanungo 1962; Rajagopalachari 1962; Shah, ed., 1968; Wadia 1954. See also Aggarwal 1982 for other references.

2

Indian English: A Sociolinguistic Profile

1.0. The linguistically and culturally pluralistic Indian subcontinent provides two primary cases of language acculturation which involve the Indianization of foreign languages. In chronological terms, the first case is that of the Persian language, and the second, that of English. The result of such acculturation is the development of two distinct non-native Indian varieties of these two languages, termed *Indian Persian* and *Indian English*. These terms are used both in a geographical sense and in a linguistic sense. In geographical terms, Indian Persian and Indian English refer to those varieties of these two languages which developed on what was traditionally called the Indian subcontinent and now includes Bangladesh, India, Nepal and Pakistan. In linguistic terms, the modifier *Indian* refers to the linguistic processes used by Indians toward the Indianization of Persian and English which then resulted in the *Indianness* of these two languages. The Persian parallel is important here, because to a large extent the processes of Indianization have been more or less identical in both the languages. I am not presently concerned with the discussion of Indian Persian, but the analogy is important in order to understand the development of Indian English.

As we have seen in the previous chapter, the linguistic characteristics of Indian English are transparent in the Indian English sound system (phonology), sentence construction (syntax), vocabulary (lexis), and meaning (semantics). There are already several studies which discuss these aspects.[1] The reasons for these transparent Indian features are not difficult to find. In India, Indian English is generally used as a second language, which is acquired after one has learnt a first language, or what is usually called the *mother tongue*. This then results in *interference* (or *transfer*) from one's mother tongue in the second language.[2] We see the same principle at work, for example, in the non-native varieties of Hindi. When we identify a person as a speaker of *South Indian Hindi* or *Kashmiri Hindi*, we are actually referring to such transferred characteristics. The problem of interference in Indian English becomes more complex, since the interference is caused by a large number of mother tongues. The Indian constitution recognizes fifteen major languages, and the Census Report identifies over 1,652 languages and dialects.[3]

The other reason, for the existence of Indian features, which is often neglected in the literature, is that in India the English language is used in a different sociocultural context than that of, say, the United States, Australia or Britain. The distinct sociocultural parameters in which English has been used in India for almost two hundred years have resulted in a large number of innovations which have been termed *Indianisms* (Kachru 1965: 405–8). This is not a unique linguistic situation; a large number of Americanisms or Australianisms are labeled as such because the English-speaking settlers in America and Australia were using the English language in a new context and had to mould that language to the context of the new world. (For Americanisms, see Mencken 1941: 113–21; for Australianisms, see Morris 1898: 160; Ramson 1966.) In our discussion of Indian English we shall, therefore, consider linguistic interference and the Indian cultural context as essential for the understanding and description of the *Indianness* of this variety of English.

2.0. HISTORY

We are concerned not with the history of the English language, but with the development of one non-native variety which we have already labeled *Indian English*. Therefore, we shall restrict this section to the introduction of bilingualism in English in India, its various stages of implementation, its various uses, and the eventual development of this 'alien' language into an *Indianized* variety.

In the previous chapter (section 2) I have marked three phases in the introduction of bilingualism in English in India. The first, the missionary phase, includes the efforts of the Christian missionaries who went to the Indian subcontinent to proselytize (see Duff 1837; Sherring 1884, Richter 1908, Law 1915). The second phase was essentially that of local demand for English, during which prominent Indians such as Raja Rammohun Roy (1772–1833) and Rajunath Hari Navalkar (fl. 1770) made efforts to persuade the officials of the East India Company to impart instruction in English, rather than Sanskrit (or Arabic), so that young Indians would be exposed to the scientific knowledge of the West. In their view, the exclusive dependence of Indians on Sanskrit, Persian, Arabic or what they termed the Indian vernaculars would not contribute to this goal. As evidence of such local demand it is customary to present the letter of Raja Rammohun Roy addressed to Lord Amherst (1773–1857) dated 11 December 1823. In his letter Roy expresses disappointment at the establishment of a Sanskrit School in Calcutta, rather than using the available funds for

employing European gentlemen of talent and education to instruct the natives of India in mathematics, natural philosophy, chemistry, anatomy, and other useful sciences, which the natives of Europe have carried to a degree of perfection that has raised them above the inhabitants of other parts of the world (Sharp 1920: 99–101; also Wadia 1954: 1–13; see also ch. 1, note 7, pp. 59–60).

It is claimed that Roy's letter was responsible for starting the well-known Oriental-Anglicist controversy which forms a fascinating chapter in the history of education in India.

This controversy resulted in the third phase and culminated in the prolonged and insightful discussion on the merits and demerits of the Oriental and Anglicist (Occidental) educational systems for India. This phase began after 1765, when the earlier political manoeuvring of the East India Company finally resulted in the stabilization of the Company's authority. At that time there were primarily two attitudes towards introducing English on the Indian subcontinent; even the administrators of the raj themselves were divided into two groups. The Anglicist group included Charles Grant (1746–1823), Lord Moira (1754-1826) and T. B. Macaulay (1800–59). The spokesman for the Orientalist group was H. T. Prinsep (1792–1878), who disagreed with the Anglicist point of view and expressed his view in a note dated 15 February 1835. The dissenting group, however, could not stop the highly controversial and far-reaching Minute of Macaulay from passing (on 2 February 1835): Macaulay's aim, as he indicates in the Minute, was to form a subculture in India:

a class who may be interpreters between us and the millions whom we govern, a class of persons, Indian in blood and colour, but English in taste, in opinion, in morals and in intellect.

On 7 March 1835, the Minute finally received a Seal of Approval from Lord William Bentick (1774–1839), and an official resolution endorsing Macaulay's resolution was passed. (For details see Clive 1973: 342–426.) This resolution formed the cornerstone of the implementation of a language policy in India, and ultimately resulted in the diffusion of bilingualism in English. It is still controversial whether this decision to impose an 'alien' language on Indians was correct. There is disagreement among Indian and Western scholars on this point, and extreme positions have been presented by both the groups. One such view is presented by J. R. Firth, in his characteristic way, when he says that the 'superficiality characteristic of Indian education is an inheritance from the superficial Lord Macaulay' (Firth 1930: 210–11). It is said that, twenty years after Macaulay wrote the Minute on education, he came across it once more and expressed the judgement that 'it made a great revolution' (Clive 1973 : 426). In retrospect, after almost one and a half centuries, one must grant him that. (See also Banerjee 1878; Chatterjee 1976; Chaudhuri 1976 and Sinha 1978.)

In the years that followed, as the raj established a firm hold on India, the Anglicization of Indian education became greater, and slowly the English language gained deeper roots in an alien linguistic, cultural, administrative and educational setting. The period between 1765 and 1947 was thus the era of British patronage and encouragement of the English language in India. The first three universities were established in India in 1857, at Bombay, Calcutta, and Madras; two more universities were added by the end of the century, at Allahabad and Punjab (Lahore). By 1928 English had been accepted as the language of the élite, of the administration, and of the pan-Indian press. Although the English newspapers claimed only a limited circulation, they had acquired an influential reading public. In addition, another phenomenon with a far-reaching consequence was slowly developing, that of Indian literature in English.

3.0. VARIATION

I have already used the term 'Indian English' within the context of South Asian English in the earlier chapter without providing the necessary definition of it. I shall attempt to define it in this section. The cover term Indian English does not mean that there is complete homogeneity in the use of English in India, nor does it imply that all the Indian users of English have uniform proficiency in understanding and performance. One might ideally desire such a situation, but in the real world of first or second-language use, one does not encounter such situations. Since, a uniformity in *standard* or in language *use* is not a characteristic of a human language, one must look for variation and determine whether such variation can be explained in terms of functional, sociocultural, or educational parameters.

The variation in Indian English may be explained basically on three parameters: region, ethnic group and proficiency. In the case of Indian English, regional or geographical variation by and large coincides with the regional language. The underlying reason for regional varieties such as Gujarati English (e.g., Harry 1962), Marathi English (e.g., Kelkar 1957), and Tamil English (e.g., Gopalkrishnan 1960) is the mother tongue of the speaker of each variety. The ethnic varieties of Indian English have yet to be studied in a serious sense, though, as I mentioned in chapter 1, claims have been made concerning special characteristics of Anglo-Indian English (e.g., in Bayer 1979, Spencer 1966 and Valentine 1978). Ethnic variation cuts across the regional language or dialect boundaries. The question of variation based on proficiency is crucial in the case of a second language, and can be better explained with reference to the *cline of bilingualism* which was first presented in Kachru (1965:393–96). I have, in the previous chapter, briefly discussed this concept and shown that there is a *cline* of Englishes in India ranging from *educated* Indian English to varieties such as *Babu English, Butler English, Bearer English* and *Kitchen English*.

It is interesting that varieties such as *Kitchen English* or *Babu English* are sometimes used by Indians with native speakers of English; in turn, native speakers use the same type of language so that the Indian speaker of such a variety can understand them. It is an attempt to communicate in a variety of language which has undergone a process of pidginization. A good example of this is given in Yule and Burnell (1903: 133–4; see also Schuchardt 1891 [1980]):

The broken English spoken by native servants in the Madras Presidency; which is not very much better than the Pigeon-English [*sic*] of China. It is a singular dialect; the present participle, e.g., being used for the future indicative, and the preterite indicative being formed by 'done'; thus *I telling* = 'I will tell'; *I done tell* = 'I have told'; *done come* = 'actually arrived'. Peculiar meanings are also attached to words.... The oddest characteristic about this jargon is (or was) that masters used it in speaking to their servants as well as servants to their masters.

We might then say that the Indian English speech community comprises all the above discussed varieties. At the one end of the spectrum we have educated (or standard) Indian English, and at the other end we have Kitchen English. Other varieties, such as Babu English, appear at various points on the spectrum. The following observation of Quirk *et al.* (1972:49) is appropriate here:

In the Indian and African countries, we find an even spectrum of kinds of English, which extends from those most like Pidgin to those most like standard English, with imperceptible gradations the whole way along.

The standard variety of Indian English is used by those bilinguals who rank around the central point on the cline of bilingualism. In numerical terms, Indian English users constitute only 3% of the Indian population; that is, out of the total population there are seventeen million speakers of Indian English. This figure is impressive, considering that the total percentage of speakers of several 'scheduled languages' in India is less than the percentage of the speakers of English, or close to that figure, for example, Assamese (1.63%), Kannada (3.96%), Kashmiri (0.44%), Malayalam (4%), Oriya (3.62%), Punjabi (3%) and Sindhi (0.31%).

English is the state language of two states in eastern India, Meghalaya and Nagaland. It is the main medium of instruction in most institutions of higher learning at the postgraduate level. It is taught as a second language at every stage of education in all states of India.[4]

As a medium for inter-state communication, the pan-Indian press and broadcasting, English has been used as a most powerful tool both before and since India's independence. The statistical profile of the role of English in the Indian press presented in the 23rd Annual Report of the Registrar of Newspapers for India (1979) demonstrates that the impact of English is not only continuing but increasing.

The English press in India initiated serious journalism in the subcontinent. Out of the seven daily papers in India which have been in existence for over one hundred years, four are published in English, the other three in Gujarati. The four English newspapers are the *Times of India*, Bombay (1850); the *Pioneer*, Lucknow (1865); the *Mail*, Madras (1867); and *Amrita Bazar Patrika*, Calcutta (1868). Out of a total of 15,814 newspapers registered in India in 1978, those in English accounted for 19.5% (3,085). The newspapers in Hindi accounted for 26.5% (4,196). The Hindi newspapers had the highest circulation (23.8%), followed by the English newspapers (22%). Of the number of periodicals published by the Central Government, those in English show the highest percentage (53%); the second highest number (16%) appear in Hindi. A comparative table of the total number of newspapers published in India during 1974–78 is instructive. This number includes dailies, tri-bi-weeklies, weeklies and others.

Indianization of English

TABLE 2.1. *Number of newspapers published in India, 1974–78.*

Language	Year				
	1974	1975	1976	1977	1978
Assamese	32	38	49	50	53
Bengali	739	771	855	1,003	1,138
English	2,453	2,559	2,765	2,892	3,085
Gujarati	569	567	580	618	634
Hindi	3,200	3,142	3,289	3,736	4,196
Kannada	331	348	392	432	473
Kashmiri	1	1	1	1	1
Malayalam	465	498	539	567	609
Marathi	717	748	806	861	913
Oriya	128	135	138	151	168
Punjabi	268	259	278	312	349
Sanskrit	22	22	23	27	27
Sindhi	59	55	58	61	62
Tamil	527	556	618	653	703
Telugu	425	418	441	463	483
Urdu	915	929	975	1,047	1,130
Bilingual	989	992	1,087	1,194	1,278
Multilingual	224	247	264	279	304
Others	121	138	162	184	208
Total	12,185	12,423	13,320	14,531	15,814

Source: Press in India, Part 1, 1975–79. Ministry of Information and Broadcasting, Government of India.

The total number of periodicals devoted to specialized areas in 1978 was 14,741. A significant number of these was published in English (2,983) and Hindi (3,878). In 1978 the English language newspapers were the second largest (3,085), as compared to 1977 (2,892), thus showing an increase of 6.7%. The English-language press represented 19.5% of the Indian press in 1978.

English newspapers are published in practically every part of India, providing evidence of the pan-Indianness of the English language. Out of 31 State and Union Territories in India, English newspapers and periodicals are published in 28, including virtually every part of the country except Arunachal Pradesh and Lakshadweep. The next two languages with an all-India spread are Hindi-Urdu and Sanskrit, in which newspapers or periodicals are published in 21 states and 13 territories.[5]

4.0. DESCRIPTION

The available descriptions of the various aspects of *educated* or *standard* Indian English are very fragmentary. One reason for this lack of research may be the language attitude which both Indian and non-Indian speakers of English have shown toward this variety of English (see Prator 1968; Kachru 1969a, and 1976a). As discussed in chapter 1, this attitude manifests itself in terms such as *Babu English* or *Cheechee English* which were earlier used for this variety. Even the term *Indian English* was used in a derogatory sense; Indians normally would not identify themselves as members of the *Indian* English speech community, preferring instead to consider themselves speakers of British English.[6] I shall present below certain selected characteristic features of Indian English. The observations made here relate to both the spoken and written forms of this variety of English.

A word of caution is in order with reference to the formations included from the written form of Indian English. A number of these formations are specifically used in particular types of writing, e.g., in legal writing, in newspaper advertisements or in Indian English fiction. In this sense, then, these are functionally restricted, and in statistical terms such formations have a low probability of occurrence in Indian English in general. In linguistic literature such functionally determined items are termed *register-bound*. One might consider, for example, the formation *salt giver* in Mulk Raj Anand's fiction to be as much a part of Indian English as James Joyce's or E. E. Cummings's linguistic innovations are a part of British English and American English respectively. The difference is that one must be careful to identify these as register-bound or author-bound.

In the spoken form, the term 'educated Indian English' is used in the same sense in which one might use 'educated British English,' 'educated American English', or 'educated Hindi.' Educated speakers of these languages do not speak in identical ways—far from it. Their spoken language shows characteristics of class, area and education, as does the spoken English of educated Indians. An Indian English user reveals other characteristics, too; his English might display certain features which show that his mother tongue is Bengali or Hindi or Punjabi. If his mother tongue is Bengali, the chances are that he will not make a distinction between [s] as in *same* and [ʃ] as in *shame*. A Hindi speaker finds [ɪsteɪʃn] easier to pronounce than the combination of *st* in the initial position in words such as *station*. One can add to this list from other Indian languages, but the illustrations are not crucial. What is important is the underlying reason for this type of pattern which a bilingual demonstrates in his or her second language. The phenomena of variation are not unique to Indian English. The homogeneity of a speech community is an ideal to which linguists aspire, but it is not a characteristic of human language. Therefore, if we say that there are American *Englishes*, British *Englishes*, or Indian *Englishes*, we are near the truth.

It is worth emphasizing that, in spite of variation of various types, there are several characteristics which the users of educated Indian English share. An Indian English speaker intuitively recognizes another Indian English speaker; at the same time he categorizes him as an 'educated' speaker, or as one who does not come up to that standard. In India, then, the concept of a standard or educated Indian English is not as elusive as purists or cynics (e.g., Prator 1968) tend to believe. But, at the same time, when we study Indian English we are essentially making a study of a *second language* in a bilingual or a multilingual context. In such a context, as we have discussed earlier, the effect of transfer, or what linguists term *interference*, cannot be ignored.

The term *bilingual* implies that such a person has two linguistic systems which he uses for communication in appropriate situations. A multilingual person has, on the other hand, more than two linguistic systems which he might use in his various spheres of activity. In bilingual (or multilingual) situations, therefore, *transfer* (see chapter 4, pp. 131–32) or *interference* takes place. The transfer (or interference) is generally from a dominant language (say, a mother tongue) to a less dominant language (say, a second language). There are also cases where the opposite might happen. In India there are several examples of this situation; specifically, one can take the case of English. The Indianization of the English language is generally discussed in the literature on the subject, but there are examples of the Englishization of Indian languages, too; this influence is seen on their sound systems, grammars and, of course, on their vocabularies (see Kachru 1978b and 1979). The extent of interference is also closely linked with the cline of bilingualism. The more interference in a person's English, the lower the person ranks on the cline.

4.1. *Sound System*

A number of observations have been made in various studies to characterize the Indianness in Indian pronunciation of English; these are crucial for understanding deviations at this level. It is due to these characteristics that one can isolate the transparent features of Indian English. As I have stated in the first chapter these and other grammatical, lexical and semantic characteristics may be considered area features and termed *South Asian English*. I shall discuss some of the important characteristics below under various categories.

The first category is that of *systemic differences*. The term *system* is used here in a syntagmatic sense and refers primarily to the differences in the consonant or vowel inventory between English and Indian English, or one of its regional dialects. In comparing the syllable structure of English and, say, Hindi, one will find that both these languages have *CVC* syllable structure. While this is a correct observation, this similarity can be misleading, since the items which comprise the total consonant inventory of one language may not be identical to the inventory of the other. The consonants [f, θ, ð] in English do not occur in the consonant inventory of any major Indian language, a fact which leads to the substitution of [ph, th, dh] for these sounds in Indian English. There is no need to elaborate on this point, since it has been discussed even in elementary textbooks.

The second category is that of *distributional differences*. The items in the consonant or vowel inventory may have some shared items which are phonetically identical, but their distribution may not be identical. Again let us take an example from Hindi-Urdu. In Hindi-Urdu and in English we find the consonant combinations (clusters) *sk*, *sl*, *sp*, but the distribution of these clusters in these languages is different. In Indian English as spoken in the Hindi area we find that English *station*, *school*, *stool*, *speech* are pronounced as [ɪsteɪʃn], [ɪsku:l], [ɪstu:l], [ɪspi:tʃ] respectively, because in Hindi the clusters *st*, *sk*, *sp* do not occur in the initial position. This is one clue which marks the Indian English speakers of the Hindi area from the Indian English speakers elsewhere.

The third category is termed *series substitution*. This means that a complete series of consonants from an Indian language may be transferred into Indian English. An often discussed example of typical Indian pronunciation of English is the substitution for the English alveolar of a retroflex series.

The fourth category may be termed *prosodic transfer*. This involves the main non-segmental characteristics of Indian English, for example, deviation in the stress system. English is a stress-timed language, as opposed to most of the Indian languages, which are syllable-timed. This difference between English and the Indian languages results in distinct rhythms : in syllable-timed languages the rhythm is based on arranging long and short syllables, while in stress-timed languages it is based on the arrangement of stressed and unstressed syllables. This seems to be one of the main linguistic factors which impedes intelligibility between an Indian English speaker and a native English speaker. Systemic differences and distributional differences do not seem to be crucial for intelligibility (see Bansal 1969 and Nelson 1982).

4.2. *Grammar*

A detailed grammatical description of educated Indian English is not yet available. The following statements, therefore, do not present an outline of the total range of the deviation in Indian English. The term *deviation* is used in a special sense here and is not to be confused with *mistake* (see Kachru 1965:396–7 and 1982a) :

A mistake may be defined as any 'deviation' which is rejected by a native speaker of English as out of the linguistic 'code' of the English language, and which may not be justified in Indian English on formal and/or contextual grounds. A deviation, on the other hand, may involve differences from a norm, but such deviations may be explained in terms of the cultural and/or linguistic context in which a language functions.

A number of these observations are *variety-oriented* and mark members of the Indian English speech community as separate from users of other varieties of English. The other type of observations are *register oriented*. These features are characteristic of the typical registers of Indian English, which are definable with reference to the functions of Indian English in typically Indian sociocultural settings. Consider, for example, the following collocations, used primarily in the Indian political context : *salt march* (*RH* 36), *salt-laws* (*HA* 55) or the much used *fissiparous tendencies* (*L* 23 November 1965). A detailed list of these and such other collocations may be found in Goffin (1934) and in Kachru (1965, 1969a, 1975a). The third type of collocations are *author oriented* and may be present only in the works of creative Indian English writers who write about typically Indian contexts. These would include, among others, Mulk Raj Anand (b. 1905), Raja Rao (b. 1909) and R. K. Narayan

(b. 1906). Such collocations provide linguistic clues to the style of a specific author (see Desai 1974). There are also features which are *text specific* and may not be generalized as features of the total literary output of a writer. For example, the style of *Kanthapura* cannot be generalized as the style of Raja Rao, just as we cannot generalize the style of 'any one lived in a pretty how town' as the style of E. E. Cummings. In both these cases it is important to understand the style of the text in order to understand the total *style repertoires* of Raja Rao or E. E. Cummings.

We find that linguistically definable Indianisms present a spectrum, and each item needs careful categorization. At one end, this spectrum presents statistically frequent Indianisms which may be generalized as *variety-oriented* features; at the other end it presents *text-specific* and statistically marginal features such as the formation *may the vessel of your life never float on the sea of existence (C 20)*. This formation is both author-restricted and text-specific, but it is a possible formation in Indian English, as are the 'deviant' formations of Cummings or Joyce in other Englishes. When it is claimed (Mukherjee 1971:214) that one cannot 'postulate Indian English' based on examples drawn from Indo-Anglian writers', one is confronting a confusion between language *use* and *prescriptivism*. It becomes more confusing when Mukherjee further claims (1971:214):

The Indo-Anglian writer should be allowed the freedom to experiment with the language for his own artistic needs rather than be heaved into a system of linguistics in search of that elusive medium—a standard Indian English.

Standard Indian English is no more 'elusive' than is standard American English or standard West African English. An individual author experiments with the style repertoire which a speech community uses, whether for 'artistic' or practical needs. In the description of language use, 'artistic needs' for creative use of language are as much a part of the total range of language use as is purely functional use (e.g., in ordering one's meal). In general observations about Indian English, the concern is not necessarily with the scope, range, and statistical frequency of formations: A judgment of that type is valid, of course, but not relevant to our present discussion.

I shall now discuss certain grammatical characteristics which mark 'educated' Indian English as deviant from the 'educated' native varieties of English. First, let us consider some features involving sentence and clause structure. There is no large-scale empirical study which would provide a detailed analysis, but intuitively, and on the basis of very restricted analyses, it is claimed that Indian English has a tendency toward using complex noun and verb phrases and rather long sentences. The following excerpt from *Kanthapura* (p. 56) is illustrative:

The day rose into the air and with it rose the dust of the morning, and the carts began to creak round the bulging rocks and the coppery peaks, and the sun fell into the river and pierced it to the pebbles, while the carts rolled on and on, fair carts of the Kanthapura fair. . . .

One cannot generalize, since R. K. Narayan's style is the opposite of Raja Rao's. But stylistic characteristics do not have to be uniform; generalizations are indicative of tendencies .

Second, in constructions at the phrase level (verb phrase or noun phrase) we find several features. Let us consider, as an example, the *be* + verb + *ing* construction in Indian English. In such constructions some Indian English users seem to 'violate' the selectional restriction applicable to such constructions in the native varieties of English, where the members of the subclass of verbs such as *hear* and *see* do not occur in the progressive tenses. This restriction, on the other hand, does not apply to Hindi-Urdu verbs *sunnā* 'to hear', *dekhnā* 'to see' (e.g., *mãi sun rahā hū̃* 'I' 'listen' 'progressive' 'am'; 'I am listening'; *mãi dekh rahā hū̃* 'I' 'see' 'progressive' 'am'; 'I am seeing'). The tendency is to extend this feature to Indian English. In the use of tenses there are several other features discussed in Kindersley (1938:25; also see chapter 1, pp. 34–36).

Third, characteristics may be defined in terms of systemic variation. An often-discussed illustration of such deviations is the use of articles in Indian English. (See Dustoor 1954: 1–70; 1955: 1–17). It is not claimed here that Indian English necessarily displays a consistently 'deviant' pattern in the use of articles. The picture is one of arbitrary use of *the*, *a/an* and ∅ article. In Dustoor (1954, 1955) very descriptive labels have been used to categorize the Indian deviations in the use of articles, such as 'missing and intrusive articles in Indian English', and 'wrong, usurping and dispossessed articles in Indian English'.

The fourth characteristic, that of reduplication, is both syntactic and semantic, entailing reduplication of items belonging to various word classes. This aspect has been discussed with illustrations in chapter 1. As an aside, it might be mentioned that Indian English users, for example, share this characteristic with the users of West African English and

Black American English. In the spoken form it is not uncommon to come across examples such as *he sells different different things, I have some small small things, give them one one piece.* In the written form one can provide a large number of examples from, among others, Raja Rao or Mulk Raj Anand, e.g., *hot, hot coffee (CB1); long long hair (CB71).* The reduplication is used for various syntactic and semantic reasons. In Hindi-Urdu, the reduplicated items fall into two main categories. In one there is a choice between selecting a reduplicated item or a non-reduplicated item, with the choice entailing no semantic difference. In the second category no such choice is involved, since the reduplicated or non-reduplicated items do not have semantically 'identical' functions. Consider, for example, the following:

(1)   rām ne khāte khāte kahā ki...
      Ram said while eating that...
(2)   rām ne khāte hue kahā ki...
      Ram said while eating that...
(3)   rām ne čalte čalte kahā ki...
      Ram said while walking that...
(4)   rām ne čalte hue kahā ki...
      Ram said while walking that...

The above (1) and (2) are understood in the same way, but there are two interpretations for (3) and (4). In Indian English reduplication is used for *emphasis* and to indicate *continuation* of a process. Raja Rao seems to use it for intensification of a situation, or to underscore an act, for example: '*With these very eyes, with these very eyes, I have seen the ghosts of more than a hundred young men and women, all killed by magic, by magic....*' (Rao 1978b: 84). In this example the reduplication of a phrase provides the effect of colloquial speech, as well as giving linguistic clues to mark a character type.

The fifth characteristic concerns the formation of interrogative constructions in which Indian English speakers do not necessarily change the position of the subject and the auxiliary items. Consider, for example, *What you would like to eat?* or *Really, you are finished?* The tag questions in Indian English also show the influence of the first languages. It is not uncommon to find either a general 'it' in all tag-questions, (e.g., *You have taken my book, isn't it? He has left, isn't it?*) or simply a negative particle in the tag question (as in *She borrowed my book, no?*).

One may also discuss here certain formations which fo--- both grammar and lexis. Some of the linguistic devices used such formations are very productive. I have earlier used the term *Indian English collocations* for such formations (Kachru 1965, 1966, 1969a, 1973a, 1975a). There is no need to provide a linguistic definition of the term 'collocation' here: it refers to the tendency of certain lexical items to keep company with a set of other lexical items. In other words, there is a mutual expectancy and a tendency of co-occurrence between certain words in a language. One might say that knowledge about the constraints of mutual expectancy of lexical items forms a part of a native speaker's competence in a language. The formation *silly ass* in English is often given as an example of a collocation. A *silly ass* means more than what the two lexical items mean individually—for a native speaker of English, these words signal a lot more than a four-legged animal.

The use of English in India for almost two hundred years has naturally nativized the company which English words traditionally keep in their non-Indian settings. The Indian linguistic and cultural context has either extended the membership of the set of items with which lexical items can co-occur, or new, typically Indian collocations have been formed. The Indian collocations naturally sound 'foreign' to native speakers; after all, these have to be understood in the Indian context (Kachru 1975a). Therefore, a large number of typically Indian collocations mark Indian English as distinct from other varieties of English. Let us now examine the process involved in the Indianization of typically Indian English collocations. A collocation might be marked as Indian either in terms of its constituent members, or in terms of its extended or restricted semantic range. I have discussed such formations with illustrations in chapter 4 (section 6).

The concept *interference*, with reference to the sound system of Indian English, has already been mentioned. The interference is not restricted to one level only; it shows in grammar, lexis, collocations and transfer of idioms from Indian languages into English. In lexis or in idioms, this process manifests itself in what is termed *translation*. The translated items vary in their assimilation in the target language—the language which absorbs the items. The list of such items in Indian English is a long one. Let us consider, for example, the following: *twice born* (*U* 14) 'dvija'; *waist-thread* (*HW* 190) 'kaṭiḍorā'; *dining-leaf* (*WM* 84) 'pattal'. At first glance these items appear to be unEnglish, but one can find several contextual arguments for their existence in Indian English, the most convincing one being that these formations make sense in Indian English—they have a meaning with reference to Indian culture. It is true that translated idioms sometimes stand out without being assimilated; they may even remain marginal in terms of use. But so did *a marriage of convenience* or *it goes without saying* when these were first translated from French into English. It is a rare scholar who would be curious to find out their ancestry, to identify their source. In Indian English the translated idioms *may the fire of ovens consume you* (*C* 78), *a crocodile in a loincloth* (*HW* 217) sound rather unusual now, but there is no linguistic reason to consider them so. The formation *pin drop silence* appears less deviant, the reason being that we have heard it often and have used it for a long time. The following comparative constructions in *Kanthapura* are translations which have a typical Indian character, and convey the Indianness which the author obviously intended to convey: *as honest as an elephant* (12), *as good as kitchen ashes* (46), *helpless as a calf* (55), *lean as an areca-nut tree* (259). A construction which is more English would perhaps sound less deviant, but then it would also be less Indian—therefore, less effective.

4.3. *Lexis*

The compilation of Indian words entitled *Hobson-Jobson* (1886) has provided linguistic entertainment for generations of Indian scholars and students of Indo-British cultural, political and linguistic relations. It was, however, not the first compilation of its kind. A number of lexical lists had been compiled before *Hobson-Jobson*, primarily to facilitate the work of administrators involved with Indian affairs. Sir Charles Wilkin appended a glossary of such Indian words to the *Fifth Report* of the Select Committee submitted in 1812. A later work by Wilson (1885; first edition 1855) entitled *Glossary of Judicial and Revenue Terms*, provided the basis for Yule and Burnell's monumental compilation, *Hobson-Jobson*. The latest additions to this aspect of Indian English are *Indian Words in English* by Rao (1954), Kachru (1975a) and the 'Supplement of Indian Words' to the *Little Oxford Dictionary* (1976).

Let me explain what we mean by Indian English lexis. The term 'lexis' is used here roughly in the sense of 'vocabulary,' [7] and refers to two characteristic types of Indian English vocabulary. A large part of the Indian English vocabulary is used essentially in Indian contexts and is restricted in use to Indian English; it is not shared with the native varieties (say, American or British English). The second part consists of those items which do not have such a variety specific constraint and have thus become part of the borrowed lexicons of other Englishes too. One might term such items *assimilated items*, that is, assimilated in the lexicon of the English language. (For details, see chapters 5 and 6.)

The earliest Indian source items to intrude into the English language were the ones used in travel literature concerning South Asia. Later, the needs of administration and the particular sociocultural context of India encouraged the use of such already established Indian words.

After the East India Company was firmly established in India and communication with India was increasing, there were two attitudes toward borrowing Indian source items into the English language; one of linguistic purism, and the other of linguistic tolerance. (See chap. 5, pp. 149-52.) However, this borrowing process could not be stopped and the attitude of linguistic tolerance prevailed. As a result, we now find that various types of lexical innovations are used in Indian English; we shall discuss some of the more important innovations here. The largest body of such items involves *single item transfer* from Indian languages into Indian English (Kachru 1975a). These items are restricted in their use to India and have not yet been assimilated into British or American English. They need not be assimilated in these varieties since the contexts for their use are exclusively Indian, and are restricted to typically Indian registers of law, politics, society and newspaper writing. The second type may be termed *hybridized items*. A hybridized (or mixed) formation comprises two or more lexical items, in which at least one is from an Indian language and one from English. Consider, for example, *lathi-charge* (*HS* 15 June 1959), *kumkum mark* (*K* 159), *tiffin carrier* (*DD* 78), *goonda ordinance* (*S* 23 December 1970). Such formations are further divided into two subgroups, i.e., *open set hybrid items* and *closed system hybrid items*. An open set item does not have any grammatical constraints on the selection of the members of a hybridized item (e.g., *kumkum mark*). On the other hand, a closed system item has certain grammatical constraints, e.g., *-wala* in *policewala* (*SMH* 61), *-hood* in *Brahminhood*, *-dom* in *cooliedom*, and *-ism* in *goondaism*. (See chapter 5, pp. 153-54.) One might make several other observations about such formations, both about their form and contextual distribution: These have been discussed in chapter 5. A reader interested in this aspect of Indian English will find detailed lists and discussions in the following works, among others: Yule and Burnell (1886), Wilson (1940 [1885]), Rao (1954), Kachru (1975a and 1980b) and Sagert (1951).

4.4. *Semantics*

The Indian semantic features of the Indian variety of English may be characterized as (1) semantic restriction of English words; (2) semantic extension of English words; (3) archaisms which have been preserved in Indian English and are no longer current in the native varieties of English; (4) register shifts which involve the use of items without register constraints in Indian English; and (5) contextual redefinition of lexical items.

In order to account for semantic restriction and extension (above 1 and 2), the Indian English lexicon has to assign [+] and/or [−] Indian semantic features to such items. The lexical items may either be from an Indian source language (e.g., *ahimsa, satyagraha*) or from English (e.g., *cousin-sister*). I have given examples to illustrate this point in chapter 5 (see esp. pp. 154-62).

An item is considered an *archaism* if it is no longer used in the same sense in the native varieties of English (cf. the use of *bosom* in Indian English). The register shift may involve items from one or more of the above categories. Consider, for example, the following items, which have high frequency of use both in spoken and written Indian English: *communal, interdine, intermarriage*. These items involve a register shift and also 'contextual redefinition' in the sociocultural and linguistic context of India.

5.0. INTELLIGIBILITY

At this point, since we have already briefly discussed some illustrations of the Indianness of Indian English at various linguistic levels, it may be appropriate to pause and ask two questions. First, in spite of regional and language-bound variations, is Indian English intelligible to Indians all over the subcontinent? Second, is Indian English intelligible to educated native speakers of English, for example, from Britain or America? As I have stated elsewhere (Kachru 1976a), very little and superficial empirical research has been done concerning the intelligibility of non-native varieties of English. It is an extremely fertile area for research, but has yet to attract the serious attention of theoretical and applied linguists.

In answer to the first question, on the basis of experience, one can claim that 'standard' or 'educated' Indian English has pan-Indian intelligibility. That does not mean, however, that an educated Indian speaker of English does not reveal some regional characteristics in his speech. These characteristics are of the same nature as one may find in the speech of an educated British or American speaker of English.

In the written medium several pan-Indian registers (such as the administrative and legal) have already developed. These are distinctly Indian in their lexical and (some) grammatical characteristics. In English newspapers one also notices regional lexical innovations, and other formations, which are language-bound and are transferred to English due to the influence of the mother tongue. In order to find such formations one has, for example, only to look through *The Mail* in Madras, *The Amrita Bazar Patrika* in Calcutta, the *Tribune* in Chandigarh or the *Searchlight* in Patna.

The intelligibility of Indian English by native speakers forms a cline; some Indians are fully intelligible, others less so. This again is an area in which very little empirical research has been done. Bansal (1969) has presented some results which are relevant to this question. In the following table I have summarized the main conclusions of his study. It presents the results of tests for measuring intelligibility between the speakers of the following varieties of English: (1) Indian English speakers and native speakers of American English and Received Pronunciation; (2) Indian English speakers and other non-native speakers of English—Germans and Nigerians; (3) Indian English speakers with other Indian English speakers.

TABLE 2.2. *The intelligibility of Indian English (Test results)*

Participants in test	Highest%	Lowest%	Average
1. Indian English & RP speakers (group)	73	67	70
2. Indian English & RP speakers (cline of intelligibility)	95	53	
3. Indian English & American English speakers	81	72	74
4. Indian English & German speakers	67	40	57
5. Indian English speakers & Nigerians	66	34	53
6. Indian English speakers with other Indian English speakers	88	54	74
7. RP speakers with other RP speakers	100	95	97

The highest and the average figures in Table 2.2 are of interest. It is evident that an educated Indian speaker of English maintains his Indianness and has not cultivated what Firth (1930 [reprinted 1966:200]) would consider 'a shameful negative English which effectually masks social and local origin and is a suppression of all that is vital in speech' (see also Nelson 1982).

6.0. INDIAN ENGLISH LITERATURE

The growth and development of *Indian English Literature* was earlier viewed with considerable skepticism, and its literary merit and contribution as an *Indian* literature was discussed with great cynicism. In recent years, however, especially since the 1950s, the attitude toward Indian English and evaluation of its literary contribution have undergone a change both in India and in other English-speaking countries. This changed attitude is succinctly summed up by Iyengar (1962:3): 'Indian writing in English is but one of the voices in which India speaks. It is a new voice, no doubt, but it is as much Indian as others.'

In the long literary tradition of India, the only other languages which acquired pan-Indian literary traditions were Sanskrit and (much later and to a smaller extent) Indian Persian, (primarily in the north of India). In recent years Hindi has been aspiring to such a role, but its national impact has not been of the same degree as that of Indian English. It should, however, be mentioned here that in India there are only three literatures which have pan-Indian reading public —although numerically very small ones—Indian English, Hindi and Sanskrit.

By the term *Indian English Literature* (or *Writing*) is meant the fast-growing body of literature which is written by Indians using English as their *second* language. As a minor digression it may be mentioned here that in this respect the English language is unique among the present world languages. In the last three or four decades, a considerable body of creative writing has developed in English written by non-native users of the language, especially in West Africa, the Philippines and South Asia. (For a detailed discussion, see Bailey and Robinson 1973, Ramchand 1973, S. Sridhar 1982 and Bailey and Görlach 1982.) Indian English literature is thus an important constitutent of the 'new Englishes' which have developed in the Commonwealth countries and other parts of the world.[8]

A brief discussion of the term *Indian English Literature* may be appropriate here, especially since this term is not unanimously accepted. As mentioned in chapter 1, there has been considerable polemic argumentation concerning a name for this body of writing. Because the use of various names with various implications has resulted in some confusion, I shall discuss some of these labels here. The term *Anglo-Indian* writing is used with reference to that body of creative writing which focuses on the Indian subcontinent as the central theme, and is written by those who use English as their *first* language; e.g., E.M. Forster, Rudyard Kipling, John Masters and Paul Scott. The Anglo-Indian writers are not to be confused with the Indian ethnic group with the same name. The contribution of this group of writers is linguistically interesting for two reasons: they coined many contextually deviant collocations in English which are relevant to the Indian sociocultural and political context, and they borrowed a number of words from South Asian languages into English, primarily to add what is termed 'local colour'. A detailed critical evaluation of such writing from a literary point is given in Oaten (1908) and Singh (1934). The awkward-sounding and semantically confusing term *Indo-Anglian* writing is used for the work of 'those who are Indian *and* who have written in English' (Mukherjee 1971: 15). During World War II the term *Indo-Anglican* gained currency; in recent literature, fortunately, it is not too often used. Another term, *Indo-English*, was alternately used with Indo-Anglican, but on the whole the battle of terms now seems to have subsided, in favour of the self-explanatory and less confusing *Indian English Literature* (or *Indian Writing in English*). In certain circles the hesitation to use this term is primarily attitudinal. The modifier *Indian* with English seems to imply a second-class status for some scholars; in linguistic literature this term has, however, been in use for a long time, though not always with desirable attitudinal connotations (see chapter 1, pp. 42-43).

The short history of Indian English literature has been one of controversy and schizophrenia in identity (Lal 1969). Indian creative writers who write in languages other than English suspect the integrity of writers who use an 'alien' language for creative purposes. Writers in other English-speaking countries treat them as marginal to the mainstream of English literature. But in spite of these controversies in recent years, especially after Indian independence, Indian English literature has steadily grown in various literary forms, e.g., fiction (Mukherjee 1971), poetry (Iyengar 1962, esp. 427-31; Lal 1969: i-xliv; Parthasarathy 1976), essays (Iyengar 1962: 344-69), and journalism (Chalapati Rau 1974). Indian political writing in English in India dates back to Rammohun Roy (1772–1833) and continued with renewed vigour during the struggle for Indian independence.

In the 1930s the attitude toward Indian English literature was much different from what it is today, as has been shown in the observations of Singh (1934:306) and Gokak (1964:162) quoted in the previous chapter.

A historical study of Indian English literature with critical comments is present in the following works, among others: Iyengar (1943, 1962), McCutchion (1968) and Mukherjee (1971). In the last decade several anthologies of poems have also been published (e.g., Daruwalla 1980, Deshpande 1974, Gokak 1970, Parthasarathy 1976, Peeradina 1971).

Indian English fiction is now being studied and discussed in the entire English-speaking world by those interested in the Indian subcontinent or in non-native Englishes, and by linguists for its thematic and stylistic Indianness. At least half a dozen Indian English novelists have created a small but slowly increasing international reading public for themselves, e.g., Mulk Raj Anand (see Sinha 1972), Anita Desai, Manohar Malgonkar (see Amur 1973), Kamala Markandaya, R. K. Narayan (see Holmstrom 1973, Sundaram 1973), Raja Rao (see Naik 1972, Narasimhaiah 1973), and Khushwant Singh (see Shahane 1972) and Nayantara Sehgal.

The position of Indian English poets seems to be rather precarious. The Bengali poet and critic Buddhadeva Bose does not present merely his own opinion when he says:

It may seem surprising that Indians, who have always had a firm poetic tradition in their own languages, should ever have tried to write verse in English. That they did so was an outcome of the Anglomania which seized some upperclass Indians in the early years of British rule. (quoted in Lal 1969: 3–4).

In the same note, entitled 'Indian Poetry in English', Bose refers to the present scene:

There are still a few Indians (both parents natives) who claim English to be their 'best' language. What circumstances led to this inconceivable loss of a mother tongue, or whether they had abjured it voluntarily, cannot be ascertained...

Then discussing their reading public, Bose continues:

The fact is that the 'Indo-Anglians' do not have a real public in India, where literature is defined in terms of the different native languages, and their claim can be justified only by appreciation in England or the United States.

Bose then concludes with an often quoted reminder of Yeats:

As late as 1937, Yeats reminded Indian writers that 'No man can think or write with music and vigour except in his mother tongue'; to the great majority of Indians this admonition was unnecessary, but the intrepid few who left it unheeded do not yet realize that 'Indo-Anglian' poetry is a blind alley, lined with curio shops, leading nowhere.

This is, of course, one view, an extreme view: this argument has been presented against the Indian English writers for a long time now. A very stimulating discussion on Bose's paper is presented in Lal (1969), and provides an overview of Indian English poetry and the reactions of several poets toward Bose's position (see esp. i–xliv, 3–7).

The tradition of Indian English poetry is not recent; it goes back to, among others, Sri Aurobindo (1872–1950), Manmohan Ghose (1869–1924), Toru Dutt (1857–77) and Sarojini Naidu (1879–1949). In Bhushan (1945a, and 1945b) and Gokak (1970) a number of other poets are mentioned (see also Bose 1968). In the last fifteen years several anthologies of such poetry and a number of single collections of poems have been published. The number of Indian English poets is fast growing, and their poetic output varies from half a dozen poems to several collections. One can mention the following, among others, as representative poets: Kamala Das (b. 1934), Keki Daruwalla (b. 1937), Nissim Ezekiel (b. 1924), Arun Kolatkar (b. 1933), Jayanta Mahapatra (b. 1928), R. Parthasarathy (b. 1934) and A. K. Ramanujan (b. 1929).

The post-independence period has initiated a split among the Indian English writers living on both sides of the sea. This has resulted in

....two different, and sometimes even hostile, streams: the Aliens and the Indigenous writers.... the Aliens (who often retain Indian nationality but prefer to stay abroad for a complex variety of reasons, chief among them being the advantage of living in close proximity to 'pure' English, U-English, and of finding a reasonably well-paying market for their work), are in the final count, contributing to the tradition of *English* literature, while the Indigenous writers are adding to the spectrum of Indian literature (Lal 1969: xviii–xix).

This point of view, of course, is not shared by all.

The use of Indian English has increased in other genres too, e.g., essays, political writing, and newspaper writing (Iyengar 1962, Ramakrishna 1980). In recent years, contrary to the earlier cynicism of some Indians and non-Indians, Indian English literature has substantially increased, its quality and range has improved, and it has established itself as one of the *Indian* literatures. It is now slowly being accepted and recognized both in India and in the English-speaking world as a whole.

7.0. ENGLISH IN INDIA'S LANGUAGE PLANNING

In the post-independence era of India, the role of English has varied from one state to another. Education and educational policy are controlled by the states, and not by the central government. However, in spite of the regional differences in the role of English in the school system, English is taught in every state as the main second language. The total number of years for the teaching of English, and the stages at which a child may be exposed to bilingualism in English are not identical in all the states. By and large, there has been less argumentation, vacillation, and change in the role of English in the central government. Each serious move to reduce the use of English in the central government and to replace it with Hindi has resulted in opposition from some southern states. The policy, therefore, seems to be to continue the *status quo*.

In present language planning in India, as in other linguistically and culturally pluralistic societies, various political, cultural, and social considerations determine the position of English at the state level or national level. There are primarily three questions which continue to be asked and discussed, and to which no generally acceptable answers have yet been found. The first question obviously concerns the position which English should be assigned in early and in higher education. The second question, not unrelated to the first, concerns the proper roles for the regional language, Hindi and English. The third, which concerns English educators, is which model of English should be presented to Indian learners, and how that presentation can be made uniformly and effectively. The answers to these questions are still being sought.

The Government of India has been primarily concerned with the first two questions, since these are directly related to language planning at both the national and at the state levels. The language questions became an explosive national problem and the Government of India has initiated various efforts to probe it. The most important efforts in this direction are listed below. Any discussion aimed at finding a generally acceptable solution to the language question invariably involves the present and future role of English in India. After 1947, the first important step in looking into the overall language question of India was the appointment of the Official Language Commission by the President of India on 7 June 1955, under the Chairmanship of B. G. Kher. It was the duty of the Commission to make recommendations to the President as to

(a) the progressive use of the Hindi language for the official purposes of the Union; (b) restrictions on the use of the English language for all or any of the official purposes of the Union; (c) the language to be used for all or any of the purposes mentioned in Article 348 of the Constitution; (d) the form of numerals to be used for any one or more specified purposes of the Union; (e) the preparation of a time schedule according to which and the manner in which Hindi may gradually replace English as the official language of the Union and as a language for communication between the Union and State Governments and between one State Government and another. . . . (See *Report of the Official Language Commission*, hereafter *ROLC*, 1956: 1.)

The *Report* provides an excellent document for the study of two basic views on the future role of English in India. One was represented by Suniti Kumar Chatterji (see his Note of Dissent, *ROLC* 1956: 271–314) and P. Subbarayan (see his Minute of Dissent, *ROLC* 1956: 315–30). The other view was represented by other members of the Commission (see *ROLC* 1956). This is a monumental report on India's language question, and the future of English in various roles is discussed in detail.

According to Article 343 (2) of the Indian Constitution, the English language was to be used for all official purposes of the Union until 26 January 1965. The Constitution (Article 343 [1]) specified that after this date Hindi was to be the official language. But due to the language controversy (and riots) in various parts of the country, especially in Tamil Nadu in May 1963, Parliament passed the Official Language Act. In order to reassure the non-Hindi groups, the Official Language (Amendment) Act was passed in 1967. The Act specifies that

Notwithstanding the expiration of the period of fifteen years from the commencement of the Constitution, the English language may, as from the appointed day, continue to be used, in addition to Hindi, for all the official purposes of the Union for which it was being used immediately before that day, and for the transaction of business in Parliament.

In the last two decades several commissions have been appointed by various agencies to study the functions of English in India, and to reorganize the curriculum at the school and university levels. We shall briefly discuss some of the more important reports here. In 1950 and 1951 the *Report of the University Education Commission* was published. The Commission was headed by S. Radhakrishnan. Its report presents an in-depth evaluation and plan for Indian education. (For the role of English, see esp. 316–26.) The following observations concerning English are relevant to this study. With reference to the past role of English in India, the report says (316):

> Now it is true that the English language has been one of the potent factors in the development of unity in the country. In fact, the concept of nationality and the sentiment of nationalism are largely the gifts of the English language and literature to India.
> . . .English has become so much a part of our national habit that a plunge into an altogether different system seems attended with unusual risks. It appears to us, however, that the plunge is inevitable. English cannot continue to occupy the place of state language as in the past. The use of English as such divides the people into two nations, the few who govern and the many who are governed, the one unable to talk the language of the other, and mutually uncomprehending. This is a negation of democracy.

Concerning the future role of English, it says that 'we must take into account our Yugadharma,' and, therefore recommends. 'That English be studied in High Schools and in the universities in order that we may keep in touch with the living stream of ever-growing knowledge' (326).

In 1955, the University Grants Commission appointed a Committee under the Chairmanship of H. N. Kunzru. The Kunzru committee submitted its report in December 1957. Its important recommendations are summarized in a later report, as follows (see *Report of the English Review Committee*, 1965 : 39):

(1) That the change from English to an Indian language as the medium of instruction at the university stage should not be hastened.

(2)   That even when a change in the medium of instruction is made, English should continue to be studied by all university students.

(3) That it would be necessary to have textbooks prepared on scientific principles and that the Government of India or the Council of Secondary Education should take up this question for consideration.

(4) That in relation to the Three Year Degree course which is now proposed to be introduced in our universities the teaching of English be given special attention in the pre-university class.

(5) That the teaching of English literature should be related to the study of Indian literatures, so that apart from its value for linguistic purposes, it could be an effective means of stimulating critical thinking and writing in the Indian languages.

(6) That it is desirable to have the question of courses of study in English and methods of teaching English at the university stage examined by an expert body and the recommendations of that body adopted by all the universities.

(7) That where English is not the medium of instruction at any university it is necessary to adopt special methods to secure an adequate knowledge of English as a second language.

(8) That far greater attention should be given to linguistics in our universities and in our teacher training colleges.

(9) That it is in our educational interest that English should be retained as a properly studied second language in our universities even when an Indian language is used as the ordinary medium of teaching.

The recommendations of the Kunzru Commission were presented before a conference of English teachers in 1958 at the Central Institute of English later renamed the Central Institute of English and Foreign Languages in Hyderabad. The recommendations of this conference were primarily concerned with methods, curriculum and textbooks. In February 1960, the University Grants Commission appointed a Committee of Experts under the Chairmanship of G. C. Banerjee to examine the issues involved in the teaching of English. The Committee was charged with the following (*Report of the English Review Committee* 1965:4):

(1) To define the objectives of teaching and learning English at the various levels of university education.

(2) To examine the standards of teaching in English language and literature both at the undergraduate and postgraduate levels.

(3) To examine the methods of teaching English used in our universities and colleges to equip students with the minimum competence required in this regard in the shortest possible time.

(4) To consider measures for reorganizing the M.A. course in English to provide for an intensive study of the language as a tool of knowledge rather than of literature.

(5) To recommend the steps that may be taken to strengthen the teaching of English in the context of the medium of instruction in the universities.

The recommendations of the Committee of Experts are not more insightful than were the recommendations of earlier committees. This report, however, presents another phase in the activity toward breaking the teaching of English away from the earlier approaches, goals and curricula. In addition to these, several other commissions and committees have directly or indirectly looked into the question of the role of English in India's language planning.[9]

In the 1960s many felt that at last a solution to India's language problem had been found in what was termed the *three-language formula*. It involved learning three languages: the regional language, Hindi and English. In the so-called Hindi area it was expected that the study of a Dravidian language would be encouraged, since in that area Hindi would be identical with the regional language. This formula has, however, not been accepted with equal enthusiasm in all states. In the *madhya-deśa* (Central India), the so-called Hindi area, the teaching of a Dravidian language was not taken seriously. In recent implementation of a language planning policy in India, the main focus has been on Hindi and regional languages: The attitude toward English has been one of vacillation and uncertainty.

The current literature on language planning in India and the various languages in Indian education provides the viewpoints and attitudes of various groups. First, there is the Union Ministry of Education, the policies of which are not always acceptable to the State governments. Second, Indian English writers (Lal 1969: i–xliv), have organized themselves in various regional and national groups. And there are anti-English groups, which include the supporters of Hindi and of regional languages. However, in certain states the supporters of the regional languages are not necessarily supporters of Hindi (e.g., in Tamil Nadu and Bengal). The English-knowing élite, traditionally pro-English, has played a very vocal role in the debate on the role of English in India. This élite also includes ethnic groups such as the Anglo-Indians, who identify themselves with the English language and sometimes even claim it to be their mother tongue (Spencer 1966 and Bayer 1979). Whatever the controversies and attitudes toward the future of English in India, one thing is certain: the diffusion of bilingualism in English, creative use of English in the country, and its use as a pan-Indian link language has continued during the post-independence years. (For detailed references see Kachru 1982d.)

8.0. CONCLUSION

The post-Independence years have brought the language controversy to the forefront. In this controversy the English language has been the main focus of argumentation. There is already a substantial body of literature which presents the various views on this controversy (For details, see Ahmad 1941, Shah 1968). This era has also been the most productive period for Indian English literature; indeed it is during this period that this body of literature has acquired the status of an *Indian* literature. The Sahitya Akademi (National Academy of Letters) has awarded several annual prizes to Indian English writers, and various journals have appeared which are specially devoted to such writing, notably *The Journal of Indian Writing in English* (Gulbarga). A number of contributions have also appeared on such writing in, among others, *The Literary Criterion* (Mysore), *The Literary Half-Yearly* (Mysore), *The Indian P.E.N.* (Bombay), and *New Quest* (Pune).

Research on various aspects of Indian English literature has finally caught the attention of Indian academicians and universities (Aggarwal 1982). The change in their attitudes and perspectives is obvious in various writings (see, for example, Lal 1969).

The earlier focus on research on English in Indian universities is changing. A realistic attitude has developed which is significantly different from the earlier tradition of research in universities. A recent survey provides some insights into this changing attitude and disillusionment (Kachru 1975b).

NOTES

This chapter is adapted from 'Indian English: A Sociolinguistic Profile of a Transplanted Language', *Studies in Language Learning* (1976:1.2).

1. A selected number of such studies has been included in the bibliography.

2. A detailed discussion of the theoretical and language-specific aspects of interference is given in Weinreich 1953 (reprinted 1966).

3. See *Distribution of Languages in India in States and Union Territories (Inclusive of Mother Tongues)*, (Mysore: Central Institute of Indian Languages, 1973), p. v. The 'family affiliations' of these languages is as follows: Unclassified, 601; Indo-Aryan, 532; Austric, 53; Dravidian, 148; and Tibeto-Chinese, 227. This list also includes the 9 languages of Sikkim, which brings the total to 1,561.

4. See, for details, *Universities Handbook*, 1979; Mehrotra 1977.

5. The statistical information of the newspapers and periodicals presented in the study is based on *Press in India 1975-1979, 19th-23rd* Annual Reports of the Registrar of Newspapers for India, Part I (New Delhi: Ministry of Information and Broadcasting, Government of India, 1976–1980).

6. In India, the British manner of speech was considered prestigious and was normally the goal of a Western-educated Indian. This goal was very rarely, if ever, attained. A recent survey has shown that even now the British model of English is preferred

by educated Indians over the Indian or American models of English (see Kachru 1976a and 1982a).

7. One can provide a large number of such examples from Indian English newspapers, or from the administrative register.

8. The language contact in India has resulted in a two-way linguistic impact. On the one hand, Indian languages and literatures have influenced foreign ('imposed') languages, the result of which is *Indian* Persian or *Indian* English. On the other hand, foreign languages have substantially influenced Indian languages and literatures (see Kachru 1979).

9. The following reports also discuss the place of English in Indian education and the problems in the teaching of English: *Report of the Secondary Education Commission* (New Delhi: Ministry of Education, Manager of Publications, Government of India, 1965) (Chairman, A. L. Mudaliar); *Report of the Education Commission* (Education and National Development) (New Delhi: Ministry of Education, Manager of Publications, Government of India, 1966) (Chairman, D. S. Kothari); this report recommended: 'As English will, for a long time to come, continue to be needed as a "library language" in the field of higher education, a strong foundation in the language will have to be laid at the school stage' (p. 197); *The Study of English in India: Report of a Study Group* (New Delhi: Ministry of Education, Manager of Publications, Government of India, 1967) (Chairman, V. K. Gokak); *Report of the Committee on Colleges* (New Delhi: University Grants Commission, 1967); *National Policy on Education* (New Delhi: Ministry of Education, Manager of Publications, Government of India, 1968); *Proceedings of the Conference on the Methodology of Teaching Indian Languages as Second Languages in Secondary Schools* (New Delhi: Ministry of Education, Manager of Publications, Government of India, 1969) (Chairman, G. K. Chandramani), see esp. pp. 27–44; *Teaching of English: Report of the Study Group* (New Delhi: Ministry of Education and Youth Services, Manager of Publications, 1971) (Chairman, V. K. Gokak); *Governance of Universities: Report of the Committee on Governance of Universities and Colleges* Part I (New Delhi: University Grants Commission, 1971).

II THE INDIANIZATION: LANGUAGE IN CONTEXT

3

Contextualization

This chapter is primarily an investigation in sociolinguistics, restricted to one aspect of the language contact situation in India.[1] It is a study of a variety[2] of the English language used as a second language (L_2)[3] by English-knowing bilinguals in an Indian cultural and linguistic setting. In order to examine the effects of such a cross-cultural situation on the language features of an L_2 we have included two types of statements: formal, and contextual.[4] A statement about context may be possible if certain categories are adopted for the contextualization of a text. The contextual categories may form part of the general linguistic theory at the (inter-)level of context. The necessity to include context as a relevant (inter-level) of description motivated the second aspect of this paper, which is a programmatic study towards the setting up of a construct for contextualization.

This chapter, then, includes both theoretical preliminaries and descriptive statements. There is no attempt to present a theory of context, although we hope that the categories suggested here may contribute towards such a theory. The categories have been set within the framework of linguistic science, the aim being, as Firth says, (1957c [Palmer 1968]:192) to 'make statements of meaning so that we see how we *use* language to *live*' (my italics). This approach has contributed towards bringing out the *Indianness* of the Indian uses of English, as opposed to the *Englishness* of British English and the *Americanness* of American English.

The illustrative material has been abstracted from the English texts written by Indians (henceforth termed Indian English).[5] The term Indian English (abb. IE) is used here as a cover-term for that variety of the English language which is used by 'educated' Indians. In terms of their proficiency in English, care has been taken to include only the users of the standard form of IE. A standard user of IE is one who ranks somewhere between the *central* and *ambilingual* points on the *cline of bilingualism*.[6] The form of English used by educated Indians could be called, alternatively, 'standard Indian English'.

English in an Indian Setting

Perhaps it should be mentioned here that in India the English language functions in the following sociolinguistic setting : (1) it is a second language used under the influence of a number of substrata, (2) it is used in cross-cultural (and cross-religious) contexts, as well as for describing both these and native contexts ; (3) it is used in IE writings (fiction, newspapers, etc.).

The above 1–3 assign specific roles to IE which, on the whole, are different from the ones assigned to English where it is used as the first language. It may then be said that Indians are bilingual in the sense that they are using English as a *complementary language* in typically Indian contexts.

In the use of the written medium of IE a distinction is possible along the lines of writer/reader relationship. An Indian bilingual's use of English may be conditioned by the reading public of his work. This is clear in the creative work of IE writers, especially the novelists and short story writers. Thus, on the basis of writer/reader relationship we have two forms of IE : one written in India, the reading public of which is exclusively Indian ; another which is written either in or outside India, for Indians or non-Indians. (The second form of IE may be written with a view to a reading public having English as L_1. This distinction is significant in the sense that these two forms vary in their degree of Indianness and in their use of Indianisms.)[7]

TRANSFER AND CONTEXT

1.0. PROCESS OF TRANSFERENCE IN AN INDIAN LANGUAGE CONTACT SITUATION

1.1. In linguistic terms a study of a language contact situation involves a study of transfer (or transference) at different levels. In such a situation there are at least two languages (L_1 and L_2) and, in certain cases, two cultures (C_1 and C_2) involved.'[8]

1.2. In IE the process of transference may result in the following : (1) items of L_1 may be transferred to L_2 to form hybridized formations ; (2) formal exponents of the contextual units (see below, section 3.2) may be transferred to L_2 (in this case, British English) at different ranks (see note 4) ; (3) extensive use may be made of the *open set* items of different L_1s to contextualize the text in Indian situations, which are part of C_2 for an English L_1 speaker (see section 7.0 to 9.6) ; (4) items of L_2 may be collocated[9] in 'unEnglish' collocations (section 6.0).

1.3. This process (cf. 1.2) involves transfer of two types : transfer of linguistic items from L_1s ; and transfer of certain non-linguistic features, i.e., the *non-belonging elements*[10] of the C_2.

1.4. The above (1–4) may be better explained if we take into consideration the 'meaning'[11] of an utterance and its *use* in actual Indian contexts, in addition, to the formal features of IE. In order to show the effects of the Indian setting of IE we shall treat one variety of English, which is spoken as the *first* language, as the norm for marking the deviations in the variety used as an L_2. There are, we think, strong reasons for treating British English as the norm for IE. A distinction may also be made between a 'mistake' and a 'deviation'. (For a detailed discussion of these two terms see Kachru 1982a.[12]

1.5. The types of transfer discussed in 1.2 may be termed : A. Transfer of context; B. Transfer of formal items; C. Transfer of form/context components.

A. *Transfer of Context*

This refers to the transfer of 'elements' of certain contexts from C_1 and L_1 to L_2. A further distinction may be made in terms of the culture of the participants. If the participants are speakers of Hindi and Marathi, or Tamil and Telugu, or French and English, there may be transfer at the formal levels only, without necessarily any transfer at the contextual level. If the participants, however, belong to different cultural and language backgrounds (e.g., Hindi-English, Tamil-English, French-Russian), this may involve the transfer of certain contextual units (see below 3.2) which may be non-belonging elements of the culture of L_2, such as the caste system of India, social and religious taboos, notions of superiority and inferiority, and the like.

In terms of the *performer/addressee* relation, in the case of IE the process may be explained as follows:

Medium	Performer	Addressee	Situation of transfer
Written and/or spoken	Indian	Indian and/or non-Indian	C_1 and L_1 items transferred to L_2

B. *Transfer of Formal Items*
This may be of two types:

(a) Formal items from different ranks may be transferred from L_1 to L_2, e.g., sentences, clauses, phrases, fixed collocations, compounds. Consider, for example, the following from IE fiction: *salt-giver* (*K* 32), *spoiler of my salt* (*U*), *sister-sleeper* (*VG* 130), *bow my forehead* (*U*), *turmeric-ceremony* (*MM* 70).

(b) L_1 meanings may be transferred to L_2 items. For instance, the term *brother-in-law* has one restricted meaning in British English as a kinship term; in IE it has acquired three distinct meanings (cf. 7.6) as a term of (a) abuse, (b) affection or intimacy, and (c) kinship. The terms *sister* and *mother* have extended collocations as terms of regard and respect used without relationship, e.g., 'Now you know what your duties are, and how to do them, sister, you will receive our instructions' (*MM* 93). In the use of the items *flower-bed*, *government*, etc. there is a change of register in IE with the result that a native speaker of English will not understand these items without understanding the defining-context. Examples are : 'On this, her *flower-bed*, her seven children were born' (*MM* 109).

'*Government*, she knows nothing about drinks. She is hardly sixteen and completely innocent' (*TP* 40). The item *government* is used here as a mode of address for a person who represents the state, and hence authority. Contextually and collocationally the items *brother-in-law*, *sister*,*mother flower-bed*, and *government* each belong to one or more lexical sets in IE. We see then that the IE creative writers have used, for example, *government* and *mother of Onu* as modes of address or reference. These two specific examples are, of course, author and text specific, but the use of the process is not restricted, and it can be generalized.

C. *Transfer of Form/Context Components*
Socially determined speech-functions (see 6.4, 7.0) such as *modes of address/reference*, *greetings*, *blessings/prayers*, *abuses/curses*, are related to the C_1 in the Indian context of culture. In Indian languages there are fixed formal exponents for these contexts, and these may be transferred to L_2 for those contextual units which are absent in the culture of L_2. (This might involve transfer at two levels, i.e., formal and contextual, since it is transfer of a contextual unit with the formal exponents which function in such a unit. Formally this may result in collocational deviation. (See also chapter 4, section 4.)

2.0. CONTEXTUALIZATION OF A TEXT

2.1. We should, however, hasten to say that a linguistic statement which takes into consideration the contextual units (see below, 3.2) of a language cannot be as precise as a formal statement, since this aspect of linguistic science has as yet no rigorous methodology. It has, however, been realized for some time now that for a complete linguistic description the (inter-)level of context (in traditional terminology, 'semantics') can be of crucial importance, and certain theories have been suggested.[13] (See especially Halliday 1964 and later; see also Kachru 1981c.)

2.2. A description which incorporates the (inter-)level of context as a relevant level for a formal statement has to ask certain basic questions, for instance: Is it possible to establish contextual categories on, more or less, the same basis on which the categories at the grammatical level are set up? Is there a methodology which could be used to relate the formal features of a text with the (inter-)level of context? This then involves both theoretical and procedural problems.

2.3. We have drawn on the theoretical work of the late J.R.Firth for an examination of the above relationship. A tentative classification for contextualization is found in his work,[14] and in the work of others[15] who further developed or discussed his concept. In his approach,[16] Firth does not accept the dichotomy of *form* and *meaning*, and he rejects the suggestion of the hierarchical direction among the linguistic levels; instead he adopts a 'hierarchy of techniques' (see Firth 1950 [1957b] :44). In Firth's view, then, the end product of linguistic analysis should be to relate the text to the *context of situation*, as language is 'not merely a process parallel with culture,' but 'an integral part of it'. (Firth 1934)

3.0. CATEGORIES FOR CONTEXTUALIZATION

3.1. A contextual statement may be made about a large text, in a general sense, in terms of the context of culture, or about delimited parts of a text. A restricted statement which marks a 'piece' of language for a specific operation is the first step towards establishing what we are here calling, for lack of a better term, a *contextual unit*.[17] This, however, is not of the same nature as the categories at the formal levels.

3.2. A contextual unit is set up in an attempt to demarcate the textually relevant features of a 'situation' in terms of the *contextual parameters*.[18] It may be viewed as an abstraction on two axes: the syntagmatic and the paradigmatic. Syntagmatically we think of a contextual unit as having clear endpoints in the time dimension; paradigmatically, it is a bundle of features comprising one or more contextual parameters.

3.3. The contextual parameters are definable, both formally and contextually, as variables which determine the effective operation of a text in a contextual unit. The value of each parameter is seen in terms of the change it entails in a language-text in a particular contextual unit. If the formal markers associated with a text are altered it should entail the change of the parameters too (barring those situations where the same parameter may operate in two or more contextual units). 'The *placing* of a *text* as a constituent in a context of situation contributes to the statement of meaning since situations are set up to recognize *use*.' (Firth 1957c [Palmer 1968] :179; his italics).

3.4. For contextual meaning, then, the relevant features of a text may be determined by two methods: *contextual substitution* and *textual substitution*. In contextual substitution we ask whether, for example, sex or the social status of a speaker is a relevant feature. Does the introduction of a participant of different sex, or a person from a higher or lower social status, entail a textual change? In textual substitution we ask: If another text is substituted, does that lead to contextual change?

3.5. A delimited text may be said to be the exponent of a contextual unit on the basis of those formal features which mark if off from other delimited texts, and which make it 'effective' in a particular context.

3.6. We may regard a contextual unit as a *frame* (in some ways analogous to a 'substitution frame')[19] and the parameters as the *distinctive* markers of the frame which determine the formal exponents for it. A sentence may be treated as the highest unit for contextualization and as a component of a restricted language (cf. 4.2); this, however, does not mean that the units of lower rank cannot be contextualized (e.g., markers of *sex*, *age*, *caste*, etc.). There are cases when pronouns, modes of reference/address, etc., may be language correlates of certain parameters, e.g., *government* (*TP* 40), *mother of Onu* (*SMH* 111), *twice-born* (*U* 14). A formal item may be correlated with one parameter and contextual unit in one culture, but in another culture that particular unit may be absent; for instance, *I bow my forehead* (*C* 14) will have no specific contextual unit in British culture, but in Indian culture, as used in IE fiction by Anand, it is a distinctive item operating in the contextual unit of *greetings*.

3.7. We have set the following parameters for this restricted study of IE, and these can be correlated with the formal exponents from the text. In fact, it is the text which is used as the basis for finding the parameters. This then gives us a frame for placing certain items in the context of culture. We have used Ellis' concept of 'wider situation' and 'immediate situation.'[20](Ellis 1966).

A. General cultural factors ('wider situation'):

1. Social status of the individual in the group. This has two dimensions:
   (a) Position in the hierarchy of caste.
   (b) Political status and economic position.
2. Religion. In the Indian setting it is important to know whether a participant is a Hindu, Muslim, etc. (cf. 9.3)
3. Speaker/addressee relationship: *wife/husband, children/parents, teacher/pupil.* For instance, in traditional circles in India a wife is not addressed by name but in a very indirect way as *mother of . . . (mother of Onu, SMH* 111). The same is true when an orthodox wife refers to her husband; instead of using his name she might only use a pronoun *he* or an honorific pronoun.

B. Individual or personal factors ('immediate situation'):

1. Sex of the participants.
2. Age of the participants.
3. Educational background of the participants—whether or not a person has received a formal education or a university education.
4. Characteristics which localize persons:
   (a) Linguistic: accent and other language features.
   (b) Non-linguistic: food habits, dress, etc.

Linguistic characteristics may link up with religion. There are religious dialects (e.g., Hindu Kashmiri, Muslim Kashmiri) as well as social dialects (e.g., Brahmin Tamil, non-Brahmin Tamil). Certain language features may thus correlate with more than one parameter.

4.0. CONTEXT VS. SUB-LANGUAGES

4.1. Contextually delimited language types may be termed *restricted languages, registers* (see e.g., Reid 1956:28–37, Halliday *et al.* 1964) and *speech-functions.* A statement about these is better considered as a statement of the *operation* of a language in specific contexts involving, at least, two participants *(performer/addressee).* The grouping is based on the language features which mark one text from the other class of texts, and the function of the text in specific contextual units.

This grouping may give us sublanguages recognized in terms of vocation, participants or attitudes: e.g., languages of (a) *administration, newspapers*, etc., (b) *wife/husband, parents/children, buyer/seller*, (c) *abuses/curses, flattery/persuasion*, etc., (d), *phatic communion*, (e) *radar, railways*, etc., (f) *Hindu rituals/Muslim rituals*, etc.

4.2. A *restricted language*, then, is a delimited 'sub-language' which is functionally and formally distinct from other sub-languages. It cuts across idiolects and regional varieties and may be used for specific functions by all the speakers/writers of a variety.[21] For instance, in IE the restricted languages of *administration* and *law* are pan-Indian in the sense that all the speakers/writers of different regional varieties of IE, with different IE backgrounds share these varieties. A restricted language is distinct from an idiolect or 'style' (cf. 4.5) in the sense that it does not necessarily show the individuality or idiosyncrasies of persons, and it does not mark just one person from another.

4.3. A *register*, in our sense, is a further step in delicacy in terms of sub-grouping. For instance, in the restricted language of newspapers one would expect that *editorials, legal reporting, women's pages*, etc., may be further subgrouped on formal grounds.

4.4. We may find that we need another term to explain certain special types of registers. While demarcating the restricted language of social roles, at first, we may include the following in it: *greetings, modes of reference/address, abuses/curses, flattery/persuasion*. Soon it will be evident that there are enough formal and contextual reasons for grouping such socially determined speech events separately. We shall use the term *speech function* for such items. By speech functions we mean those items (a) which reveal the personal attitude of a speaker/writer in a particular culture (e.g., *abuses/curses*); (b) which convey social attitudes in favour of or against a person or persons (e.g., *greetings, modes of address/ reference*); (c) which are repetitive and socially determined; and (d) which mark a person as 'inside' or 'outside' the culture of a speech fellowship or a speech community.

4.5. We may now ask: In the restricted language of newspapers, to take one example, shall we consider editorials, legal reporting, etc., in *The Times* and the *Guardian*, and in the *News of the World* and the *Daily Express* as the same registers? In such cases perhaps it would be useful if we accept a 'style scale' on which we mark different registers according to different styles. We may then have one register in different styles; for instance, following Joos (1960) we may have *intimate, casual, consultative, formal* and *frozen* styles for one register operating in a specific contextual unit. The difference in the above newspapers would then be a difference in style if two papers are reporting the same event. Two texts may belong to the same contextual units and be distinguished only in style.

4.6. In selecting a register for a particular contextual unit a person makes a *register choice* out of his total *register range* (see also Ellis 1966). A register range is the repertory of registers at the command of a person at a given time. This distinction is useful in a language contact situation, since a wrong choice of a register may lead to *register confusion*. By register confusion we mean the use of a register which does not belong to a particular contextual unit. There are many Indian formations which stand out as deviations because the items do not normally function in the register concerned when used by a native speaker of English.

4.7. The other manifestation of this 'confusion' is at the lexical level: it may be explained as the use of a lexical item in a restricted or extended sense by an L_2 user of a language. (For example, the Indian use of lexical items like *thrice, nice, purchase, shift, bawl*).

Lexico-Grammatical Transfer

5.0. TYPES OF TRANSFER

5.1. In IE the lexico-grammatical transfer may be of the following types:

A. Lexical transfer (or borrowing): This is what is usually termed *lexical borrowing*. It may be explained as the use of L_1 lexical items in L_2, not necessarily involving any formal change. This includes Indian loan words in IE (see chapter 5).

B. Translation: Translation is establishing equivalent, or partially equivalent, formal items at any rank in L_2 for the formal items of L_1. For instance, in IE in translating the following items an attempt has been made to establish equivalent items in L_2: *dvija* 'twice-born' (*U* 14); *namak-harām* 'spoiler of my salt' (*U*); *īshwar-prem* 'god-love' (*U* 205).

C. Shift: *Shift* (or adaptation) is distinguished from translation in the sense that in a shift there is no attempt to establish formal equivalence. The 'new' formation may be an adaptation of an L_2 item or may provide the source for an elaborate adaptation. The motivation in this case is that the contextual unit in the L_2 demands a formal item and a bilingual uses an L_1 item as the source for it. For example, *may the vessel of your life never float on the sea of existence* (*C*); the source item for this shift is *terā beṛa garkho*. It may sometimes involve the shift of fixed collocations (idioms) of L_1, e.g., *a dog is a lion in his own street* (*ABW* 71), *a crow tried to strut like a peacock* (*BH* 224), *speak to the sky* (*PD* 107).

D. Calques: *Calques* are those items which have L_2 phonology and grammar, but involve transfer of the contextual meaning from the C_1, in addition to the transfer of the collocation from L_1. e.g.; *flower-bed* (*MM*). In other words, a calque may be defined as rank-bound translation which may be parallel in terms of the units of L_1 and L_2, but may also be item bound. That is, an attempt may be made to find equivalence in the open-set items which operate in the structures concerned. Sometimes, this may result in *register confusion* or formal (collocational) deviation from the norm. For instance, *flower-bed* (*MM*) is rank-bound in the sense that the L_1 and L_2 items belong to the same unit ('word', compound), but, in addition to this, it has another characteristic: it is item-bound, too. That means that the writer, B. Bhattacharya, has translated the lexical items *phūl* (flower) and *shɔjjā* (bed) and has used *flower-bed* in the same contextual unit in which *phūl-shɔjjā* operates in Bengali culture. This results in contextual ambiguity in English, since the item *flower-bed* is restricted to the register of gardening in English. This difficulty of *register confusion* could be resolved by translating it as *nuptial-bed*, which would be rank-bound translation but not item bound; hence there would be no contextual difficulty.

5.2. Lexical borrowing in IE has been discussed by Yule and Burnell (1886 [1903]) and Rao (1954). A detailed discussion on this aspect of Indian English is presented in chapters 5 and 6 of this book. We shall now discuss the process of translation with special reference to the language contact situation in IE. It should be made clear here that translation in a language contact situation is different from contextual translation from a source language to a target language.[22]

5.3. In a language contact situation translation may be of the following two major types (further delicate analysis, however, is possible in terms of the structures involved).

A. Rank-bound: In rank-bound translation a writer translates formal items of L_1 at the 'same' rank into L_2. (That is if we presuppose that the number of units in the two languages is the same.)

In the following examples in IE the unit 'word' (compound) in L_1 has been translated at the 'same' rank into L_2: *rathyātrā* 'car-festival' (*OR* 15 July 1959); *gopūjā* 'cow-worship' (*VG* 122); *grih-devatā* 'family-protector'; *īshwar-prem* 'god-love' (*U* 205); *kaṭidorā* 'waist-thread' (*HW*

190) ; the unit 'group' (class 'nominal') has been transferred as follows: *ghōṛārḍim* 'horse's egg'; *moṭiyamdā bādshah* 'king of pearls' (*TP* 90).

A few examples are given below from the formal items of higher ranks from speech-functions and phatic communion.

(1) *May the fire of your ovens consume you (C)*, (*bhaṭṭhī mẽ jā*);
(2) *Where does your wealth reside? (TP)*, (*āpkā daulat khānā kahā hai?*);
(3) *What honourable noun does your honour bear? (TP)*, (*āpkā shubh nām kyā hai?*);
(4) *Beat me on my head till I go bald (C)*, (*kūṛ kūṛ ke mainū ganjā-karde*).

These are the examples of what may be termed *ornamental style* and are restricted to IE creative writing. The sources again are the L_1 items. The above (2) and (3) respectively mean: 'Where do you live?' and 'What is your name?'

B. Rank-changed.[23] In rank-changed translation the items of L_1 are translated at different ranks into L_2. This may be transfer at a higher rank or a lower rank. The following items of the word rank have been transferred into L_2 at the rank of group (nominal): *bhaiyā-dūj* 'brother-anointing ceremony' (*HW* 160); *yajnopavīt* 'nine-stranded thread' (*HW* 45); *shuddhī* 'cleansing-bath'; *godhūli* 'cow-dust hour'; *mundan samskār* 'hair-cutting ceremony' (*K* 56); *bad-baxt* 'you of evil star' (U).

There are other items which do not involve a rank change. In such items words of L_1 are transferred as compound words: e.g., *pattal* 'dining-leaf' (*WM* 84); *tilak* 'forehead-marking' (*MS* 206); *janeo* 'holy-thread'; *čoṭī* 'tuft-knot' (*C* 180); *dvija* 'twice-born' (U 14).

6.0. INDIAN ENGLISH COLLOCATIONS

6.1. Further, the process of Indianization of the English language has formally resulted in Indian collocations, which are sometimes termed in a derogatory sense *Indianisms* (cf. note 7). These include those compounds and collocations which may have one or more of the following characteristics:

(1) they deviate grammatically from British English compounding;
(2) they are 'loan shifts'[24] from Indian languages; (3) they are collocationally Indian; and (4) they have contextual units assigned in Indian culture which are absent in British culture.[25]

6.2. By Indian collocations we mean those formations which are contextually Indian, and/or which are collocationally uncommon in British English. In both these cases there is deviation from the norm.

In the first case it is contextually determined deviation, and in the second, it is formal deviation in terms of the sets which operate in the structure of a collocation.

We may then say that collocationally IE deviations have the following possibilities:

Item	Collocation of items	Contextualization of items	Deviation
(1) Usual	Usual	Unusual	Contextual
(2) Usual	Unusual	Unusual	Formal/Contextual
(3) At least one unusual	Unusual	Unusual	Formal/Contextual

In (1) we consider forms like *flower-bed* (*MM* 105), which have normal collocation of two items, and are accepted by a native speaker as 'usual', but whose contextual meaning, as used by Bhattacharya is entirely different from what a native speaker of English would understand. The meaning of such formations is intelligible only when they are related to appropriate contextual units in Indian culture.

In (2) a collocation is formally 'unusual' in the sense that the items used in IE to form such a collocation do not collocate in British English. It may be contextually deviant in the sense that in British culture it would not function in the same contextual unit which is assigned to it in India; or in certain cases, there may be no contextual unit at all for such collocations in British culture. For example: *sister-sleeper* (*VG* 130), *separate-eating* (*K* 51), *dining-leaf* (*WM* 84).

The collocations like *sister-sleeper* are not deviant in terms of the structures, but only in terms of the class assignment of the items. The construction N + V is very productive in English compounding (e.g., *fan dancer*, *body sitter*) and structurally, it falls under this class,[26] but the item *sleeper* in IE sense is unEnglish and (in this sense) cannot occur alone in British English or IE. On the other hand, *rape-sister* (*BH* 46), which has V + N construction, is no longer productive in English although we have examples like *cutthroat*, *cutwater*, *do-nothing*, *spoilsport* (Lees 1960: 148–52).

In (3) an 'unusual' item is collocated with an item which is normal in that context; for instance, *mango-breast* (*TP* 15). In this item the deviation is in the sense that *mango* does not collocate with *breast* in British English. Perhaps the reason is that contextually *mango* as a fruit is exotic in Britian. Hence the 'secondary' meaning of this lexical item is absent in British English.

6.3. In addition to the collocational differences there is another formal difference which has resulted in many Indianisms. In IE there is a very productive device by which a syntactic unit of a higher rank is 'reduced' so as to create a compound word. In other words, at places where a native speaker of English tends to use a group or a clause, an IE user might choose a unit of word rank. Thus many nominal formations with qualifiers are reduced to endocentric nominal compounds. Another point here is that many forms which are register-restricted[27] in British English may be used in IE without such restrictions.

6.4. In the 'reduction' of the item the order of the components is changed, e.g., *an address of welcome* ∽ *welcome address* (*IE* 14 August 1959); *a bunch of keys* ∽ *key-bunch* (*AD* 178); *a box of matches* ∽ *matchbox* :[28] *lady from the mission* ∽ *mission-lady; strength of class* ∽ *roll-strengh; the basis of caste* ∽ *caste-basis* (*H* 25 November 1963).

It is difficult to be dogmatic about the cases of 'reduction' as some of the following formations might not be regarded as 'reduction' by British English speakers, e.g., *caste-proud* (*HW* 17). This might be regarded simply as collocationally and contextually IE, though formally equivalent to such an item as *house-proud*.

6.5. The contextually deviant formations are those formations which function in IE contextual units, and would perhaps be unintelligible to a native speaker of English only because he is not acquainted with Indian contexts of culture. A parallel to this linguistic situation is found in America (see, e.g., Mencken 1941) and Australia (see, e.g., Morris 1898, esp. 160), where the English-speaking settlers had to coin a large number of words to name various types of local items, which resulted in such forms as *friar-bird, frogs-mouth, ground-lark, thousand jacket*, etc. In India the situation is, however, different: It is not a group of new settlers using their L_1 in a new country, but an L_2 being used by the natives in their own contexts. The early English travellers to India borrowed a number of Indian words and hybrid forms into English for such contexts. But on the whole the IE formations (hybrid or non-hybrid) were coined by the Indians themselves. A few examples of such formations are : *alms-bowl* (*HW* 44), *alms-taker* (*MS* 154), *bangled-widow* (*K* 233), *bath-fire* (*K* 45), *bath-milk* (*HW* 130), *betel-bag* (*K* 31), *betel-case* (*VG* 20), *car-festival*[29] (*OR* 5 July 1959), *dung-cake* (*NS* 47), *leaf-bag* (*C* 149), *sacred-ash*[30] (*FE* 52), *sacred-tuft* (*TN* 142), *upper-cloth* (*AD* 223). (For a detailed discussion see chapter 5.)

6.6. We have not considered here those hybridized (or mixed) formations which comprise elements from English and an Indian language. A large number of such formations warrant a detailed separate treatment. These include two types of items:

(1) Open set: e.g., *lathi-charge* (*HS* 15 June 1959), *bidi-smoking* (*SR* 198), *city-kotwali* (*HIS* 261), *congress-pandal* (*U* 212), *police-jamadar* (*K* 29), *rail-gadi* (*BH* 75).

 (2) Closed system: e.g., *cooliedom* (*C* 44), *goondaism* (*H* 2 March 1964), *piceworth* (*SMH* 161), *policewala* (*SMH* 61), *sadhuhood* (*U* 59), *Upanishadic* (*SR* 25).

The 'mixed' forms may be classified on the basis of their function in a context or on the basis of their form. In a formal classification the categories of lexis may be adopted to classify such items. (See Halliday 1966).

INDIAN ENGLISH IN INDIAN CONTEXTUAL UNITS

7.0. INDIAN ENGLISH AND RESTRICTED LANGUAGES

The other interesting aspect of the English language in India is its use by Indians in typically non-British contextual units of Indian culture. This use has evolved an Indian 'idiom' of English different from British English; and, what is more important, this 'idiom' is now used even outside India to refer to such Indian contexts. In this section we shall describe briefly the language features of three restricted languages of IE which are used in the Indian socio-cultural context: i.e., speech-functions (7.1); the Indian caste system (8.0); and social roles (9.0). The description that follows is neither exhaustive nor fully illustrated; it does, however, suggest further research possibilities in this area. (See Kachru 1982b.)

7.1. *Speech-functions.* In (4.4) we have suggested that the term *speech-function* may be restricted to special language types with particular characteristics. An IE text may provide us one or more of the following types of contextual data about which linguistic statements can be made:[31]

(a) text of attitudes, e.g., *modes of address/reference, blessings, flattery*.
(b) text of status and social position, e.g., *superiority/inferiority, caste*.
(c) text of social roles, e.g., *rituals, ceremonies*.

(d) text of individual habits (which are not socially determined).

7.2. In describing speech functions we have first to 're-create' the non-linguistic environment; this should provide us with the 'situational data' from which the relevant definable contextual features for a speech-function may be abstracted. The 'situational data' may be related to the context of culture in which a speech function operates. In the following we have described three speech functions (i.e., *abuses/ curses, greetings* and *modes of address/reference*) to illustrate this point. These examples have been taken primarily from IE fiction, therefore these are both register-specific, and in some cases, author-specific (see chapter 2, section 4.0).

7.3. The following variables have been used for abuses/curses: (1) the geographical location; (2) the L_1 of the writer; (3) the speaker/addressee relation; (4) distinctive points about the participants, i.e., age, status (economic and social), position in the caste hierarchy, sex; (5) religion.

By *geographical location* we mean localization of a text in terms of the north or the south of India. This is the first broad division. The second step would be to localize the text more specifically, say in terms of Punjab, Uttar Pradesh, Bihar, Bengal. This is important on formal grounds, as it will be found that the item *eater of your masters* (*C* 18) is common in Punjab only. Again, the abuses *eater of your masters* and *would that you had died in my womb* (*HW* 195) can be further identified. In the first, the position and the status of the participants are involved (i.e., *master/servant* relation). The text also shows that it is a feminine abuse. The second abuse involves the relationship of *mother/child*. Another example, *keep to the side of the road, you low-caste vermin* (*U* 39), involves two persons, an upper-caste Hindu and a low-caste Hindu. It is not difficult to guess the geographical location of the text. *You circumcised son of a pig* (*DD* 202) may result in Hindu-Muslim discord in India if it is used by a non-Muslim to a Muslim. *May thy womb be dead* (*HW* 212) is obviously limited to women addressees.

7.4. A further subgrouping is possible on the basis of some formal (lexical) exponents. We have divided the *abuses/curses* under the following heads:

(a) From masters to servants:
you eater of your masters (*C* 18); *you spoiler of my salt* (*U*); *you of the evil star* (*C* 16); *son of a concubine* (*K*); *you donkey's husband* (*K*).

(b) From parents to children:
   you have eaten my life (*C*) ; *would that you had died in my womb* (*HW* 159) ; *why did I rear a serpent with the milk of my breast* (*HW* 159) ; *oh . . . you dead one* (*C* 24) ; *when you are married I shall drink a seer of frothing warm milk, you widow* (*SR*).

(c) Addressed to women only:
   may thy womb be dead (*HW* 212) ; *eater of my child* (*HW* 212) ; *ari . . . you prostitute* (*U*) ; *oh you prostitute of a wind* (*K* 170) ; *go and lie with a licking male dog* (*CB*).

(d) Used by men to men:
   the incestuous sister-sleeper (*VG* 13) ; *you lover of your mother* (*C* 119) ; *that penis of a pig who sleeps with his mother, pimps for his sister and daughter* (*TP* 144).

(e) Mostly used by women:
   may the vessel of your life never float in the sea of existence (*C* 20) ; *may you never rest in peace neither you nor your antecedents* (*C* 78) ; *may the fire of your ovens consume you* (*C* 78) ; *you cock-eyed son of a bow-legged scorpion* (*U* 38).

(f) Used between members of different religious groups:
   you circumcised son of a pig (*DD* 202) ; *a lecherous cow-eater* (*C* 226).

(g) Addressed to one's own self:
   I am a leper if there is a lie in anything I say (*AD* 54) ; *may my limbs be paralysed and my tongue dumb and my progeny forever destroyed* (*K*).

(h) Showing repentance, friendship, intimacy or affection:
   father of fathers, I could kill that man (*U*) ; *brother-in-law, you are lucky* (*U*) ; *give, obey, brother-in-law, give us some of sweets* (*U*).

(i) Used for threat and challenge:
   that incestuous lover of your sister (*TP* 25) ; *what seducer of his mother can throw bangles at me* (*TP* 72) ; *if I don't spit at his bottom* (*TP* 186) ; *if I do not spit in Mali's mouth my name is not Juggat Singh* (*TP* 187) ; *a crocodile in loin cloth* (*HW* 217).

(j) Showing jealousy (man/woman relationship):
   call yourself a priest with so filthy a heart? The sacred thread is blackened by the sweat of your pores (*HW* 93–4).

(k) Of neutral type (as to participants):

this heartless blackguard (AD 50) ; *filthy brute (AD)* ; *heartless devil (AD* 50) ; *dung-eating curs (K* 220) ; *you son of my woman (K* 129).

7.5. For contextualizing greetings in IE we need roughly the same parameters which we need for abuses/curses. The speaker/addressee relationship is more revealing here since it helps us to classify greetings according to a person's religion, his caste, and his position in the caste hierarchy and social status.

We have grouped greetings under the following heads:

(a)   Greetings addressed to elders and upper-class :
      bow my forehead (C 14) ; *I bow at his feet, I lick the dust of the road on which he passes (SMH* 70) ; *fall at your feet (C* 14) ; *touch your feet (U).*

(b)   Greetings addressed to persons of equal status but elders :
      jay-deva (C 126) ; *long live the gods (C* 14).*

(c)   Greetings addressed to superiors (officer/subordinate relationship) :
      salam Huzoor (TP) ; well, inspector sahib, how are things? : God is merciful, we only pray for your kindness (TP 19).

(d)   Greetings used by prostitutes and sycophants:
      welcome, my eyes have gone blind looking at the way along which you were to grace my house (C 202) ; *you have blessed my hovel with the good dust of your feet (SMH* 55).

Further points to note about the greetings are:

(a)   In different social relations, e.g., *master/servant, age/youth,* a greeting does not evoke the same echo response in India as in English society, e.g., *good morning—good morning.* In Indian society the response may be as follows: 'Salam, Havaldarji.' 'Come, ohe, Bakhia, how are you?' *(U).*

(b)   The verbal exponents have other nonverbal cues which help us to assign a text to a contextual unit. For greetings used in *master/servant* relations the non-verbal cues may be *joining hands, dusting his feet,* etc.; but in the greetings addressed to people who are of equal status but elders, the *folding hands* are the exponents of the same social position although the participant who is greeted is senior in age.

(c)   The markers of caste, religion, occupation, etc., indicate further context restrictions : 'Ram, Ram, Panditji.' 'I touch your feet, Panditji.'

(d)   Greetings may precede or follow markers denoting caste, profession, religion, sex or the kinship of the participants. These may further be followed by honorific suffixes (e.g., *ji*) as in Table 3.1.

TABLE 3.1. *Showing markers with greetings* [32]

Caste	Profession	Religion	Kinship (cf. 7.7)
pandit	*babu*	*khwaja*	*brother-in-law*
thakur	*havaldar*	*sardar*	*mother*
			sister
			grandmother
jamadar	*inspector*		*father*

7.6. The *modes of address* and *modes of reference* are essentially determined by the systems of L_1 and the social pattern in which that system
functions. A term restricted to the kinship system of a language may
be used with extended meaning in another culture and transferred to
an L_2. The extended use of the term in L_2 may cause contextual ambiguity.

The following items have been used in non-English contexts in IE.

1. Superiority/inferiority:
   (a) *Cherisher of the poor:* 'Cherisher of the poor, what does your
       honour fancy?' (*TP* 37)
   (b) *King of pearls:* 'King of pearls, you can say what you like but
       this time I am innocent.' (*TP* 90).
   (c) *Government:* [33] 'Government, she knows nothing about drink.
       She is hardly sixteen and completely innocent.' (*TP* 40)
   (d) *Huzoor:* 'Would huzoor like to sleep on the verandah?'
       (*TP*99)
   (e) *Ma-bap:* 'The government are just and bounteous, they are
       your ma-bap (mother-father).' (*SMH* 48)
   (f) *Friend of the poor:* 'Take care of yourself, friend of the poor.'
       (*SJ* 228)

2. Professional: [34]
   (a) *Inspector sahib:* 'Come along, inspector sahib,' said Hukum
       Chand. (*TP* 128)
   (b) *Deputy sahib:* 'The deputy sahib has already sent orders to all
       police stations to keep a lookout for Jugga.' (*TP* 55)
   (c) *Policewala:* 'Policewala, badman, wildman, burn-face man.'
       (*SMH* 61)

3. Caste/religion:
   (a) *Pandit:* 'Hey, Pandit, can't you remain at peace with yourself for a moment?' (*FE* 185)

4. Kinship:
   The IE kinship system has been discussed elsewhere (7.7). The following examples, however, show that items operating in British English kinship terms may be used with an extended meaning in IE; for instance, *mother* as a term of respect, *sister* of regard, and *father-in-law* in the sense of abuse. *Bhai* (brother) is used for any male of equal age, *father* for all elder persons, and an uncle may be referred to as *father*:
   (a) *Mother:* 'Mother, a betel-leaf for you,' she hailed. (*SMH*) (Shopkeeper addressing a customer.)
   (b) *Father:* 'Father,' said the old man as he held out his card .... (*SMH*165) (Addressing a social worker.)
   (c) *Sister:* The coolie said: 'Are you travelling alone, sister?' 'No, I am with my master, brother.' (*VG* 19)
   (d) *Mother of my daughter:* 'Oh, I say, the mother of my daughter,' said the burra Babu, in the archaic conversation of Indian family life. (*C* 29)
   (In certain circles this is the normal mode of address or reference.)

   The third person pronoun *he* may be used referring to one's husband. In orthodox circles it is not modest for a lady to refer to her husband by name; in such cases the pronoun *he* is used, e.g., 'He, now in jailhouse, would not have eaten.' (*SMH*90)[35]

5. Flattery/affection:
   (a) *Jewel of jewels:* 'You will hear the jewel of jewels screaming.' (*SMH* 1)
   (b) *Mother of:* 'Why do you stick your eyes to my kitchenpot, mother of Onu ...' (*SMH* 111)
   (In certain situations a woman may be referred to or addressed as *mother of* . . . followed by the name of her child.)
   (c) *Brother-in-law:* (i) 'Brother-in-law, you are lucky.' (*U*)
   　　　　　　　　　(ii) 'Give, obey, brother-in-law, give us some of the sweets,' said Chota. (*U*)

6. Neutral (as to participants):
   - (a) *Babu-sahib:*[36] 'Where does your wealth reside, Babu sahib?' (*TP* 53)
   - (b) 'No, Bhai, no. If I knew, why would I not tell you?' (*TP* 99)
   - (c) *Master:*[37] (i) 'Yes, master, I do pay.' (*EE* 4)
     - (ii) 'Do not take my boat, master, you have taken all. Spare this one, master'. (*SMH* 48)
   - (d) *Dada:* (M) 'Dada, I am dead serious.' (*SMH* 3)
   - (e) *Didi:* (F) 'Speak didi,' he moaned. (*SMH* 130)
   - (f) *Sab:*[38] 'The proprietor, a genial Bombay man, was a friend of his and cried: "Ishwarsab, the results were announced today."' (*AD* 85)

7.7. In the speech functions in IE the effect of culture on the use of kinship terms is contextually significant and, as mentioned earlier, may differ from the use of kinship terms in British English. In British English the lexical set of kinship terms may comprise, among other items, the following items: *brother, brother-in-law, cousin, father, mother.* In IE these terms need different formal and contextual statements since (1) the members of one British English set operate in three sets in IE; (2) the members of a set, in IE, have been increased; (3) the meaning of the items has been extended. The extension of items of one British English lexical set to more than one lexical set in IE means that items like *brother, sister, mother, brother-in-law,* may operate in any of the following sets: (1) modes of address/reference; (2) terms of endearment; (3) terms of regard and respect as well as in the usual British English sense as (4) terms of kinship.

In British English the item *cousin* has no marker of sex; in IE, however, *cousin* may be followed by a sex marker, i.e., *cousin-sister* (*RH* 29), *cousin-brother* (*FF* 131).

8.0. CASTE IN INDIAN ENGLISH

8.1. References to the Indian caste system in English (not only in IE) show how the items of a foreign language may be used to describe an entirely alien contextual unit. The contextual unit of caste in the typical Indian sense is absent in British culture, and any reference to it may mean either a lexical borrowing from Indian languages or an extension of the collocability of the lexical items of British English. It may also entail a rank-bound (cf. 5.3. [a]) or rank-changed (cf. 5.3. [b]) transference from Indian languages.

In IE fiction or newspapers (especially legal and administrative reporting) we observe that, over the years, a restricted language of the caste system has evolved. This would be a topic for an independent study : here we have only touched upon a few features of this restricted language.

8.2. In English the item *caste* or the *caste system* is used in any of the following senses: [39]

(1) for reference to the hereditary classes of the Hindu society (i.e., *Brāhmaṇa, Kṣatriya, Vaiśya, Śudra*);

(2) for reference to social grouping, in any culture, on the analogy of the Indian caste system; and

(3) for reference to the sub-castes in any of the four castes in (1).

In IE the item *caste*, when treated as a node of a collocation, collocates with the following items:

Items following 'caste':

-basis (*H* 25 November 1963); *-brotherhood* (*BH* 125); *dinner* (*K* 89); *-distinction* (*U* 210); *-domination* (*L* 19 March 1961); *-elders* (*HW* 17); *-feast, -feeling* (*U* 193); *-following* (*L* 19 March 1961); *-less* (*U* 143); *-mark* (*RH* 204); *-proud* (*HW* 171); *-sanctity* (*HW* 155); *-well* (*U* 33); *-union* (*MM* 190); *-vermin* (*U* 68); *-waif* (*HW* 203).

Items preceding 'caste':

high- (*HW* 94); *inter-* (*MM* 190); *low-* (*MM* 163); *lowest-* (*U* 35); *out-* (*U* 39); *professional-* (*MM* 142); *sub-* (*AD* 10); *upper-* (U 33).

In *modes of address/reference* in the caste system the following items are used:

(a) for upper caste: *high-born*; *high-caste* (*HW* 94); *twice-born* (*U* 14),[40] *upper-caste* (*U* 33).

(b) for lower caste: *caste-less* (*U* 229); *low-caste* (*U* 67); *lower-caste* (*CB* 9); *untouchable* (*U* 177).

In the social roles also items of different ranks in IE are used for the two main castes, the upper caste and the lower caste. For example, there is an *ordered series of words* restricted to the upper caste in which the item *Brahmin* precedes:

Brahminhood (*SR* 20); *-corner* (*K* 106); *-guru* (*SR* 223); *-house* (*SR* 28); *-priest* (*RH* 106); *-land* (*SR* 285); *-quarter* (*K* 132); *-restaurant* (*SF* 161); *-role* (*HW* 109); *-street* (*K* 21); *-section* (*SR* 50).

Then we have another series in which *Brahmin* is modified by words like *sacred*, e.g., *sacred brahmin* (*SR* 11). In the context of the upper caste a large number of items are assigned restricted semantic areas: e.g., *forehead-marking* (*MS* 206); *nine-stranded thread* (*HW* 45); *red-paste trident* (*HW* 98).

The following sets are used for the lower caste:

(a) *chamar woman* (*HW* 107), *-people* (*HW* 107);

(b) *pariah children* (*K* 225), *-girl* (*K* 219), *-kids* (*K* 219), *-looking* (K 242), *-mixer* (*K* 63), *-polluter* (*K* 127), *-quarter* (*K* 19), *-street* (*K* 219), *-woman* (*K* 219);

(c) *sudra corner* (*K* 118), *-lines* (*K* 242), *-street* (*K* 31), *-woman* (*K* 24), *-quarter* (*K* 25).

8.3. In some formations one component may be the item *caste* which may help in contextualizing a text and assigning it to the proper contextual unit. The difficulty arises when L_2 items like *defile, pollute, touch*, etc., are used contextually and collocationally in an unEnglish sense. The following three 'sets' will make this clearer:

1. Defile : *touched me and defiled me ; the defiled one ; defiled by contact ; defiled my house ; defiled my religion ; . . . feet become defiled ; defiling distance.*

2. Touch : *the touched man ; touch-purify ; fear of touch ; untouchable ; touched the dust of his feet ; touched me and defiled me ; touched each other while dining ; touched our low-caste feet.*

3. Pollute : *polluting myself ; polluting kitchen ; fear of pollution ; pollution of progeny ; our community polluted ; pollute the food ; polluting distance.*

These items could then be termed *context-specific items* (cf. 9.7) since their meaning is essentially determined by the contextual unit in which they operate. Once the contextual unit is changed they become unintelligible to a native user of English.

8.4. As a preliminary study in quantitative method for classification of deviations in a variety of a language we took one text (*Untouchable*, a novel by Mulk Raj Anand, London, 1935) of an IE writer. A selected number of items (*caste, defile, high, highest, low, lowest, out, pollute, touch, upper*) were abstracted and the following study made:

(i) the total range of collocations (cf. Table 3.2); and

(ii) the frequency of 'usual' and 'unusual' lexical environments of these items.

9.0. INDIAN ENGLISH IN INDIAN SOCIAL ROLES

9.1. In treating social roles separately in this section we are not creating a dichotomy between (1) restricted languages, (2) speech-functions, and (3) the language of social roles. These may cut across each other, and this distinction is made for classificatory convenience. There is, however, some difference between the speech functions and the lan-

TABLE 3.2. *Degrees of Indianness or casteness of certain items in Indian English*

Item	Total frequency	Usual collocations (i.e., as in British English) Frequency	Unusual collocations (i.e., special Indian English collocations) Frequency
caste	99	—	99
defile	20	—	20
high	9	2	7
highest	2	1	1
low	12	5	7
lowest	3	2	1
out	42	18	24
pollute	35	—	35
touch	84	15	69
upper	2	1	1

guage of social roles in general: social roles do not necessarily include the socially determined repetitive events; and social roles are not limited in the same sense as the speech functions are.

9.2. The division of social roles into contextual units is very arbitrary. In order to find language correlates in language contact situations we may define social roles as those demarcated 'areas' of activity which are brought under the focus of attention of the linguist, and for which there are formal exponents in the text under description.

9.3. The following are some of the contexts in which IE is used in India: (a) religion, (b) cremonies and rituals, (c) dress and ornaments, (d) food and food habits, (e) marriage (f) politics.

We shall consider here only a few collocations which show the religious attitude of the two major Indian communities, Hindus and Muslims. As the item *caste* has become the node of all the caste collocations in IE, in the same way the item *communal*[41] is used in Hindu-Muslim relations. It may be used with the suffixes -*ism* (*BJ* 7 June 1959) and -*ist* (*TN*140). The range of collocability of *communal* is entirely different in IE from what it is in British English (in *OED* and other dictionaries of English one Indianized meaning of *communal* is usually given). The following formations with *communal* as node have been abstracted from various *ordered series of words* (which in this case are also lexical sets) of IE:

communal attitude (*L* 9 April 1951); *-bodies* (*IN* 8 July 1961); *-col-
ouring* (*IN* 7 February 1964); *-consideration* (*IN* 7 February 1964);
-disturbance (L 26 March 1961); *-distinctions* (*TN* 141); *-parties* (*L*
26 March 1961); *-passion* (*L* 26 March 1961); *-press* (*L* 26 March 1961);
-riots (*VG* 84); *-trend* (*HS* 1 July 1961); *-unity* (*IN* 8 July 1961). (Also
communally named (*L* 9 April 1961); *inter-communal* (*IN* 8 July 1961);
communal leader.)

Reference to any clash between the religious communities, especially
Hindus and Muslims, is made by the item *communal riots* (*VG* 84) or *riots*
(*TN* 121). In IE, the item *riot* has more or less a restricted meaning
referring to the disturbances of a 'communal nature.'

This difference may come up not only in the register of politics, but
also in other social roles like eating and marriage, and in speech functions, such as abuses/curses (cf. 7.4 f), modes of reference/address, and
greetings (cf. 7.5). In the relationship of two religious groups in eating
we have terms like *inter-dine*, *separate-eating* (*K* 51), *cow-eater* (*VG* 124),
cow beef eater (*FF* 157), *cow-worship*, *forbidden meat* (*MM* 31), and in
social relations *inter-marriage* (*MM* 11). (*Inter-marriage* is also used
for marriages between two castes, but is less frequent for what are
called international marriages—those between an Indian and a
foreigner.)

9.4. The ceremonies may be of two types, (1) individual, and (2)
social.

  (a) Individual: *hair-cutting ceremony* (*K* 56); *rice-eating ceremony* (*K*
     171); *turmeric-ceremony* (*MM* 70); *naming ceremony* (*SMH*).
  (b) Social: *aroti-time* (*HW* 207); *bath-milk* (*HW* 130); *car-festival*
     (*OR* 15 July 1959); *shagan-ceremony* (*BH* 124); *brother-anointing
     ceremony* (*HW* 160); *rain-bringing ritual* (*FF* 88); *vinayaka-festival*
     (*ET* 21).

9.5. In the restricted language of politics in IE the problem is not of
'redefining' the items: what interests us here is that some lexical items
and formations have acquired specific meanings. In a Gandhian context the following lexical items are used: *ahimsa*, *satyagraha*, *khadi* or
khaddar. These items have now been borrowed in British English, too,
and are listed in the *OED*. These three give us the following lexical
sets, which, incidentally, are also ordered series of words:

ahimsa camp, *-leader*, *-soldier* (*WM* 78); *-sweeper* (*U* 218);
ashram disciple (*MM* 82); *-camp* (*WM* 82); *-khadi board* (*SL* 8 June
1959); *-clad* (*SL* 6 June 1959); *-competition* (*WM* 97); *-coat* (*K* 148);
-cloth (*K* 109); *-shop* (*K* 135); *khaddar clad* (*TN* 14); *-jibba* (*WM* 44);

-*sari* (*WM* 48); *swadeshi movement, -cloth* (*U* 208); *satyagraha movement*[42](*SMH* 73); *satyagraha campaign* (*BJ* 7 June 1959).

9.6. The following formations are used in connection with village parties or village politics, trade unions, and other societies:

Congress-panchayat committee (*K* 119); *Dehati Janata Party* (*SL* 15 June 1959); *Grain Gola Committee* (*OR* 15 July 1959); *Gram Sahayak Refresher Course* (*Hit* 28 December 1959); *Kisan Candidate* (*VG* 13).

9.7. In describing social roles in IE it will be useful if we treat certain items as *context-specific items* (cf. 8.3). A contextual item, in our sense, would be a formal item of any rank the meaning of which is entirely dependent on the Indian context. We have taken a few excerpts to illustrate this point.

(a) 'She pulled a dining-leaf out of the bundle in the kitchen rack, spread it on the floor...' (*WM* 84).

(b) '... called for coffee ... brought in brass tumblers ... poured it back and forth ... forth and back in the perpetual concertina motion.' (*DD*)

The above (a) is contextually parallel to what in the English society would be *she took a plate and laid it on the table*. In this case, then, there is unintelligibility for an L_2 speaker of English because the items and the collocations that fill the structure are not usual, and because this contextual unit is absent in British English. The unintelligibility at the cultural level may leave the following 'meanings' uncomprehended:

(1) that the person is from the south of India (because the *dining-leaves* are not, normally, used in the north of India); and

(2) that it is a middle-class orthodox Hindu speaking about a conventional household.

10.0. CONCLUSION

In the preceding sections we have attempted to illustrate briefly how the Indian socio-cultural and linguistic setting has affected features of the English language in India. It has been argued that a statement which includes context as a congruent level for such a language contact situation is not only more insightful, but it also helps in the classification of those formations which some scholars, in India and elsewhere, have termed *Indianisms*. Indianisms have wrongly been considered 'substandard' as such items are not used in British English, and hence should not form part of 'standard English'.

In a comparative description of the variety of a language, what is important is that in addition to the comparison of the structures and systems, at one or more levels, the contextual units in which the varieties function should also be considered as crucial for a complete description. A comparison involving the contextual units of a variety may be explained as a study of the effects of the context of culture (both 'wider situation' and 'immediate situation') on a variety of a language.

We have considered some selected and restricted formal and/or contextual aspects of I E to illustrate how I E has acquired an Indian characteristic which manifests itself at other than the phonetic or the phonological levels. In the spoken medium I E has by now established itself into an Indian variety of English (which, however, varies significantly on the cline of bilingualism). At the other levels too the Indian contextual units, in which the English language has been increasingly used even after 1947, have influenced the formal features of I E. I E has ramifications in Indian culture, and is used in India toward maintaining appropriate Indian patterns of life, culture and education. This, in short, we might call the *Indianness* of Indian English, in the same way as we speak of the *Englishness* of British English.[43]

NOTES

This chapter is based on 'Indian English: A Study in Contextualization' in C. E. Bazell, J. C. Catford, M. A. K. Halliday and R. H. Robins, eds., *In Memory of J.R Firth*. London: Longman, 1966. The idea of this study, in the present form, originally came from the late J.R. Firth. I am indebted to him for the encouraging interest he took in my work (a part of which is presented here), during 1958–60, first at Edinburgh, and later at his home at Haywards Heath (Sussex).

1. A detailed discussion of the theoretical framework briefly outlined in this chapter is given in Kachru 1981c.
2. By *varieties* of a language we mean two or more forms of a language as 'developed' in different cultural settings. A good example is the English language in the U.S., Australia, Canada, etc. The varieties of English used essentially as second languages (L_2s) would include English in India, parts of Africa, Malaysia, etc. Another example is Hindi as developed in South India, especially Hyderabad, and other non-Hindi speaking regions of India. See Ferguson and Gumperz 1960.
3. The terms L_1 and L_2 have been suggested by Catford as abbreviations for a primary language and a secondary language (see Catford 1959). It should, however, be made clear here that the relative status of a bi- or multilingual person's language is difficult to establish. For most multilinguals, one language is clearly dominant, in the sense that it is used with greater facility, most of the time, in the widest range of situations. The dominant language is the primary language (L_1)—other languages are secondary languages (L_2s). For some Indians, perhaps, English has equal status with an Indian language. Even so, there are important spheres of language use—notably in the private and emotional life of such persons—where an Indian language

is L_1. For most, English is clearly L_1. In any case English functions as L_1, and can for the purpose of this study generally be regarded as such.

In the Indian context we find the distinction between *first language*, *second language* and *foreign language* useful. A *first language* may be defined as the mother tongue, or broadly, the regional language. A *second language* is a language which belongs to India both culturally and linguistically: for instance, Tamil or Kannada in Uttar Pradesh, or Hindi in Andhra Pradesh or Tamil Nadu. A *foreign language* is any language which is not used as the *first language* in any part of India. The case of English in India is, however, different, as I have explained in the Introduction. English has already acquired the status of an 'Indian' language, and functionally it is a second language for educated Indians.

4. The terms *context level*(s), *inter-level*, *rank* and other technical terms (excluding *exponent* and *exponence*) have been generally used in the sense in which these are used in Halliday 1961. See also Halliday's use of the terms *formal* meaning and *contextual* meaning in Halliday 1961 (244–45).

5. The term *Indo-Anglican* (or *Anglian*) writing has been used by some scholars. (See e.g., Iyengar, 1945 and later.) We prefer the term *Indian English writing*, as it makes clear that L_1 speakers of Indian languages are using IE as an L_2, and, more important, the English language is operating in Indian contexts which are unEnglish. In our use there is no value judgment attached to the term as there is in the use of Whitworth (see Whitworth 1907).

6. The term *cline of bilingualism* has been explained in chapter 2 (section 3). See also Halliday 1961 (248–49).

7. *Indianisms*, as used traditionally, include those formations which are rejected by some scholars as 'substandard' though these are widely used by educated Indians. The examples given are: *pin-drop silence*; *B.A. pass*; *England-returned*; *Himalayan blunder*; *nation-building*; *change of heart*; *dumb millions*; *to marry with*; *to make friendship with* etc. (cf. Goffin, 1934, Mathai, 1951:99). Note that in their use Indianisms include not only formally deviant items, but contextually deviant items, too.

8. C_1 is used here as an abbreviation for the native culture of an L_1 speaker, and C_2 for the culture of the native speaker of an L_2. These are used as parallel terms with L_1 and L_2 at the contextual level.

9. Firth originally suggested 'collocation' as a technical term (see Firth 1951a: 11–13), and discussed it further in Firth 1957c: 11–13. Also see Mitchell 1958: 108.

10. See, e.g., Weinreich (1953) 'The non-belonging elements can be separated as "borrowed" or *transferred*. This is one manifestation of linguistic analysis' (7). In this study, 'transfer' includes non-linguistic features too, for instance, transfer of the contextual units which are foreign to the culture of the native speaker of an L_2 (in the Indian situation these would be British speakers of English).

11. Used as a technical term.

12. A 'mistake' includes items generally rejected by a native speaker of a language as out of the linguistic code of that particular language; such items may not be justified on formal or contextual grounds. A 'deviation' may involve differences from the norm, but may be necessary in the cultural context in which a language functions (See also Kachru 1980a, 1982a and 1982b).

13. Of special interest is Katz and Fodor, (1963), which presents a semantic theory of language on the basis of Chomsky's linguistic theory. For more recent references see Kachru 1981c.

14. See Firth 1930 (38–45), 1937 (126–30) and the relevant papers in 1957b and 1957c: Bursill-Hall 1961, Langendeon 1968.

15. e.g., Mitchell 1957 (31–71); Halliday 1959; Ellis 1966 and Kachru 1981c.

16. See Firth 1957c (Palmer 1968). 'In the most general term the approach be described as monistic' (169).

17. A contextual 'unit', however, is not of the same nature as a 'unit' at the formal levels, Earlier the term 'sector' was suggested for it; cf. Kachru, 1961:89.

18. The use of this term in this context was suggested to me by Firth in August 1960 after he visited the PAT (speech synthesizer) laboratory in the Phonetics Department of the University of Edinburgh.

19. The concept of 'substitution frame' has been used by Metzger and Williams in their ethnolinguistic work. See Metzger and Williams 1963.

20. Firth used this term for those sub-languages which are 'restricted by scientific method conforming to functions of language in life'. See Firth 1959 (Palmer 1968):207.

21. See Hill, 1958 'The word *tongue* will be used as a neutral term for any of the entities commonly styled dialect, language ....' (442).

22. The categories of a general theory of translation may, however, be applied to the process of translation in a bilingual situation.

23. Note that the use of *rank-changed* is not the same as Halliday's *rankshift*. (See Halliday 1961:251).

24. This term is used here both for compounds and collocations.

25. Note that (3) and (4) are not mutually exclusive. What is contextually 'unEnglish' is often 'collocationally unEnglish'.

26. Lees has described such cases in Lees 1960: '. . . in a great many cases it will be possible to construct on the basis of the given transformations an indefinitely large number of compounds which do not occur in any corpus of English not because they are excluded by the grammatical rules of English, but rather because of various conventions of usage and of historical vicissitudes' (121).

27. A register-restricted form is one which is accepted in a specialized register, but would not be accepted in common speech or writing: for example, *dying declaration* may be used in a legal document but not in non-legal registers.

28. In British English *match-box* is used for a box without matches. In IE it is substituted for what in British English would be a *box of matches*.

29. The reference is to annual *ratha-yātrā* of Lord Jagannatha, a deity in Puri, Orissa. The image of the deity is carried in a procession on an enormous car adorned with paintings.

30. This item is a member of an ordered series of words which also form a lexical set. The other members are: *sacred lamp*; *sacred thread*; *sacred paste*; *sacred tuft*; *sacred fan*.

31. Firth has used this term in his work, but there is no suggestion about the specific use and its distinction from 'restricted language'.

32. The categories in the table are not mutually exclusive; for instance, 'pandit' is an exponent of both religion and caste.

33. This term is used here for a person representing official authority, i.e., one who is a symbol of the government. This is a transfer of Hindustani *sarkār*.

34. Sometimes peddlers may be addressed by naming the goods they are selling, for instance *tooth-powder* in 'Hey, tooth-power come here, give me a packet.' (*FE* 80)

35. Consider, another example: 'He (You wouldn't speak your groom's name even in your heart, you said he)' (*SMH* 76).

36. Spelled as *bābū* or *bāboo*. A term of respect used frequently in the north of India. In the south, it is used for *sir, your honour*. In many parts of India it is used as a mode of address for a native clerk. (Cf. Yule and Burnell 1886 [1903]: 44)
37. May be used as a mode of reference by orthodox women for their husbands.
38. In colloquial language, *sāb* is used as the weak form of *sāhib*. It is equivalent to *master* and may be used without religious or status restrictions when one wants to show respect. Originally it was used for Europeans in India.
39. A lucid and brief explanation of the Indian caste system is given in Basham 1954: 137–87).
40. This is a loan-shift from Sanskrit *dvija*. See Basham 1954:138. Also see, fn. 1, Introduction p. 14.
41. In *OED* and other standard dictionaries of English the extended Indian meaning is normally found. See also chapters 5 and 6.
42. *Satyāgraha* is usually translated into English as 'non-cooperation'. This is not the correct translation, *satya* is 'truth' and *āgraha* 'demand'.
43. The crucial questions such as how much 'deviation' from the norm is 'allowable' in an L_2 variety at the different formal levels, and the necessity (and problems) of standardisation of a variety, have not been discussed here. These, of course, are directly linked with the interpretation and classification of a 'deviation' or a 'mistake' in a L_2 variety (cf.n. 12). See also Kachru 1982a and 1982b.

4

The Indianness

1.0. In chapter 3, a programmatic framework had been presented, drawing upon the Firthian concept of the context of situation toward a theory of contextualization. The concept was applied to some Indian English texts which were demarcated in terms of the *contextual units*. A contextual unit was defined as an abstraction on the syntagmatic and paradigmatic axes. Syntagmatically it was viewed as having definite end-points in the time dimension, and paradigmatically it comprised bundles of 'features' which were termed the *contextual parameters*. The contextual parameters were tentatively defined, following Firth, as those formal and contextual variables which determine the effective operation of a text in a contextual unit. I adopted the *contextual substitution* and the *textual substitution* as procedural devices at the *(inter-) level* of context for marking the relevant features of a text.

In this chapter, using the earlier theoretical framework, I shall concentrate mainly on the *linguistic performance* [1] of IE users in Indian social contexts. First, I shall consider a restricted body of IE writing essentially from a linguistic standpoint following a sociologically oriented linguistic model. [2] At the formal levels I shall consider IE collocations, and some of the more noticeable syntactic devices used by IE writers. My aim is to draw attention to some of those formal features of IE which mark it distinct in its *Indianness* from the *Englishness* of British English, or from the *Americanness* of American English. [3] My second aim is to consider briefly the linguistic significance of the sociological and cultural factors in a bilingual's use of English as L_2, and more important, the impact of such cultural factors on the formal features of his English.

It will be argued that the use of the terms *mutual intelligibility* or *acceptable/unacceptable* in the case of varieties [4] of a language may be better explained if the formal and contextual levels are interrelated. This applies more to those varieties of a language (in this case, English) which are used as the foreign or second languages (say, e.g., Indian English, Malaysian English, Filipino English).[5]

This study is based on some selected features of IE fiction and newspaper writing of those Indian bilinguals who use English as a second language (L_2). I have further restricted it to a group of bilinguals whom I consider standard (or educated) IE users. In order to define a standard IE user I have earlier (in chapter 2) suggested a scale of proficiency termed the *cline of bilingualism* to rank bilinguals in terms of their proficiency in English.

2.0. THE CLINE OF BILINGUALISM

As mentioned in chapter 2 (section 3.0), the cline has three 'measuring points', i.e., the *zero* point, the *central* point, and the *ambilingual* point.[6]

An English-speaking bilingual who ranks just above the zero point is considered a *minimal* bilingual. Such bilinguals may have some knowledge of the written and/or spoken mediums of English, but they will not be considered proficient in the language (as, e.g., the competence of postmen, travel guides, and 'bearers' in India).

The central point is again an arbitrary point: a bilingual who has adequate competence in one or more registers of IE (say, for instance, the register of the law courts, administration, science), may rank round the central point. This would then include a large number of those Indian civil servants and teachers who learn English as their major subject of study and are able to make use of the language *effectively* in those restricted fields in which the English language is used in India.

A standard (or educated) IE bilingual may be defined as one who is intelligible not only to other Indians in different parts of the subcontinent, but ideally speaking, to the educated native speakers of English, too. But, intelligibility does not necessarily imply that the user's command of English equals that of the native speaker. The term *intelligibility* may be used in a wider sense to imply an Indian bilingual's capacity to use English effectively for *social control* [7] in all those social activities in which English is used in India. And, most important, it does not mean that a person is ambilingual. I consider ambilingualism a rare, if not impossible, phenomenon, and to become an ambilingual may not necessarily be the goal of a bilingual.[8]

In IE we may then imagine a scale of bilingualism running from almost monolingualism at one end, through varying degrees of bilingualism, to absolute ambilingualism at the other end. It can be safely said that the IE writers considered in this study rank high on this scale, approaching a point where they may be termed *standard* IE writers.[9]

In an Indian context one has also to consider a bilingual's command over the registers and restricted languages [10] of IE if one wishes to classify typically Indian collocations of English and to rank a bilingual on the cline. In certain cases the deviation of a collocation lies in the fact that an Indian user does not have command over a wide register-range in English, and this, naturally, results in register-confusion. By register-confusion I mean the use of a register-bound item in another register of English where such an item is not normally used in the natively used varieties of English.

3.0. DEVIATIONS IN INDIAN ENGLISH. [11]

In India an *idiom* of English has developed which is Indian in the sense that there are formal and contextual exponents of Indianness in such writing, and the *defining context* (see Hockett 1956:233) of such idiom is the Indian setting. I believe that the Indian deviations can be better understood after one takes into consideration the linguistic and cultural setting of India. [12]

It is by interrelating the socio-cultural and linguistic factors of India that we may be able to make a crucial distinction between (1) those formations which are *deviations* from other L_1 varieties of English, and (2) those formations which are termed *mistakes* [13] or substandard formations.

One might then ask: In what sense is Indian English 'distinctive' (to use Raja Rao's term (1938: 9–10); see chapter 1, section 4.[14]), and has a distinctive form of Indian English really evolved? There is no clear yes-no answer to this question since it depends on the language attitude of a person. In order to trace the distinctive characteristics of IE, at other than the phonological level, I shall focus attention on some typically IE formations and term these *Indianisms*. The Indianisms will include the following types of formations:

    a. those which are transferred from Indian languages into IE: e.g., *the confusion of caste* (*K* 51), 'varṇa sankara'; *dung-wash* (*SD* 101), 'lepan';

    b. those which are not necessarily transferred but are only collocationally unusual according to an L_1 user of English e.g., *salt-giver* (*K* 32), *rape-sister* (*BH* 46);

c. those which are formed on the analogy of natively used forms of English, and hence, in a lesser degree, are collocationally deviant (e.g.. *black money* (*TN* 43) on the analogy of *black market*); and

d. those which are formally nondeviant but are *culture-bound*. Such formations amount to an introduction of a new register by writers in IE, and extend the register range of such items (e.g., *flower-bed* (*MM* 109), *government* (*TP* 40); see 4.2 and 4.3).

It may then be said that an Indianism is an item of any *rank* used by a standard IE writer, which may involve either formal and/or contextual deviation.

4.0. THE SOURCES OF INDIANISMS

The linguistic factors which generally determine the Indianness of IE are not different from those in any other language-contact situation. In such a situation, we are mainly concerned with what we have termed in chapter 3, the process of *transfer*.

In linguistic literature transfer is essentially used in the sense of *interference* at any linguistic level. I propose to make a broader use of the term and to include under it certain *non-linguistic* elements as well. I shall consider the process of transfer in IE in terms of the following three types.

1. *Transfer of context*: This involves transfer of those cultural patterns (units[15]) which are absent or different in those cultures where English is used as L_1. For instance, in IE fiction the following cultural patterns, which repeatedly occur in typically Indian plots, come under such transfer: the caste system, social attitudes, social and religious taboos, superstitions, notions of superiority and inferiority.

2. *Transfer of L_1 meanings to L_2 items*: This may either be restricted to the lexical level, or it may involve transfer of higher units of description. If it is only lexical transfer, it may be of two types: In the first case the meaning of an item of an Indian language may be transferred to an item of English. A good example is the use of *flower-bed* in the sense of a *nuptial bed* by B. Bhattacharya. (e.g., 'On this her *flower-bed* her seven children were born.' (*MM* 109)). In this case Bhattacharya has transferred the meaning of Bengali lexical item *phūl shɔjjā* to a lexical item of English. Thus the transfer of meaning may result in the extension of register-range of an item of L_1. In English *flower-bed* is restricted to the register of gardening, but in IE (at least, as used by Bhattacharya), the register-range of the item has been extended. Formal transfer may

involve units like the sentence, clause, phrase, collocation or compound.
For example, consider the following:

> *rape-sister* (*BH* 46) ; *sister-sleeper* (*VG* 130) ; *turmeric ceremony* (*MM* 70) ;
> *salt-giver* [16] (*K* 32) ; *three-eyed* [17] (*K* 209) ; *the eater of your masters* (*C* 18) ;
> *fall at your feet* (*C* 16) ; *a dog is a lion in his own street* (*ABW* 71).

3. *Transfer of form-context component*: This is essentially determined
by those contextual units which are typically Indian and which are
not normally used in the L_1 varieties of the English language. Such
contexts may be called Indian contexts, as opposed to purely English
or American contexts. This situation is not unusual: In Indian languages
(which IE writers use as their L_1's) there are specific formal
items which function in such Indian contexts, and while writing in
English about such contexts these items are transferred to IE. These,
naturally, stand out as Indianisms. At the lexical level such Indianisms
may result in collocational deviation, or what McIntosh terms (1961:
333) 'unusual collocations and normal grammar'. This process involves
Indianization of the *speech functions* such as *abuses, curses, greetings,
blessings, flattery*, and so forth as discussed in chapter 3 (pp. 113–18).

The following four *speech functions* are selected to illustrate the transfer
of form-context components:

(a) *Abuses and curses: You eater of your masters* (*C* 18) ; *you of the evil
stars* (*C* 16) ; *you goose-faced minion* (*K* 31) ; *may thy womb be dead* (*HW*
212) ; *oh, you prostitute of a wind* (*K* 170) ; *the incestuous sister-sleeper* (*VG* 13) ;
may the vessel of your life never float in the sea of existence (*C* 78) ; *you cock-eyed
son of a bow-legged scorpion* (*U* 38) ; *you circumcised son of a pig* (*DD* 202) ;
a crocodile in a loin-cloth (*HW* 217).

(b) *Greetings: bow my forehead* (*C* 14) ; *fall at your feet* (*C* 16) ; . . . *blessed
my hovel with the good dust of your feet* (*SMH* 55).

(c) *Blessings and flattery: thou shalt write from an inkwell of gold* (*TP*) ;
draw a hundred lines on the earth with the tip of my nose (*C*) ; *your shoe and my
head* (*U*) ; *Oh Maharaj, we are all lickers of your feet* (*HW* 179) ; *let the sindur-
mark ever trace the parting of your hair* (*MM* 99).

(d) *Modes of address and reference: cherisher of the poor* (*TP* 37) ; *king
of pearls* (*TP* 90) ; *government* [18] (*TP* 40) ; *policewala* (*SMH* 61) ; *inspector
sahib* (*TP* 128) ; *mother of my daughter* [19] (*C* 29) ; *jewel of jewels* (*SMH* 1) ;
master [20] (*FE* 4).

The above 1 (transfer of context) and 3 (transfer of form-context
components) are different in the following sense. The transfer of
context involves an extension of the register range in IE and adds a
new contextual unit to the language. On the other hand, the transfer

of form-context components does not necessarily involve an extension of register or addition of an Indian contextual unit. It involves the use of Indianisms in those registers (and contextual units) which already exist in L₁ varieties of English (for example, the above speech functions). Consider the use of *government* (transfer of Hindi/Urdu *sarkār*) which involves a change of register, in '*Government, she knows nothing about drinks. She is hardly sixteen and completely innocent.*' (*TP* 90)

5.0. FORMAL EQUIVALENCE AND INDIANISMS

I shall consider here mainly the formal features of some of the transferred Indianisms. It is useful to describe Indianisms in more than one way. In terms of lexical structure and grammatical structure the transfer may result in collocational and/or grammatical deviations.

The transfer of Indianisms in IE may involve equivalence of formal items of L₁ and L₂ in two ways.

(a) It may be *translation* (see below 1) of an Indian item, or

(b) It may be a *shift* based on an underlying Indian source item (see below 2).

1. *Translation*: Translation may be defined as establishing equivalent or partially equivalent formations (= items) in IE for the formation in Indian languages.[21]

In translation there is not necessarily a one-to-one correspondence between the items of L₁ and L₂. An item of word rank in L₁ may be transferred at group rank into L₂. For instance, *namak-harām*, a *bahuvrihi* type compound from Hindi, has been translated by Anand as the *spoiler of salt* and not as *salt-spoiler*. Yet another compound, *iśwar-prem* has been translated by the same author as *god-love* (*U* 205). Also, note the following examples, *twice-born* (*U* 14), '*dvija*'; *waist-thread* (*HW* 190), '*kaṭiḍorā*'; *cow-worship* (*VG* 122), '*go-pūjā*.'

In terms of structural equivalence in IE, translation may either be *rank-bound* or *rank-shifted*. In *rank-bound* translations I include those Indianisms in which a writer has attempted to translate at the same rank in IE (that is, of course, if we take it that the units of description in the languages involved are identical). For instance, the following Indianisms belong to the same rank ('word') in the two languages: *car-festival* (*OR* 15 July 1959); *caste-mark* (*RH* 204); *caste-dinner* (*K* 86); *cow-worship* (*VG* 122); *cousin-sister* (*RH* 29); *cousin-brother* (*FF* 131); *nose-screw* (*NS* 10); *waist-thread* (*HW* 190).[22]

On the other hand, in rank-shifted translation no such structural equivalence is found between an Indianism and an Indian source item. Consider the following rank-shifted translations:[23] *ankle-bell* (*TP* 37); *brother-anointing ceremony* (*HW* 160); *cow-dung cakes* (*SMH* 113); *dining-leaf* (*WM* 84); *dung-wash* (*NS* 181); *eating-leaf* (*K* 57); *forehead-marking* (*MS* 206); *hair-cutting ceremony* (*K* 171); *nine-stranded thread* (*H* 45); *rice-eating ceremony* (*K* 171); *sacred-paste* (*MM* 182); *schooling-ceremony* (*FE* 106); *sitting planks* (*MS* 53).

In certain cases the rank-shift does not involve the change of a unit of one rank into another, but a monomorphemic item of an Indian language is transferred as a polymorphemic item into IE. Such items have been included in the above list, e.g., *pattal*: 'dining-leaf' (*WM* 84); *tilak* : 'forehead marking' (*MS* 206); *pīṛhā*: 'sitting planks' (*MS* 53).

It should be made clearer here that while transferring items from L_1's to Indian English, an Indian writer of English is not necessarily thinking in terms of parallel or semi-equivalent units in IE. A creative writer may mainly be interested in 'building up' a native contextual unit in L_2, and, for that, translation from L_1 may be used as a language device. Thus, in translation, another distinction may be found useful, namely, between 'unconscious' and 'conscious' translation. The process of 'unconscious' translation, perhaps, applies at the lower end of the cline of bilingualism, where a bilingual does not always realize that he is using a transferred item of an Indian language.

Furthermore, this applies to those transferred items which have been completely assimilated into the borrowing language. For instance, consider the following in English : *a marriage of convenience, I've told him I don't know how many times*, or *it goes without saying*. These are, as Bloomfield says (1938:457), 'word for word imitations' of French phrases and by now have been completely adapted as transferred items in English.

The conscious Indianisms, on the other hand, are those which are used in IE writing with the purpose of establishing one-to-one correspondence, or partial correspondence, between the formal items of the L_1 and IE, in order to make the dialogue 'realistic,' to Indianize the situation or to adopt typically Indian speech functions in IE (e.g., *greetings, blessings, modes of reference*, and/or *address*).

It is, of course, difficult to put one's finger unmistakably on the above-discussed types of translations. One clue to conscious translation is when a writer purposely transfers items from the Indian language and accepts it as a linguistic device for stylistic effect.[24]

2. *Shift:* A *shift* (= adaptation) is different from translation in the

sense that in a shift no attempt is made to establish formal equivalence. An Indianism classified as a shift is usually an adaptation of an underlying formal item of an Indian language which provides its source. Shifts are better explained and understood if considered with their appropriate contextual units from Indian culture. The following types of Indianisms may be treated as shifts: *may the vessel of your life never float in the sea of existence (C 20); may the fire of ovens consume you (C 78); a crocodile in a loin-cloth (HW 217)*. Generally, the underlying Indian source item for a shift is a fixed collocation of an Indian language.

6.0. INDIAN ENGLISH COLLOCATIONS

The types of transfer discussed above (see 4.1 to 4.3) result in Indianisms which may be defined as collocationally deviant from the native varieties of English and described as IE collocations. An IE collocation includes those formations which have Indian characteristics in the following three senses. First, they may deviate grammatically from American and British English formations. Second, they may involve loan shifts from Indian languages. Third, they may be formally nondeviant and only contextually deviant (that is, if they have those contextual units assigned in Indian culture which are absent in those cultures where English is spoken as the L_1).

The collocational deviation of Indianisms, then, may be of two types: formal and contextual. By formal deviation is meant the deviation in terms of the lexical items which operate in the structure of a collocation. Contextually deviant formations include those formations which are formally nondeviant.

A. *Degrees of Collocational Deviation*. By definition a collocation must have at least two members. In an IE collocation there are the following possibilities of deviation from L_1 varieties of English: (a) the members of a collocation may be 'usual' in the sense that in L_1 varieties of English that collocation is possible, but the contextual use of that collocation may be typically Indian: e.g., *flower-bed (MM* 105); (b) the lexical items of a collocation may be collocated in non-native collocations. Thus we get lexically and contextually Indian collocations: e.g., *sister-sleeper (VG* 130), *dining-leaf (WM* 84), *rape-sister (BH* 46); (c) the contextual use of collocation may present no difficulty to L_1 users of English, only the collocability of an item with the *node* of a collocation may be 'unusual'; (e.g., *mango-breast (TP* 15)). This then is violation of a selectional rule of a language.

A node of a collocation may be defined as that lexical item in a collocation which is in focus to determine the range in terms of the *sets* following and preceding the node.

Note that the collocations like *sister-sleeper* are deviant only in terms of the class assignment of the lexical items. They are not structurally deviant from L_1 varieties of English. The construction N + V is a productive structure in English compounding (e.g., *fan dancer, babysitter*). (See also Lees 1960: 167.) The main point of deviation, however, is that in IE *sleeper* is used in a particular sense in which it is not used in English.

There is a small number of Indianisms, like *rape-sister* (*BH* 46), which have V + N construction and are parallel to *carry-all, killjoy, spitfire*, etc., but as Lees says (1960: 152–53), this construction is no longer productive in English.[25]

B. *Deletion in Indian English Collocations*. It is interesting to note that there is on the whole an underlying regular syntactic process involved in forming IE collocations. In a large number of Indianisms a syntactic unit of a higher rank in English is reduced to a lower rank in IE. There are cases where an L_1 speaker of English tends to use a group or a clause, but in many such cases an Indian user of English uses a unit of a lower rank. Note, for example, many nominal formations of modifier + head + qualifier structure are reduced in IE to formations of modifier + noun structure.

In many such Indianisms the rank reduction involves first the process of deletion and then permutation of the lexical items. Consider, for instance, the following nominal groups of English: (1) *an address of welcome*, (2) *a bunch of keys*, and (3) *love of God*. In IE these are reduced to: (1) *welcome address* (*IE* 14 August 1959), (2) *key bunch* (*AD* 178), and (3) *God-love* (*U* 205).

In formations such as *America-returned* (*FF* 105) or *England-returned*, the process involved is more complex. Though the process is complex the underlying structures are nondeviant, but the realized structures (e.g., *America-returned* or *England-returned*) are deviant and would need both semantic and grammatical explanations in the Indian variety of English.

On the other hand, we need extra semantic feature assignment in order to realize semantically deviant and formally non-deviant *salt giver*. The use of this item in the sense of 'one who feeds or protects' and the use of *salt-spoiler*[26] in the sense of 'one who is not grateful' create semantic problems[27] which one has to face in describing such Indianisms.

Indianisms like *caste-mark* (*RH* 204), *nail bed* (*DD* 55), *well-pot* (*FE* 10), *plough-pair* (*SMH* 48), *forehead marking* (*MS* 206) are acceptable only after the defining-context is understood.

Note that the tendency towards deletion in IE results in many such Indianisms which vary not necessarily grammatically but only in the *acceptability* by a native speaker of English. The reasons for the *non-acceptability* are varied and will not be discussed here. The acceptability of IE collocations forms a scale, and the native speaker's reaction toward such Indianisms may be *acceptable, unacceptable,* or *more-or-less acceptable.*

One cannot, however, be dogmatic about the rank-reduced formations. There are many formations of this type in the L₁ varieties of English, too. The IE formation *caste-proud* (*HW* 17) might be regarded simply collocationally and contextually an Indianism; structurally it is equivalent to a formation like *house-proud* (or *purse-proud*) which is common in some L₁ varieties of English.

Whitworth considers the rank reduced formations 'wrong compounds' (1907) for the reason that Indians are following the process of analogy of Sanskrit *tatpuruṣa* compounds, like *deva-putra* 'a son of god', and transfer such formations into IE (say, for example, *deva-putra* as 'god-son'). This, as he mentions, may also result from loan-shifts, as in *bride-price*, which is from *kanyā śulkam.*[28]

Goffin (1934), without trying to explain the underlying reasons (or process) of rank-reduced Indianisms, suggests that such formations show a tendency in IE of 'phrase-mongering'. The examples given by him (e.g., *Himalayan blunder, nation-building, dumb millions*) are not different from the above examples and show clearly that there is a regular underlying pattern in such formations.

7.0. INDIANISMS AND INDIAN CONTEXT

Those Indianisms which have specific meaning (and function) in Indian culture may be termed contextually determined (or contextually loaded) Indianisms. These will include those formations which have a specific function (or associations) in IE contextual units. Contextually determined Indianisms may be 'deviant' in the sense that they are unintelligible to the user of other varieties of English because they are not acquainted with those typically Indian contexts in which such formations are used by Indians.

Contextually determined Indianisms involve the transfer of meaning from the native culture of IE writers, in addition to the transfer of collocations from Indian languages: e.g., the use of *flower-bed* (*MM* 90) in the sense of *nuptial-bed* which has already been mentioned.[29]

To illustrate this point, a short list of such (non-hybrid) Indianisms is given below. The list includes two types of formations: (a) those which involve a semantic shift in IE, and (b) those which do not necessarily involve a semantic shift (but are simply contextually Indian).

The formations have been abstracted, among others, from the following contexts: *material objects, flora-fauna, socio-religious and political systems, relationships of the castes and social hierarchy, speech-functions, social roles:*[30]

alms-bowl (*HW* 44), *ankle-bells* (*TP* 37), *anklet-bells* (*TN* 50), *ash-marks*[31](*K*·65), *bamboo-stretcher* (*ET* 95), *bangle-man* (*SD* 13), *bangle-seller* (*MM* 55), *bangled-widow*[32](*K* 233), *bath-fire* (*K* 45), *bath-milk*[33] (*HW* 130), *bedding-rolls* (*DD* 191), *betel-bag* (*K* 31), *betel-woman* (*SMH* 158), *black-money*[34](*TN* 43), *blessing-ceremony* (*K* 64), *bridal-bath*[35](*MM* 68), *bride-showing* (*MM* 48), *bullock-proof* (*DD* 5), *burning-ground*[36](*Hit* 28 December 1959), *car-festival*[37](*OR* 15 July 1959), *cart-man* (*K* 13), *cook-woman* (*MM* 15), *cowdung cakes* (*SMH* 113), *cow-worship* (*VG* 112), *cousin-sister* (*RH* 29), *cousin-brother* (*FF* 113), *dining-leaf* (*WM* 84), *dung-basket* (*K* 32), *dung-washed* (*SD* 121), *eating leaves* (*K* 57), *flower-bed*[38] (*MM* 105), *forbidden-meat*[39] (*MM* 31), *forehead-marking* (*MS* 206), *invitation-rice* (*K* 173), *leaf-bag* (*C* 149), *leaf-plate* (*C*), *leaf-pot* (*C* 66), *marriage-drums* (*DD* 29), *marriage-festival* (*SMH* 17), *marriage-month* (*SF* 50), *marriage-season* (*FF* 122), *milk-bath*[40](*HW* 124), *nine-stranded-thread*[41] (*HW* 45), *nose-screw* (*HW* 95), *procession-throne* (*K* 143), *red-paste trident*[42] (*SMH* 50), *reed mat* (*HW* 71), *rice-eating ceremony* (*K* 171), *rice-initiation ceremony* (*SMH* 30), *rope-cot* (*WM* 241), *sacred ash*[43](*FE* 52), *saucer-lamp* (*C* 207), *separate-eating* (*K* 51), *seventh-month ceremony* (*K* 37), *sitting-planks* (*MS* 53), *tuft-knot* (*C* 180), *upper-cloth* (*AD* 223), *village-elders* (*MM* 133), *well-pot* (*FE* 10), *wedding-bangles* (*RH* 158), *wedding-house* (*FE* 49), *wrist-band* (*TN* 152).

8.0. HYBRID INDIANISMS

Hybrid (or mixed) formations are those Indianisms which comprise two or more elements, and in which at least one element is from an Indian language and one from English. We shall, for instance, consider the following types of formations as hybrid Indianisms: *attar-bottle*

(*SR* 266), *Congress-pandal* (*U* 212), *kumkum-mark* (*K* 159), *nazul-land* (*HT* 1 February 1961), *police-jamadar* (*K* 29).

Hybrid formations, like non-hybrid Indianisms, need description in terms of the composition of the elements, and also in terms of the contexts in which such formations function in India. These formations have been discussed in chapter 5.

9.0. LANGUAGE VARIETIES AND CULTURE

It has been argued here that the use of varieties of a language in different cultures raises interesting sociolinguistic problems. The term *English language* may be used as a cover-term for L_1 varieties of English and also for the *other Englishes* which have slowly developed in West Africa, India, Malaysia, and so forth because of political, commercial, and educational contacts of these countries with the English-speaking countries.

In India the English language has blended itself with the cultural and social complex of the country and has become, as Raja Rao says, the language of the 'intellectual make-up' of Indians. It is the only language, except perhaps Sanskrit, which has been retained and used by Indian intellectuals in spite of political pressures and regional language loyalty. In certain ways the use of English as a link language (and the growth of IE) has for the first time created a pan-Indian literature (except, of course, the earlier use of Sanskrit) which symbolizes cultural and socio-political aspirations of Indians. Thus, a foreign language has become culture-bound in India more deeply than Persian and Arabic were in the times of the Muslim rulers.

The linguistic implications of such acculturation of IE are that the more culture-bound it becomes the more *distance* is created between IE and other varieties of English. This is well illustrated by the extended semantic domain of the kinship terms of the natively used varieties of English in IE[45] or by contextually determined Indianisms which are deviant as they function in those contextual units of India which are absent in British culture (although formally the formations may be nondeviant). This, then, would imply that in any semantic study of Indianisms, the significant fact that these formations operate in Indian culture and not in British culture cannot be ignored. In fact, it is important to take the contextual units into consideration if one is interested in the study of a language in actual situations.

10.0. LEXICAL CATEGORIES AND CONTEXT

The study of the interrelation of context and the language features in different cultures may further be extended to the lexical level. Considering collocation as the basic lexical category, it might be useful, again, to define the collocations of the varieties of English in terms of *association* and *mutual expectancy*. By association I mean statements of the habitual places of a given lexical item in a collocational order. It is, as Firth says (1957b:196), an abstraction and does not involve a conceptual approach to the meaning of the lexical items. The use of association will be restricted to formally determined items. By formally determined, I mean restricted in terms of the structure of a collocation and the items of sets which may precede and/or follow the node of a collocation.

The mutual expectancy, on the other hand, is the probability of a collocation in a contextual unit of that specific culture in which a variety of a language functions. For instance, when we hear the IE collocations (*I*) *touch your feet* or (*I*) *bow my forehead* in an Indian context, we know that these collocations function in the speech functions of *greetings* in India. If the text is substituted, for instance, by *you eater of your masters*, we naturally change the context of the collocation to the speech function of *abuses* and *curses*.

This distinction, I think, helps us to relate the concept of collocation to two levels: the formal level and the (inter-) level of context. We can then draw a distinction between *a formally determined collocation* and *a contextually determined* (*or culture-bound*) *collocation*. What is formally *normal* and *expected* in one contextual unit in one culture, may be *unusual* and *unexpected* in the same contextual unit in another culture.

11.0. CONCLUSION

In this chapter I have attempted to illustrate that the *distance* between the natively used varieties of English and IE cannot be explained only by comparative studies of phonology and grammar. The deviations are an outcome of the Indianization of English which has, gradually, made IE culture-bound in the socio-cultural setting of India. The phonological and grammatical deviations are only a part of this process of Indianization. I think this is also true of the other South Asian varieties of English.

NOTES

This chapter is adapted from *Word*, 21 : 391–410. This is an abridged and revised version of parts of my two earlier papers presented to the Linguistics Group, University of California, Berkeley, 10 March 1965, and the First Regional Meeting of the Chicago Linguistic Society, 3 April 1965.

1. The term 'linguistic performance' is used in the Hallidayan sense (see Halliday 1964) and not in the sense in which Chomsky uses it in Chomsky 1965. Halliday says: '…the explanation of linguistic performance can also perhaps be regarded as a reasonable goal and one that is still, as it were, internal to linguistics' (1964:13).
2. See Halliday (1964:fn 4,17) : 'The interest is focused not on what the native speaker *knows* of his language but rather on what he does with it : one might perhaps say that the orientation is *primarily textual* and in the wider sense, sociological.' (My italics.)
3. Ellis uses the term 'the Englishness of English' in order to emphasize the 'individuality of language'. (See Ellis 1961).
4. The use of the term *variety* has been explained in chapter 3, fn 2. See also Kachru 1982a, and Kachru and Quirk 1981.
5. In recent years the socio-cultural impact and the linguistic settings of many non-English speaking countries have contributed toward the growth of a *new idiom* of English especially in West Africa, India, the Philippines, etc. The new idiom, naturally, involves the problem of intelligibility with other varieties of English which are used either as first languages or foreign (or second) languages. For a detailed discussion see chapter 2 (sec. 4.5). See also Kachru 1976a, 1977 and 1979 and 1982a.
6. A number of linguistically interesting examples from various points on the cline are given in Hunt 1931 and 1935 and Gokak 1964.
7. The term has been suggested by Abercrombie 1956.
8. There are some Indians who have 'native-like control' (Bloomfield 1938:56) at one level, but at the other levels their English may show marked influence of the substratum. For example, at the grammatical level one may attain an ambilingual's command, and at the same time show marked Indianness at the phonological and lexical levels.
9. Note that the term IE writing may be used for the whole mass of English writing in India on different subjects, or in a restricted sense, only for 'standard' creative writing and newspaper writing.
   The history of creative writing in English in India is fairly old. It may be traced back to 1830 when a volume of poems, *The Shair, or Minstrel and Other Poems* by Kasiprasad Ghose, was published. But the impact of IE creative writing in India, and its recognition by the wider English-speaking world is, strictly speaking, a post-Indian Independence phenomenon. See chapters 1 and 2.
10. The following further distinction may be made in a bilingual situation. A bilingual may make *alternate* use of one or more languages, other than his L $_1$ either for restricted communication, or for unrestricted communication. On the basis of the functional use of a language we may then have restricted *bilingualism* and *unrestricted bilingualism*.
    Restricted bilingualism is restricted in the sense that an L $_2$ is used only for some specific purposes, e.g., (1) administration, (2) legal proceedings, (3) education,

(4) rituals. The above (1, 2 and 3) include the use of English in India, and (4) includes the use of Sanskrit in India and the use of Latin in certain parts of Europe.

An example of unrestricted bilingualism is the use of Hindi in Uttar Pradesh, Bihar, Madhya Pradesh, etc.,—the so-called Hindi-speaking areas of India—where people speak dialects or varieties at home and use Hindi as a common medium outside their homes. The bilingualism of a Hindi speaker, in the above case, is of a different degree from that of a Tamil or a Kashmiri Hindi speaker (see also Gumperz 1964a and 1964b.).

11. The writings of those 'educated' Indians who use English as a foreign language and write for the Indian and or foreign reading public, have been termed by some *Indo-Anglian, Indo-Anglican,* or *Indo-English* (see, for example, Iyenger, 1954 and later). I shall, however, use the term *Indian English* writing for the writings of such Indian bilinguals. This term has been used earlier in roughly the same sense by the following: Anand 1948, Dustoor 1968 and Jha 1940. See also chapter 1 (sec. 4) and chapter 2 (sec.5).

H.A. Passé and some other scholars, too, object to the use of the term. According to them, it implies a status for IE which equates it with those varieties of English which are used as L_1s (see Passé 1947).

I think the term IE is contextually self-explanatory, and linguistically significant. Furthermore, it makes clear that the English language is used as a non-native language by the users of Indian languages, and more important, that it functions in those contexts which are 'non-English' or 'non-American'. The term *Anglican* is misleading in another sense, too. It has a theological connotation connected with the Church of England which does not fit in an Indian context. Perhaps it should be made clear here that the term IE is not used in this study in the same sense in which it has been used by Whitworth (1907) and other scholars. Whitworth uses it in the sense of a 'sub-standard' variety of English.

12. As mentioned in chapters 1 and 2, it may be argued that the factors which mark IE as separate are not much different from those factors which justify the differences in Australian English, Canadian English, Scottish English, etc. This analogy, however, cannot be taken too far since IE is used as an L_2 in contrast with the above varieties of English which are, by and large, used as L_1s. For further discussion see Kachru 1982a, Strevens 1977 and Kachru and Quirk 1981.

13. A *mistake*, as explained in Introduction (pp. 2–4), is rejected by a native speaker of English as out of the linguistic 'code' of the English language, and therefore may not be justified in Indian English on formal and/or contextual grounds. A deviation, on the other hand, may involve differences from a norm, but such deviations may be explained in terms of the cultural and/or linguistic context in which a language functions (see also Kachru 1982a).

14. Rao was not alone when he pleaded for an Indian variety of English. In 1940, addressing the Conference of English Professors, Playwrights and Critics, in Lucknow, India, A. N. Jha went a step further. He said:

May I, in that respect, venture to plead for the use, retention and encouragement of Indian English? . . . Is there any reason why we need be ashamed of Indian English? Who is there in the United Provinces [Uttar Pradesh] who will not understand a young man who had enjoyed a *freeship* at college, and who says he is going to join the *teachery* profession and who after a few years says he is engaged in *headmastery*? Similarly, why should we accept the English phrase *mare's nest*, and object to *horse's*

The Indianness 143

egg, so familiar in the columns of *Amrita Bazar Patrika*? Why should we adhere to *all this* when *this all* is the natural order suggested by the usage of our own language? Why insist on *yet* following *though* when in Hindustani we use the equivalent of *but*? Must we condemn the following sentence because it does not conform to English idiom, even though it is a literal translation of our own idiom? *I shall not pay a pice what to say of a rupee.* Is there any rational ground for objecting to *family members* and adhering to *members of the family*? ... A little courage, some determination, a wholesome respect for our own idioms and we shall before long have a virile, vigorous *Indian English.* (Reported in the *Ceylon Daily News*, 28 September 1940).

Jha's tone is perhaps rhetorical, and the arguments not very clear, but what he is aiming at is to emphasize the distinctive characteristics of IE, which, as he argues, are determined by the transference.

15. Unit is used here both for the units of description as used in Halliday (1961) and for contextual units. The second use of the term is non-Hallidayan and is discussed in chapter 3.
16. Used in the sense of a *provider* or *helper*.
17. Mode of reference to Lord Siva in Hindu mythology.
18. Also see chapter 3, p.101.
19. In certain circles it is the normal mode of address or reference used for one's wife. Note that in Indian orthodox circles a woman is not expected to refer to her husband by his name. In such situations, a third person pronoun may be used.
20. It is, however, difficult to say whether, on the part of a writer, the attempt to establish equivalence is 'conscious' or 'unconscious'.
21. Frequently used in southern India as a term of address.
22. Rank-bound translation applies to the higher units of description too, Consider, for example, the items 'horse's egg' *ghōṛārḍim* (Bengali) and 'king of pearls' *motiyamdā bādshah* (Punjabi); both of these are nominals belonging to unit group in the native languages.
23. Only the English equivalents are given here.
24. For instance, Anand (1948:23) '... for now I literally translate all the dialogues in my novels from my mother tongue and think out the narrative mostly the same way'.
25. Note also the following three-item collocations: *brother-anointing-ceremony* (*K* 56); *inter-district criminals* (*SL* 6 June 1959); *inter-caste-unions* (*MM* 190); *nine-stranded-thread* (*HW* 45); *red-paste-trident* (*HW* 98); *rice-initiation ceremony* (*K* 37); *thousand-and-eight flames ceremony* (*K* 142).
26. The formation *salt-giver* is used in a metaphorical sense of referring to one who is a provider (of food, etc.). It is a translation of *annadātā*.
27. Also consider *strength of class* → *roll strength*; *a box of matches* → *match box*.
28. He also lists the following formations under this class: *state subject, government-member, sandal-wood pieces, bride-price, bridegroom price, English-educated, England-goers, foreign-travelled, tea-cups, grape-bunches, grass-blades*.
29. In terms of the structure, it is a rank-bound and item-bound transfer. It is rank-bound in the sense that structurally in Bengali and English it belongs to the same unit ('word', compound) and item-bound in the sense that *phūl* has been equated with *flower* and *shэjjā* with *bed*. The collocation has been used in the same contextual unit in which *phūl shэjjā* operates in Bengali culture. As mentioned earlier, in this case the register-confusion could be avoided by the use of an item like *nuptial bed*.

30. As discussed in earlier chapters, a parallel to this cross-cultural linguistic situation is not difficult to find. A significant number of *Americanisms* or *Australianisms* have been so named because the English-speaking settlers in America and Australia had to coin new expressions for the contextual items of the new world. Hence the following Americanisms: *bull-frog, razor-back, turkey-gobbler, egg-plant, Jimson-weed, fox-grape, apple-butter* (Mencken 1919 [1941]: 113–21). For Australianisms see Morris (1898: 160).

    The case of Indianisms, however, is different in the sense that in India it is not a group of new settlers using their L_1 in new situations in a new country. In this case, a second language is used by the natives in their own native contexts. The introduction of such Indianisms may be traced back to early foreign travellers to India, who borrowed a large number of Indian words into English, or coined many hybrid formations for Indian contexts. See also chapters 5 and 6.

31. Reference to a caste-symbol on one's forehead, cf. '*A fine thing too, it is, you with your broad ash-mark and your queer son and his ways.*' (*K* 65).

32. Showing social attitude toward a widow in Hindu society, cf. '*What to that bangled widow? She will lead us all to prostitution*'. (*K* 233.) (A Hindu widow is not supposed to wear any ornaments.)

33. Restricted to ceremonies in Hindu temples.

34. On the analogy of *black-market*, cf. . . . '*and he had more than a hundred thousand rupees of black money in the locker.*' (*TN* 43).

35. A special ritual performed in the Hindu wedding ceremony.

36. Used in the sense of 'cremation-ground'.

37. Reference to the famous Hindu festival in Puri, Orissa.

38. '*On this, her flower-bed, her seven children were born.*' (*MM* 109).

39. '*Heera Lal knowing the caste injunctions would not touch the forbidden meat.*' (*MM* 31).

40. Restricted to the religious register. '*I will make a milk-bath offering to the deity.*' (*HW* 124).

41. Reference to the holy thread (*janeo*) worn by Hindus. '*That white . . . nine-stranded thread shall gleam across your chest.*' (*HW* 45).

42. A crimson mark of trident shape on the forehead of Brahmins.

43. '*His forehead smeared with red vermilion and a splash of sacred ash.*' (*FE* 52).

    Furthermore, note that in many cases affixation is used to form Indianisms for Indian contextual units. Consider, for example, the following: *inter-dine, inter-marriage* (*MM* 11), *inter-marry* (*HS* 15 June 1959), *sub-caste* (*AD* 10), *casteless* (*HW* 203).

44. For instance, the term *brother-in-law* has one restricted meaning in British English as a kinship term; in IE it has acquired three distinct meanings as a term of (1) abuse, (2) affection or intimacy, and (3) kinship. The terms *sister* and *mother* have extended collocations as terms of regard and respect without relationship: '*Now you know what your duties are, and how to do them, sister, you will receive our instructions.*' (*WM* 93).

    In IE, then, as discussed in chapter 3 (section 3), the members of the English kinship system, e.g., *brother-in-law, cousin, father* and *mother*, need different formal and contextual statements since: (1) the members of one British English set operate in three sets in IE; and (2) the meaning of items has been extended.

45. In IE the members of the BE kinship system may operate in any of the following sets: (1) modes of address/reference, (2) terms of endearment, (3) terms of regard and respect, (4) markers of attitude (*brother-in-law*); and, in the normal BE sense, (5) terms of kinship.

III   LEXICAL EXTENSION

5

Lexical Innovations

1.0. In this chapter I propose to discuss certain characteristic lexical features of South Asian English (hereafter abbreviated SAE) which to a large extent are peculiar to this variety of English as opposed to its other native and non-native varieties. The examples discussed here are drawn primarily from Indian English texts. However, on a closer study it becomes apparent that it is more meaningful to consider these as SAE innovations, since historically the whole subcontinent had almost an identical impact of the English language. The underlying linguistic and sociocultural motivations for these lexical innovations are thus essentially shared by India, Pakistan, Bangladesh, Sri Lanka and Nepal. Therefore, it is both contextually and linguistically significant not to treat these innovations merely as Indian but as South Asian. That provides a better understanding of the *South Asianness* in this variety of English (see also Kachru 1982e).

In my earlier studies on SAE (e.g., Kachru 1961 and 1965 and later) I have focussed attention on a number of productive linguistic processes characteristic of Indian English. This chapter is essentially data-oriented and is restricted to those lexical innovations which, in terms of their constituents, may be termed 'hybrid innovations.'

The studies by Bansal (1969) and Kachru (1969a and 1973a) have shown that in order to determine and, if possible, 'measure' the intelligibility of SAE with other varieties it is crucial to analyze SAE data at various linguistic levels. It seems to me that the lexical aspect has serious implications for intelligibility—both in the written and spoken modes—between SAE users and the users of other varieties of English. The deviations at this level are especially evident in the texts of SAE creative writing and journalism.

The peculiar South Asian contexts in which these lexical items function have been taken into consideration in some earlier lexicographical studies (e.g., Wilson 1940 [1855]; Yule and Burnell 1886; Rao 1954). In other varieties of English, too (e.g., Australian, West African), contextual differences play an important role not only by adding new items to the lexical stock of the language, but also in giving extended semantic markers to certain lexical items (see, e.g., Ramson 1966). This then leads to problems in intelligibility and lends distinctive characteristics to each variety.

2.0. EARLIER RESEARCH

Interest in the compilation of lexical lists for SAE dates back to Sir Charles Wilkins's appending of a glossary of such items to the *Fifth Report* of the Select Committee of 1812 (see Yule and Burnell 1886:xv).

Before this attempt, as Yule and Burnell have stated, early travellers to India had compiled some fragmentary lexical lists.[1] One of the first 'register-oriented' studies in this direction is Wilson's *Glossary of Judicial and Revenue Terms* (1855), 'which leaves far behind every other attempt in that kind' (Yule and Burnell 1886:xv). About fifteen years later such a list was also compiled for Sri Lankan English, entitled *Ceylonese Vocabulary: Lists of Native Words Commonly Occurring in Official Correspondence and Other Documents* (Colombo, 1869).

The culmination of such research is found in the highly readable and interesting lexicon *Hobson-Jobson: A Glossary of Colloquial Anglo-Indian Words and Phrases, and of Kindred Terms, Etymological, Historical, Geographical and Discursive.* Originally compiled by Henry Yule and A. C. Burnell in 1886, the work was reissued in a new edition edited by William Crook in 1903[2] and has recently been reprinted.[3] Because of the immense value of the work in terms of its lexicographic method and data, it may not be out of place to include a brief discussion of it here.

Attempts prior to the publication of *Hobson-Jobson* were mainly 'intended to facilitate the comprehension of official documents by the explanation of terms used in the Revenue department, or in other branches of Indian administration' (Yule and Burnell 1886 [1903]: xv-xvi). *Hobson-Jobson*, on the other hand,

... was intended to deal with all that class of words which, not in general pertaining to the technicalities of administration, recur constantly in the daily intercourse of the English in India, either as expressing ideas really not provided for by our mother-tongue, or supposed by the speakers (often quite erroneously) to express something not capable of just denotation by any English term. A certain percentage of such words have been carried to England by the constant reflux to their native shore of Anglo-Indians, who in some degree imbue with their notions and phraseology the circles from which they had gone forth. This effect has been still more promoted by the currency of a vast mass of literature, of all qualities and for all ages, dealing with Indian subjects; as well as by the regular appearance, for many years past, of Indian correspondence in English newspapers, insomuch that a considerable number of the expressions in question have not only become familiar in sound to English ears, but have become naturalised in the English language, and are meeting with ample recognition in the great Dictionary edited by Dr Murray at Oxford. [4]

The growth of South Asian lexical stock in British English has rightly been treated as a 'study of Indo-British cultural and linguistic relations' by Rao (1954). In his 'Introductory Note' to Rao's study, W.A. Craigie emphasizes this aspect. In Craigie's opinion, the lexical study of Rao is of value and interest for the following reasons: 'It brings together the history of the British in India and the result of this in enriching their own language during a period of three centuries and a half.' (Rao 1954:v).

Rao's study, *Indian Words in English*, is the first serious study in SAE lexicography which discusses the Indian element in the English language from cultural, historical, phonetic, grammatical and semantic angles.

If viewed in the framework of their goals, the earlier lexical studies were successful: their aim was to provide vocabulary lists for the use of the civil servants of the raj. On the other hand, in terms of lexicographical sophistication, these studies were rather amateurish. Nonetheless, in later years these works were used as dependable source material for selecting South Asian borrowings for the standard lexicons of British and American English.

In this study the term *lexis* is used in a rather restricted sense, referring to single lexical items which have either found their way into the mainstream of the English language or which form a special class in the sense that they are register-restricted and are used only in South Asian contexts in SAE.

I shall briefly refer to the single lexical items (see below, section 3.1) but shall mainly focus attention on certain productive processes employed by educated SAE users at the lexical level in producing hybrid lexical items.

3.0. SOUTH ASIAN ELEMENT IN ENGLISH

The earliest of the South Asian language items to intrude into the English language were essentially those lexical items which came through travel literature. The second phase developed with the register-restricted items whose history is not different from American Indian items in American English and aboriginal language items in Australian English. Wilson (1855 [1940]: i) has succinctly shown the need for such items:

Ryot and *Ryotwar*, for instance, suggest more precise and positive notions in connection with the subject of the land revenue in the South of India, than would be conveyed by cultivator, or peasant, or agriculturist, or by an agreement for rent or revenue with the individual members of the agricultural classes.

As the East India Company became established in India, first in commercial terms and later in political terms, its orders towards the use of South Asian items in the English language began to reflect a specific language attitude. Perhaps it was a trend of the times which is reflected also in Jonathan Swift's letter to 'the Most Honourable Robert, Earl of Oxford and Mortimer, Lord High Treasurer of Great Britain', which contained *A Proposal for Correcting, Improving, and Ascertaining the English Tongue*. In the letter, Swift suggests (1883 : v. 9 : 147 [written in 1712]):

The persons who are to undertake this work, will have the example of the French before them, to imitate where these have proceeded right, and to avoid their mistakes. Besides the grammar part, wherein we are allowed to be very defective, they will observe many gross improprieties, which, however authorized by practice, and grown familiar, ought to be discarded. They will find many words that deserve to be utterly thrown out of our language, many more to be corrected, and perhaps not a few long since antiquated, which ought to be restored on account of their energy and sound.

The following excerpt further displays this attitude:

We have forbidden the severall Factoryes from wrighting words in this language and refrayned itt our selves, though in books of coppies we feare there are many which by wante of tyme for perusall we cannot rectefie or expresse. [5]

As Rao (1954) has stated, '. . . the natural tendency to borrow could not be completely checked by official command' (see Rao 1954: 4). The following letter, written by Robert Young and John Willoughby at Lahore to the President and Council at Surat, 26 October 1624, is an illustration of the profuse use of South Asian lexical items:

Their last was of the 15th present, with a copy of the king's 'furmand' [*furmān:* command]. Since then they have procured the dispatch of two 'haddies' [*ahadi:* a royal messenger], who are ordered to carry to them the royal farmān, in company of John Willoughby, 'Cojah [Kwaja Abul Hasan] havinge given them his parwanna [*parwana*: a written order] to see all things restoored unto you and re-established againe in youre formar trad and priviolidges.' The messengers should therefore be acquainted with all moneys unjustly taken from them, either by Safi Khān, 'Chuckedares [chaukīdār: here, a custom-guard] or radarries' [*rāhdār*: a road-guard]. . . . [6]

The frequency of South Asian lexical items kept increasing and about one hundred and fifty years later the multitude of these terms in use prompted Edmund Burke's observation:

This language is indeed of necessary use in the executive department of the company's affairs; but it is not necessary to Parliament. A language so foreign from all the ideas and habits of the far greater part of the members of the House, has a tendency to disgust them with all sorts of inquiry concerning this subject. They are fatigued into such a despair of ever obtaining a competent knowledge of the transactions in India, that they are easily persuaded to remand them . . . to obscurity.[7]

It seems that during this period two distinct attitudes regarding South Asian language items in English prevailed. First, a large number of documents reveal that the administrators of the raj in Britain did not necessarily approve of the South Asian elements in the administrative register of the Indian Civil Service. Second, the administrators of the raj in India—both Indians and perhaps non-Indians—considered such borrowings from South Asian languages crucial for effective administration in India. However, in later years, through a variety of registers, South Asian items were borrowed into the English language. Consider, for example, the following items which came to English in the seventeenth and eighteenth centuries. Administration: *batta* (1632), *cadi* (1608), *chit* (1608), *crore*, *dawk* (1623), *firman* (1614), *kotwal* (1623), *sunnud* (1759), *rahdaree* (1623); Agriculture: *bigha* (1763), *hashish (hasheesh)* (1598, 1613), *jumma* (1781), *jowar* (1636), *ryotti* (1772), *zamindar* (1656), *zamindari* (1757). According to the sources listed below, the extent of South Asian items in English varies from 188 items to 26,000 items.

(1) Fennell (1892: xi)   399 [8]
(2) *Oxford English Dictionary*   900 [9]
(3) Wilson (1940) [1855]   26,000 [10]
(4) Serjeantsen (1961: 220-60)   188

These figures do not include South Asian items in various registers of SAE, as no survey of such items has been made.

It seems to me that in order to find the structure of such items in SAE, an analysis of the following SAE registers is desirable : (1) SAE creative writing; (2) SAE journalism; and (3) SAE officialese.

4.0. TYPES OF LEXICAL INNOVATIONS

Lexical innovations in SAE are essentially of the following types:

4.1. *Single Items*

By single item innovation I mean the transfer of South Asian lexical items into SAE. These items are to be separated from hybrid items and other innovations, such as *shifts* or *loan translations* (cf. chapter 4, pp. 133–35). By shifts we mean those South Asian items which are an adaptation of an underlying formal item from a South Asian language which provides the source for the South Asian English item. A loan translation involves a formal equivalence between a South Asian language item and SAE. These items are further to be subgrouped into two additional categories. There are, first, those items which have become part of the lexical stock of the English language and are used both in British and American English, and may, therefore, be termed 'assimilated items'. For administrative, cultural, and political reasons the borrowing of South Asian items is higher in British English than in American English. Second, there are those items which have not necessarily been included in the lexicons of the native varieties of English, but have high frequency in various registers of SAE. I shall use the terms 'non-restricted lexical items' (or 'assimilated items') for the first type and 'restricted lexical items' for the second type. The first are non-restricted in the sense that they do not occur only in SAE. However, note that a large number of lexical items in the above-discussed types have certain semantic constraints which they do not have in the South Asian language from which they have been borrowed. These constraints are either in terms of extended semantic features or restricted semantic features (e.g., the use of *purdah* in SAE; cf. p. 155). A study of such lexical items shows that only a few South Asian words have found their way into the native varieties of English. On the other hand, considerably more are used in SAE writing, especially in journalism.

It seems that the borrowing of lexical items from South Asian languages into SAE is not arbitrary ; these are register-restricted and may be classified according to their semantic fields (cf. 4.7).[11] A need to list

such register-restricted items was one reason for earlier lexicographical work in SAE. Yule and Burnell (1886[1903] xv–xvi) gives a large
number of words 'expressing ideas really not provided for by our
mother tongue.'

Those lexical items which are restricted to SAE and which are frequently used in SAE writing (especially in journalism) provide an
interesting example of the distinctiveness of SAE at the lexical level.
The following excerpts from standard SAE newspapers are illustrative
of register-restricted items:

He set the pace for the recital with a briskly rendered Pranamamayakam in
Gowlai, a composition of Mysore Vasudevachar. One liked the manner in
which he and his accompanying vidwan built up the Kriti embellishing it with
little flourishes here and there.... Then came Kamboji alapana for Pallavi.
...with Vedanayagam Pillai's Nane Unnie Nambinane in Hamsanandi,
the recital came to a glorious end (*The Statesman*, New Delhi, 14 December
1969).

Again:

This is clear from the results of the panchayat elections announced yesterday.
The elections were held on Sunday and some 170,000 villagers cast their
votes to elect 180 pradhans and 1500 odd members of gaon sabhas. Pradhans
and members of 15 gaon sabhas were elected unopposed (*The Hindustan Times*,
New Delhi, 17 December 1969).

One can add such examples from other registers, too. Consider, for
example, the following from Pakistani English and Lankan English:

He [Major General S. D. Khan Niazi] was addressing various detachments
of Mujahids who participated in the Mujahids mela held at Kasur (*Dawn*,
Karachi, 4 February 1970).

Among those who called at the avasa of the new Mahanayke of the.... (*The
Times of Ceylon*, Colombo, 26 November 1969).

4.2. *Hybridized Items*

By a hybridized lexical item is meant a lexical item which comprises
two or more elements, at least one of which is from a South Asian
language and one from English. The elements of a hybrid formation
may belong either to an *open set* or to a *closed system* in lexis. An open-set
item is considered 'open' in the sense that there are no grammatical
constraints on the selection of the elements of the item. Consider, for
example, the following: *lathi-charge* (*HS* 15.6159); *kumkum mark* (*K*
159). A closed-system item is 'closed' in the sense that at least one

element belongs to the closed system of a South Asian language; for example, the suffix-*wala* in *policewala* (*SMH* 61).

4.2.1. *Constraints on Hybridized Items*

It seems that there are certain structural and contextual constraints on hybridized items. By structural constraint is meant the possibility of 'element' substitution. Let us consider *lathi-charge*. In this item *daṇḍā* is not substitutable for *lathi*, although the two items are semantically 'identical.' It is also very rare that *lathi* is replaced by *baton*. On the other hand, there are other hybrid formations which are used interchangeably (cf. *police thana* and *police station*). The question of contextual constraints on South Asian items in SAE is further discussed below, in 4.3.2. In a sense, many of these items have become fixed collocations in their specific registers.

4.3. *Types of Hybrid Innovations*

There are the following main types of hybridization in SAE: (1) hybrid collocations, (2) hybrid lexical set (s), (3) hybrid ordered series of words (OSW); and (4) hybrid reduplication.

4.3.1. *Hybrid Collocations*

In contrast to a non-hybrid collocation, a hybrid collocation has these additional characteristics: it is composed of elements from two or more different languages; it is formally and contextually restricted; and its operation is generally restricted to one register in SAE, though the South Asian element may have a wider range of functions in the South Asian source language(s). Consider, for example, *khilafat committee, Sarvodaya leader, satyagraha movement, Swatantra Party, swadeshi cloth, halqua president*.

4.3.2. *Hybrid Lexical Sets*

A hybrid collocation and a hybrid lexical set are not necessarily mutually exclusive. As stated above (see 4.3.1), a hybrid collocation is register-restricted (or bound) in SAE. In the South Asian source language(s), on the other hand, a South Asian lexical item does not have contextual constraints in the same sense in which it has these constraints in SAE. These may, therefore, also be termed hybrid lexical sets. The following examples may clarify this distinction. In the SAE texts which I examined, the item *purdah* (in Indian and Pakistani English) preceded only *-women, -system, -lady*. It therefore is register restricted in SAE and has a limited semantic range as it occurs only in one register. On the other hand, in Hindi-Urdu *purdah* does not have any such register restriction. Consider, among others, the following contexts in which it occurs: *drapes; curtain (of a movie, theatre); screen; hindrance; veil; wall; layers; oar;* 'a fret of a musical instrument such as a guitar.' In addition to these, it may also be used in the following fixed collocations: *pardā kholnā* 'to expose a secret'; *pardā ḍālnā* 'to cover up a secret or an act'; *pardā rahnā* 'to remain unexposed'; *pardā lagānā* 'to remain under the veil'; *parde mẽ baiṭhnā* 'to remain under protection'. In SAE it has only one semantic marker and no idiomatic uses. Other items such as *ahimsa, satyagraha, sarvodaya* are again restricted to one register (that of politics), while in Hindi-Urdu they have no such register-restriction.

4.3.3. *Hybrid Ordered Series of Words* [13]
A hybrid lexical set, as discussed above, is abstracted on the basis of the function of items in particular registers. We may make quantitative statements about their lexical environments and possibilities of occurrence in various registers. The members of an OSW are not necessarily contextually restricted. An OSW has certain formal and contextual characteristics which distinguish it from a lexical set. In terms of context, the members of an OSW may belong to one or more registers; and, formally, all the members of an OSW have one element in common, as well as a common structure.

The members of an OSW may or may not form a lexical set, since they can operate in different contexts. The basis for abstracting them is essentially their structural similarity. Consider, for example, the following set: *angrezi-chair,-furniture,-proverb,-race,-sweet,-teapot,-women*. The names of days in Hindi and Kashmiri form an OSW; but the names of months in Hindi, Kashmiri, and English form a lexical set. It may so happen that the members of an OSW are also members of a lexical set—just as are the analogous categories in grammar ('class' analogous to a lexical set, 'paradigm' analogous to OSW)—since these are not mutually exclusive.

4.3.4. *Hybrid Reduplication*
In a language contact situation sometimes two or more components with an 'identical' lexical meaning in the languages from which they

are taken are used as single formations. Such formations may be termed
'hybrid reduplication.' Consider, for example, the following: *lathi-
stick* (*K* 210); *cotton-kapas* (*M* 1 January 1959); *curved-kukri* (*SIF* 61).

4.4. *Lexical Diffusion and Hybridized Items*

There are also some hybrid formations which may start as area-bound
and then slowly cut across the linguistic isoglosses into another language area. These are, by and large, contextually determined and
refer to material objects, customs, fauna-flora, or religious practices
which are part of the culture of a specific area or a group; and they
gain currency by use in SAE writing, debates in Parliament, or in the
state assemblies. These formations are pan-Indian in the sense that
they form part of South Asian writing in English. Consider, for example, the following formations which are, by and large, restricted
to the south of India: *coconut paysam* (*AD* 8; *M* 1 January 1959); *jibba
pocket* (*WM* 19); *jutka driver* (*BA* 101); *kuruvai harvest: kuruvai straw* (*M*
1 January 1959); *potato bonda* (*WM* 222). Note also that items such as
yakka carriage (*BH* 55) and *yakka driver* are mostly used in north India,
though contextually these are identical to *jutka carriage* of south
India. *Religious diwan* (*IN* 12 June 1959) is limited to the Sikh community in the Punjab, and *dadan money* (*HS* 11 June 1959) has been
found in the restricted language of agriculture used in West Bengal.

4.5. *Classification of Hybrid Formations*

In the following classification I have discussed hybrid formations according to the units and the elements which operate in their structure.

A large number of hybrid formations belong to the nominal
group, with two or more elements in the structure. I have divided
these into the following two subgroups: (1) South Asian item as
head, (2) South Asian item as modifier.

4.5.1. *South Asian Item as Head*

The first group includes those formations in which there are two elements and the relationship is that of a modifier and a head. The first
component—the modifier—is from English and the head is from a
South Asian language, e.g., *British sarkar* (*BH* 192). The second group
also belongs to the class nominal but the order of elements in the
group is reversed. In this case, a South Asian lexical item functions

as a modifier, and an English lexical item as the head, e.g., *ayurveda-system* (*MM* 99).

In the first group the formations of modifier-head (MH) relationships have been further subgrouped according to the position of the components, i.e., (i) NN type, (ii) AN type, and (iii) *-ing* as H type.

1. NN type: In these the first element belongs to the class noun, e.g., *babu English* (*SR* 33), *-mentality* (*IN* 3 December 1960), *canal-bund* (*SR* 281); *Christian sadhu* (*FF* 257); *city kotwali; coconut paysam* (*AD* 8); *college babu* (*F of F* 33); *Congress pandal* (*Un* 212); *-raj* (*SR* 31); *copper pie* (*SMH* 91); *cotton kapas* (*M* 1 January 1959); *-pajama* (*HA* 139); *-sadri* (*BH* 147); *-sari* (*RH* 153); *-satranji* (*HW* 222); *doctor sahib* (*HJ* 590); *evening -bhajan* (*K* 186); *-puja* (*HW* 170); *flower bazaar* (*HA* 56); *gang coolie* (*AD* 181); *glass choorie* (*HW* 211); *gold mohar* (*TN*); *gram khir* (*K* 43); *marriage pandal* (*NS* 34); *onion pecoras* (*RH* 17); *police jamadar* (*K* 29); *-lathi* (*K* 162); *-thana* (*SMH* 85); *rail gadi* (*BH* 75); *ration ghat* (*V* 10 May 1960); *Saturday haat* (*SMH* 52); *solar topee* (*VG* 10); *string charpoy* (*SF* 151); *tamarind chutney* (*SR* 244); *tank bund* (*AD* 61); *vermicelli paysam* (*K* 18); *village panchayat* (*Hit*); *zamindari system* (*IN* 28 December 1959).

2. AN type: In these the first element belongs to the class adjective, e.g., *British sarkar* (*BH* 192); *ceremonial pronom* (*HW* 195); *counterfeit kismet* (*BH* 182); *double roti* (*C* 261); *eternal upavasi* (*SR* 386); *evil sarkar* (*BH* 51); *holy mantra* (*MN* 64); *imperial raj* (*HA* 141); *landless kisan* (*SMH* 18); *religious diwan* (*IN* 12 June 1959); *swadeshi cloth* (*K* 63); *-shroud* (*TN* 154); *yakka* carriage (*BH* 55).

(3) *-ing* H type: In a restricted number of formations the *-ing* form functions as a modifier, e.g., *burning-ghaut* (*BH* 207); *burning-ghee* (*BA* 66).

4.5.2. *South Asian Item as Modifier*

In terms of structure, the items discussed below are also of the unit group (class nominal), but the difference is that the position of the modifier is reversed. In this case, an English item functions as a head. This group has been further subdivided into the following: (1) derivative N, (2) *-ing* as head, (3) agentive, (4) verb as head, (5) noun + noun.

1. Derivative N, e.g., *anjali salutation* (*FF* 84); *bazaar musician* (*FF* 16); *haldi invitation* (*K* 152); *kashi pilgrimage* (*K* 199); *vilayati mixture* (*BH* 102); *yakka carriage* (*BH* 55).

2. *-ing* as head, e.g., *beedi-smoking* (*SR* 198); *durri weaving* (*SL* 8 June

1959); *goonda-looking* (*TN* 129); *kirtan singing* (*FF* 221); *pan-spitting* (*SR* 31); *puja-offering* (*HW* 127).

3. Agentive, e.g., *ashram scavenger* (*U* 217); *-sweeper (U)*; *beedi-seller* (*AD* 52); *charas smuggler* (*IE* 12 June 1959); *harikatha performer* (*K* 23); *jutka driver* (*BA* 101); *palki-bearer* (*MM* 214); *paria-mixer* (*K* 63); *sarangi player* (*SJ* 106); *sarvodaya leader, senai player* (*HW* 159); *sherbet-dealer* (*BH* 34); *tiffin carrier* (*VG* 19); *tom-tom beater* (*AD* 111); *tonga driver* (*VG* 36).

4. Verb as H, e.g., *guru ridden* (*FF* 171); *ghee-fried* (*HW* 205); *khadi-bound* (*K* 41); *khaddar-clad* (*TN* 14); *sari-clad* (*SMH* 81).

5. N + N: This class is most productive; such formations are frequently seen in the newspapers and other pieces of creative writing. These hybrid formations are used in various socio-cultural contexts in South Asia (see 4.7): *ahimsa soldier* (*WM* 78); *-spell* (*SMH* 84); *akashti holiday* (*BH* 162); *akkulu paddy* (*M* 1 January 1959); *anna coin* (*AD* 123); *aroti ceremony* (*HW* 113), *-time* (*HW* 207); *aruni-field* (*SR* 282); *asirvad ceremony* (*WM* 115); *ashram camp* (*WM* 82); *-disciple* (*MM* 82); *attar bottle* (*SR* 266); *ayurveda system* (*MM* 166); *baran rite* (*MM* 98); *basar chamber* (*MM* 85); *-room* (*MM* 73); *basavana bull* (*SR* 293); *bhajan song* (*SMH* 171); *chit-book* (*RH* 71); *choli-piece* (*SR* 58); *dadan money* (*HS* 11 June 1959); *dak bungalow* (*TP* 56); *-edition* (*HT* 2 March 1956); *durbar hall* (*AD* 224); *halqua committee* (*V* 19 May 1960); *harikatha-man* (*K* 23); *hookah party* (*VG* 108); *janta express* (*Hit* 30 December 1959); *jibba pocket* (*WM* 19); *kartik light* (*K* 127); *kharif season* (*OR* 15 July 1959); *khilafat committee* (*TN* 153); *khus-khus blind* (*SF* 19); *kumkum mark* (*K* 159); *kumkum -rice* (*SR* 123); *lathi-charge* (*HS* 15 June 1959); *mela festival* (*Hit* 28 December 1950); *mela-ground* (*HS* 11 June 1959); *mofussil town* (*TN* 69); *mondal Congress* (*HS* 15 June 1959); *nautch-girl* (*FF* 13); *-party* (*SR* 289); *pan shop* (*DD* 25); *-stall* (*RH* 80); *panchayat hall* (*K* 116); *pheni dinner* (*SR* 227); *punkah-boy* (*SR* 90); *rudrakshi bead* (*K* 136); *sainik school* (*IN* 1 July 1961); *sanai music* (*MM* 72); *sandhi rites* (*AD* 53); *sarvodaya conference* (*HT* 9 June 1959); *shagan ceremony* (*BH* 124); *sherbet shop* (*BH* 98); *shirshasana posture* (*HA* 30); *sindur mark* (*MM* 99); *Swatantra Party* (*FPJ* 11 June 1959); *taccavi loan* (*HT* 1 September 1958); *taluk magistrate* (*K* 201); *-office* (*AD* 61); *tehsil school* (*HE*); *toddy shop* (*HS* 15 June 1959); *upanayanam ceremony* (*SR* 323); *vinayaka festival* (*ET* 21); *zari work*; *zenana affair* (*FF* 66); *-life* (*SR* 181).

4.5.3. *String Formations*

In a string formation we have more than two elements, one of which may be a compound modifying a head, which may be from a South Asian language or from English. Consider the following: *four-anna class* (*AD* 84); *high-class lallas* (*BH* 125); *hillman coolie* (*BH* 86); *homespun khaddar* (*BH* 48); *pot-bellied bania* (*TN* 112) ; *state-wide hartal* (*BH* 7 June 1959).

4.6. *Hybridization and Derivative Suffixes*

The hybrid formations with derivative suffixes from the South Asian languages or English are grouped into the following three categories: (1) non-English head and English derivational suffix; (2) English head and non-English derivational suffix; and (3) non-English head and English prefix of negation.

The following English derivative suffixes are used with South Asian lexical items: *-dom, colliedom* (*C* 94); *-hood, sadhuhood* (*U* 59); *chaprasi-hood* (*C* 10); *-ism, goondaism* (*HK* 413); *-ship, patelship* (*K* 144); *-worth, piceworth* (*SMH* 161); *-ic, upanishadic* (*SR* 25).

In the texts I found only one South Asian suffix, *-wallah*, which is used with a large number of nouns to denote an *owner*, or *possessor*, or *master*, for instance, *higher-type-wallah* (*HT* 10 June 1959); *factory wallah* (*C* 82); *Congress wallah* (*RH* 119); *five rupee wallah* (*BJ* 7 June 1959); *police wallah* (*SMH* 61).

The English prefix of negation *non-* has a high frequency and is used with a large number of items, e.g., *non-Brahmin* (*OR* 15 July 1959); *non-adivasi* (*ABP* 26 October 1959).

The above taxonomy provides some indication of SAE hybrid formations in terms of their surface structures.

4.7. *Contextual Distribution of Hybridized Items*

The following contextual classification of hybrid items lists the semantic areas in which these formations occur. This classification is based on restricted data.

(1) Administration: *city kotwali; halqua committee* (*V* 19 May 1960); *-president* (*V* 19 May 1960); *kotwali police* (*P* 10 June 1959); *mofussil town* (*TN* 69); *nala scheme* (*FPJ* 11 June 1959); *police thana* (*SMH* 85); *ration ghat* (*V* 18 May 1960); *taluk magistrate* (*K* 201); *-office* (*AD* 61).

(2) Agriculture: *akkulu paddy* (*M* 1 January 1959); *basungi paddy* (*M* 1 January 1959); *dadan money* (*HS* 11 June 1959); *kharif season OR* 15 July 1959) (also *-crop, -production*); *kuruvai harvest* (*M* 1 January 1959);

nazul land (*HT* 1 February 1961); *rabi crop, samba straw* (*M* 1 September 1958); *sonamukhi rice* (*SMH* 77); *taccavi loan* (*Hit* 1 September 1958).

(3) Animals/reptiles: *basavana-bull* (*SR* 293); *dhaman snake* (*MM* 201); *jantri bird* (*FF* 53).

(4) Arms: *curved kukri* (*SF* 61).

(5) Articles of use: *angrezi furniture* (*C* 95); (also *-teapot*); *attar bottle* (*SR* 266); *chit-book* (*RH* 71); *cotton kapas* (*M* 1 January 1959); *-satranji* (*HW* 222); *glass choorie* (*HW* 211); *khus fibre* (*TP* 109); *khus khus blind* (*SF* 19); *-grass* (*SF* 13); *lotah shelf* (*Hit* 30 December 1959); *pashmina jacket* (*HA* 173); *-robe* (*HA* 176); *punkah rope* (*TP* 28); *taffeta curtain* (*RH* 97); *tiffin carrier* (*DD* 78); *toddy-pot* (*K* 194).

(6) Art/music: *bazaar musician* (*FF* 16); *damaru drum* (*FF* 237); *mithuna image* (*FF* 270); *nautch girl* (*SR* 289); *-party* (*FF* 13); *ragmala paintings* (*SJ* 34); *senai music* (*MM* 72); *-player* (*HW* 159); *veena solo* (*RH* 205).

(7) Buildings: *dak bungalow* (*TP* 56); *durbar hall* (*AD* 224); *panchayat hall* (*K* 116).

(8) Clothing/dress: *choli-piece* (*SR* 58); *coolie-hat* (*SF* 95); *durbar turban* (*K* 167); *himru jacket* (*SR* 344).

(9) Concepts: *counterfeit kismet* (*BH* 182); *kismet idea* (*BH* 78).

(10) Edibles/drinks: *angrezi sweets* (*C* 36); *coconut paysam* (*AD* 8); *dal mixture* (*NS* 195); *-soup* (*K* 43); *-water* (*SR* 295); *double roti* (*C* 171); *ghee-fried* (*HW* 205); *gram khir* (*K* 43); *madhobi vine* (*SMH* 15); *mango-chutney* (*RH* 157); *onion-pacoras* (*RH* 171) (also *-pecoras*); *pan leaf; pheni dinner* (*SR* 277); *potato bonda* (*WM* 222); *tamarind chutney* (*SR* 244); *vermillion paysam* (*K* 18).

(11) Education: *dakshina fund* (*HE*); *janta college* (*HE*).

(12) Evaluation (attitude): *babu-mentality* (*IN* 3 December 1960); also *-like* (*IN* 3 December 1960); *chamar people* (*HW* 106); *goondaism* (*H* 2 March 1964); *-looking* (*TN* 129) (also *-like*); *guru-ridden* (*FF* 171); *natu habits* (*U* 28); *paria-mixer* (*K* 63); *sarkari spy* (*BH* 51); *vilayati fashion* (*BH* 185); *-mixture* (*BH* 102).

(13) Furuniture: *angrezi furniture* (*C* 95); *cotton satranji* (*HW* 222); *nawari bed* (*BH* 28); *string charpai* (*SF* 151); *veranda chair* (*HA* 160).

(14) Habits: *beedi-smoking* (*SR* 198); *pan-spitting* (*SR* 31).

(15) Medicine: *ayurveda system* (*MM* 166).

(16) Modes of address/reference: *ahimsa soldier* (*WM* 78); *angrezi women, babu manager, brahma admirer* (*FF* 253); *British sarkar* (*BH* 192); *charas smuggler* (*IE* 12 June 1959); *college babu* (*FF* 253); *doctor sahib* (*DD* 247); (also *colonel sahib, foreign sahib*); *factory wallah* (*C* 82); *five-rupee- wallah* (*BJ* 5 June 1959); *high-class lallah* (*BH* 125); *higher-type*

wallah (*HT* 10 June 1959); *memsahib* (*DD* 231); *miss sahib* (*VG* 81); *police jamadar* (*K* 29); *pot-bellied bania* (*TN* 112); *punkah-boy* (*SR* 90); *sentry sahib* (*TP* 138); *tom-tom beater* (*AD* 111).

(17) Money/banking: *anna-coin* (*AD* 123); *copper pie* (*SMH* 91); *pice-worth* (*SMH* 161).

(18) Occupations: *beediseller* (*AD* 52); *chaprasihood* (*C* 10); *durrimaking*, *-weaving*, (*SL* 8 June 1959); *gang-coolie* (*AD* 181); *ghee merchant* (*DD* 6); *jutka driver* (*BA* 101); *palki bearer* (*MM* 214); *paan making* (*RH* 160) (also *pan*); *sarangi player* (*SJ* 106); *sherbet dealer* (*BH* 34); *tonga driver* (*VG* 36).

(19) Place names: *jungle path* (*SR* 121); *kutchery road* (*BH* 54); *loh-garh gate* (*BH* 132); *mela ground* (*HS* 11 June 1959); *rambugh gate* (*BH* 175); *thothi house* (*K* 19).

(20) Politics: *ahimsa soldier* (*WM* 78); *ashram camp* (*WM* 82); *-disciple* (*MM* 82); *Congress pandal* (*U* 212); *-raj* (*SR* 31); *field-satyagraha* (*K* 240); *imperial raj*; *khadi board* (*SL* 8 June 1959); *-competition* (*WM* 97); *khaddar clad* (*TN* 14); *-leader*, *-movement* (*SMH* 73); *khilafat committee* (*TN* 153) (cf. also *-movement*, *-leader*); *kisan candidate* (*VG* 13); *lathi-charge* (*HS* 15 June 1959); *mondal congress* (*HS* 15 June 1959); *Sarvodaya leader*; also *-conference*); *satyagraha campaign* (*BJ* 7 June 1959); *-movement* (*SMH* 73); *shahid day* (*IE* 12 June 1959); *swadeshi cloth* (*U* 208); *-shroud* (*TN* 154); *Swatantra Party* (*FPJ* 11 June 1959) (also *-candidate*).

(21) Religion and rituals: *akashti holidays* (*BH* 162); *anjali salutation* (*FF* 84); *aroti ceremony* (*HW* 113); *-time* (*HW* 207) (also *-song*); *asirvad ceremony* (*MM* 115); *bhajan song* (*SMH* 17); *burning-ghat* (*BH* 207) (also *-ghaut*); *ekadashi day* (*K* 42); *evening puja* (*HW* 170); *gurdwara committee* (*HT* 2 September 1961); *harikatha performer* (*K* 23) (also *harikathaman*); *kaliyuga flood* (*K* 50); *kalpavasa austerities* (*MM* 193); *kashi pilgrimage* (*K* 199); *kirtan singing* (*FF* 221); *korbani meat* (*HS* 15 May 1959); *puja day* (*SD* 45); *-festival* (*ABP* 28 October 1959); *-offering* (*HW* 127) (also *-room*); *religious diwan* (*T* 12 June 1959); *rudrakshi band* (*SR* 272); *-bead* (*K* 136); *sandhi rites* (*AD* 53); *sankrati fair* (*Hit* 28 December 1959); *satyanarain procession* (*K* 240); *shirshasana posture* (*HA* 30); *upanayanam ceremony* (*SR* 323); *upanishadic ancestors* (*SR* 7); *-sages* (*SR* 25); *vinayaka festival* (*ET* 21); *yagna ceremony* (*HW* 113) (also *-fire*); *yoga exercise* (*HA* 29) (also *-philosophy*).

(22) *Social* (general): *aam session* (*IN* 10 June 1959); *baran rites* (*MM* 98); *basar-chamber* (*MM* 85); *-room* (*MM* 73); *brahminhood* (*SR* 20); *brahminic corner* (*K* 106); *-priest* (*RH* 106); *-quarter* (*K* 132); *-restaurant* (*SF* 161); *-role* (*HW* 109); *-street* (*K* 21); *-thread* (*HW* 174); *communal hookah* (*TN*); *durbar turban* (*K* 167); *haldi invitation* (*K* 152); *hookah*

party (*VG* 108); *kumkum box* (*SR* 213); *-mark* (*K* 159); *-rice* (*SR* 123); *marriage pandal* (*NS* 34); *mela-festival* (*Hit* 28 December 1959); *-ground* (*HS* 11 June 1959); *paria-mixer* (*K* 63); *-polluter* (*K* 127); *-quarter* (*K* 19); *-street* (*K* 31); *shajan ceremony* (*BH* 124); *sindur mark* (*MM* 99); *zenana affair* (*FF* 66); *-life* (*SR* 181).

(23) Speech/language: *angrezi speech; babu-English* (also *baboo*) (*SR* 33).

(24) Trees/flowers: *aruni field* (*SR* 282); *darbha-grass* (*SR* 194); *gold mohar* (*TN*) : *kunda blossom* (*MM* 106); *-bush* (*HW* 1118); *mallika garland* (*MM* 106); *sheeshum trunk* (*SR* 9); *toddy trees* (*HS* 15 June 1959) (also *-branch, -grove*); *tulsi plant* (*SMH* 117).

(25) Villages (general) : *panchayat board* (*MI* June 1961) ; *village panchayat* (*Hit* 28 December 1959).

(26) Vehicles/carriages: *coolie-car* (*K* 265); *janta express* (*Hit* 30 December 1959); *rail gadi* (*BH* 75); *tonga carriage, yakka carriage* (*BH* 55) (also *-stand*, *BH* 60).

The frequency of occurrence of hybridized forms differs in different contexts. In a restricted study (Kachru 1970: 133) the highest frequency of hybrid formations was found in the contexts of religion/rituals (11.0%), social (general functions) (10%), and flowers/trees (8.9%), and the lowest in the contexts of arms, medicine, and weights/measures (each 0.2%).

In chapter 1 of this study (p. 47), I have given the frequencies of South Asian languages in hybridization. It is interesting that Hindustani and (High) Hindi items constitute 38.6% of the total. The lowest percentage (0.4%) is of Gujarati items.[14]

5.0. CONCLUSION

In this chapter I have concentrated on a data-oriented taxonomic analysis of SAE lexical innovations of one type, namely hybridization. The development of hybridization in the SAE lexis has been accomplished over two hundred years of administrative, cultural, political and educational contact with the English-speaking world. This feature of SAE is therefore interesting both from the point of language acculturation and from that of language contact. The implications of this linguistic and cultural contact are significant since it has influenced both SAE and South Asian languages in a serious sense. The influence is obvious on phonology, syntax and lexis; and hybridization at the lexical level is only one minor manifestation of this language contact situation.

NOTES

This chapter is a slightly modified version of 'Lexical Innovations in South Asian English', *International Journal of the Sociology of Language*, 1975, 4:55–72.

1. See also Yule and Burnell 1886: xv. 'Several of the old travellers have attached the like to their narratives; whilst the prolonged excitement created in England, a hundred years since, by the impeachment of Hastings and kindred matters, led to the publication of several glossaries as independent works; and a good many others have been published in later days.'
2. See chapter 6 (esp. section 2.0) for a discussion of this work.
3. 'In this edition of the *Anglo-Indian Glossary* the original text has been reprinted, any additions made by the editor being marked by square brackets. No attempt has been made to extend the vocabulary, the new articles being either such as were accidentally omitted in the first edition, or a few relating to words which seemed to correspond with the general scope of the work. Some new quotations have been added, and some of those included in the original edition have been verified and new references given. An index to words occurring in the quotations has been prepared' (Yule and Burnell 1903:xi).
4. Yule and Burnell 1903 [1886]: xv-xvi. The alternative title of the book *(Hobson-Jobson)* is significant. The term *hobson-jobson* is 'a typical and delightful example of that class of Anglo-Indian *argot* which consists of Oriental words highly assimilated, perhaps by vulgar lips to the English vernacular . . .' (Yule and Burnell 1903 [1886]: ix).
5. Surat Factors to Court, 26 February 1617, India Office Records, O. C. No. 450, quoted in Yule and Burnell 1886: ii; also in Rao 1954: 4.
6. See William Foster, *The English Factories in India, 1624-1629*, quoted in Rao 1954: 4-5.
7. Edmund Burke, 'Ninth report from the select committee of the House of Commons appointed to take into consideration the state of the administration of justice in the Provinces of Bengal, Behar, and Orissa, 25 June 1783, quoted in Rao 1954:5.
8. Fennell further breaks this number into the following categories: Hindoo [*sic*], 336; Sanskrit, 32; Dravidian, 31.
9. This number includes only words of Indian origin. It does not include many thousands of derivatives from these items.
10. See Rao 1954: 3.
11. In a recently compiled lexicon of (American) English, *The Random House Dictionary of the English Language*, the following South Asian items have been included: They include encyclopaedic items in accordance with the American lexicographical tradition: *achar, advaita, ahimsa, ahir, almirah, Andamanese, Aryanyakas, Aryan languages, ashram, Assamese, aumildar, Avestan, ayurveda, bahuvrihi, bania, batta, bawarchi, beedi,*

begar, bel, bhajan, bhakti, bhanji, Bharat, Bhavabhuti, bhikku, bhudan, Bodhisattva, Brah-
manas, buggy, cakra, chamar, chapaatie, chaprasi, charkha, chinar, choky, choli, dastur, de-
vadasi, Dewali, Dharama Śastra, Dharma Sutra, dhobi, Durga, durri, Dusehra, eagle-wood,
gadi, Gandharaa, Gandhiism, Ganesa, garu, Gondi, goonda, gotra, Gurdwara, guru, hackery,
holwa, Harijan, havaldar, Hinayana, holi, jaggery, jagir, Jataka, jawan, jizya, kacha, kali,
Kamasutra, kama, Kannada, Kashmiri, khaddar, khadi, khalsa, khansamah, kharif, khatri,
khichri, khidmatgar, khoja, khus, kisan, kotwal, kotwali, kukri, kutchery, Laksmi, lashkar,
lathi, lingam, Lingayats, lota, lungi, madrasah, mahal, Mahavira, Mahayana, mahout,
maidan, Malayalam, Mantra, matha, maya, mazdoor, mela, mimamsa, mofussil, molvi, mu-
dra, mukti, Munshi, munsif, mussuck, Nagari, nala, namastee, Nanak, naya paisa, Om, Oriya,
pagri, pakka, palki, Pancqtantra, panchayat, pandal, Panini, paria, pasmina, peepul, pooja,
pronom, purree, raga, Rajasthani, rasa, rishi, sadhu, Śakuntala, Sankara, Sannyasi, sarangi,
Saraswati, śastras, sati, Shaivite, shalwar, shamiana, shanti, Sindhi, sitar, smrti, sola, soma,
Sudra, sufi, svarabhakti, talwar, tantra, tatty, Thakur, thana, tilak, topkhana, Vaiśeśika,
Vaiśya, vakeel, varna(s), veena, vihara, sillah.

12. Firth (1957b:228) uses this term in a wider sense: 'Ordered series of words (OSW)
     include, for example, paradigms, formal scatter, so-called synonyms and antonyms,
     lexical groups by association, words grouped by common application in certain
     recurrent contexts of situation, and groups by phonesthetic association.' I have,
     however, used this term in a different sense since a distinction on the formal and the
     contextual levels has been made; for us, 'words grouped by common application
     in certain recurrent contexts of situation' are *lexical sets*.

13. Note that in this study the distinction between Hindi, Hindustani, and Urdu was
     not very clear. Certain items (e.g., *tiffin-carrier*) were treated as of doubtful source.
     For further discussion and references see chapter 1 (pp. 38–39 and 46–49) and
     chapter 6. Also see Sagert 1951 for the study of Indian words in English.

6

Toward a Dictionary

1.0. This chapter is essentially a case study of lexicographical research in one non-native variety of English:[1] namely, Indian English. But throughout this study, in what may be considered asides, I have attempted to present the state of lexicographical research, and a plea for initiating such research, in non-native Englishes. It has been shown that these varieties generally share a number of underlying formal and contextual characteristics with Indian English. Therefore, the theoretical and methodological observations made about the Indian English data are relevant to most of the institutionalized non-native varieties of English (see Kachru, ed. 1982). I have therefore included data not only from Indian English, but also from studies of other varieties—for example, for Africa in general from Bokamba (1982); for the Caribbean from Allsopp (1971, 1972, 1978) and Craig (1982); for Ghana from Sey (1973); for Kenya from Zuengler (1982); for Nigeria from Bamgbose (1971 and 1982) and Kirk-Greene (1971).

In the post-colonial period, it has at last been realized that the non-native users of English account for almost 35 per cent of the English-using population in such diverse linguistic and cultural areas as Africa, South Asia, the Far East, and the Philippines. The linguistic and literary contributions of these areas toward nativizing the English language have been discussed in several studies. (For a full discussion, see Kachru 1981a and 1982b.) However, as yet few serious attempts have been made to emphasize the importance of lexicographical research on these varieties of English. (Exceptions are, for example, Allsopp 1972 and Kachru 1973a).

In the past, references have occasionally been made to such world varieties of English at lexicographical conferences. For example, consider the following comment of Allen W. Read at the Conference on Lexicography held at Indiana University, Bloomington in 1960 (Read 1962:222):

Other parts of the world have branches of the English language with characteristic developments—New Zealand, the Philippines, India, South Africa,

Ghana, the Caribbean, etc.—and each offers a challenge for the lexicologist to assemble the material that can be drawn upon by the general lexicographer.

Whatever earlier dictionaries are available (for example, for South Asia), the main motivation for their compilation seems to have been to provide word lists or register-bound glossaries, specifically for Englishmen or Americans visiting Asia or Africa for administrative, commercial, or missionary purposes. These word lists were meant to serve as manuals for explaining un-English 'lexical exotica', or specific nativized lexical meanings of English lexical items. The recent lexicographical research on these varieties is insufficient, however, considering the magnitude and importance of the task.

The compilation of dictionaries for the non-native varieties of English is a crucial first step toward their standardization. Such dictionaries are also important for comparative descriptive (and historical) analysis. The contextualized lexical items in a dictionary provide an index to the extent of influence of (non-native) culture on a variety of English; in this sense they permit a study in the acculturation of language. Such a dictionary should also help in determining formally and contextually motivated innovations. Finally, lexical research is a step toward recognizing these varieties as contextually and linguistically definable distinct world varieties of English.

In the first part of this chapter I shall briefly discuss some of the more important lexicographical works on an institutionalized non-native variety—namely, Indian English. In the second part I shall discuss the theoretical and methodological questions which one encounters in any serious lexicographical work on this and other varieties of English, and also present a case for further lexicographical research on these varieties.

2.0. NATIVIZATION OF ENGLISH

A claim for dictionaries of the non-native varieties of English presupposes that the process of nativization of the English language manifests itself formally more or less as do the processes of Americanization, Australianization, or Canadianization of the English language. I shall not elaborate on this point here, since the contextual and linguistic parameters of one such non-native variety of English have been discussed in earlier studies. (See, for pronunciation, Bansal 1969; for overall discussions, see Kachru 1965 and later.

Also see below, section 3.0.) In these studies it is argued that the Indianization has resulted in distinct Indian characteristics at all linguistic levels, i.e., phonetic, grammatical, lexical and semantic. These deviations may result from the culturally and linguistically pluralistic context of India, and from the specialized uses of English in India as a language of administration, education, the legal system, and mass media (see chapters 3 and 4).

Some earlier studies on the native varieties of English (see, e.g., Baker 1945; Morris 1898; Ramson 1966) indicate that their distinctness developed for roughly the same reasons that are responsible for the nativization of other new varieties of English. Thus the non-native varieties of English have identical linguistic developments, though the formal manifestations of the social and linguistic context of each variety are obviously not identical. In 1828, presenting a defence for an American dictionary of the English language, Noah Webster gave the following arguments (see Sledd and Ebbitt 1962:32–3):

It is not only important, but, in a degree necessary, that the people of this country, should have an *American Dictionary* of the English language; for, although the body of the language is the same as in England, and it is desirable to perpetuate that sameness, yet some differences must exist. Language is the expression of ideas; and if the people of one country cannot preserve an identity of ideas, they cannot retain an identity of language. Now an identity of ideas depends materially upon a sameness of things or objects with which the people of the two countries are conversant. But in no two portions of the earth, remote from each other, can such identity be found. Even physical objects must be different. But the principal differences between the people of this country and of all others, arise from different forms of government, different laws, institutions and customs. . . . A great number of words in our language require to be defined in a phraseology accommodated to the condition and institutions of the people in these states, and the people of England must look to an American Dictionary for a correct understanding of such terms.

The necessity therefore of a Dictionary suited to the people of the United States is obvious; and I should suppose that this fact being admitted, there could be no difference of opinion as to the *time*, when such a work ought to be substituted for English Dictionaries.

In several native varieties of English (e.g., American, Australian, Canadian, and Scottish) the distinctiveness of a variety has been claimed on grounds of contextual differences which eventually manifest themselves in independent linguistic innovations. These innovations have been used as a justification for distinct dictionaries for Australian, American and Scottish English. It seems to me that, using the same arguments, one can make a case for a dictionary of Indian English or for other institutionalized varieties of English.

One might then say that distinct non-attitudinal dictionaries of nonnative Englishes can be justified on many grounds; for example, for semantic extension or restriction of lexical items in new contexts, and for additions to the corpus from the local languages. By 'extension and restriction' is meant assigning [+]or[–]semantic feature(s) to a lexical entry in a dictionary. I shall return to this point later. By 'addition to the corpus' is meant inclusion of those lexical items which are not normally found in the standard dictionaries of the English language. Since 1976, the Oxford University Press has produced editions of *The Little Oxford Dictionary*, with a 'Supplement of Indian Words' (pp. 709–756) by R. E. Hawkins. This Supplement is

... intended for those who, because they live in the region or are interested in it, read current books and periodicals and older literature about India, Pakistan, Bangladesh and Sri Lanka. The majority of the words included are culled from the *Oxford English Dictionary* and its Supplements but the compiler has also taken many from Yule and Burnell's *Hobson-Jobson* and from G. C. Whitworth's *Anglo-Indian Dictionary*. The last two books appeared nearly a century ago, however, before the time of satyagrahis, razakars, naxalites, gheraos, dosas, idlis, bosons and jhuggies. (709)

In the case of South Asia, a substantial number of such lexical items have been included in earlier dictionaries (e.g., Carnegy 1877; Robarts 1800; Whitworth 1885; Wilson 1855 [1940]; Yule and Burnell 1887).[2]

The other feature which provides a number of lexical items is a matter of historical accident, but linguistically it marks what may be termed *variety distinction*. This feature demonstrates an unawareness about the contemporary usage of English and the linguistic change on the part of the non-native users of English. The result is that some Africanisms, Filipinoisms, or South Asianisms, for example, are out of tune with synchronic usage and stand out as archaisms in the nonnative varieties. This characteristic is found not only in non-native Englishes, but is present in native Englishes such as American English as well. Read (1962: 218) claims that such lexical items are crucial for separating the American varieties from British English:

But decisions on origin, fascinating as they are, do not seem to me as important in lexicography as the building up of bodies of typical usage. I regard it as unwise and unfortunate that both Sir William Craigie and M. M. Mathews chose place of origin as their criterion for an Americanism rather than currency in usage. Thus they have ignored one of the most important types of Americanisms, that caused by survival in America with obsolescence in England.

In their dictionary, Yule and Burnell (1886 [1903:xxi]) have drawn attention to this aspect of Indian English:

> Within my own earliest memory Spanish dollars were current in England at a specified value if they bore a stamp from the English mint. And similarly there are certain English words, often obsolete in Europe, which have received in India currency with a special stamp of meaning; whilst in other cases our language has formed in India new compounds applicable to new objects or shades of meaning. To one or other of these classes belong *outcry, buggy, home, interloper, rogue (-elephant), tiffin, furlough, elk, roundel* ('an umbrella', obsolete), *pish-pash, earth-oil, hog-deer, flying-fox, garden-house, musk-rat, nor-wester, iron-wood, long-drawers, barking-deer, custard-apple, grass-cutter*, etc.

The above discussion, I hope, has shown that a dictionary of a non-native variety such as Indian English is nativized in several respects. It is basically a dictionary of English with an added dimension of area-bound, context-bound, and language-bound features which separate one variety of English from others. In a sense, one might, for example, claim that an Indian English dictionary has certain characteristics of a dialect dictionary. Note, however, that the term *dialect* is not used here in the conventional sense, and the term *dialectalisms(s)* is to be used in a wider sense—more in the sense of variety features. In African or South Asian English the range of differentiating parameters may be abstracted from the linguistic network of the region, and also from the cultural network. These two provide the formal exponents at various linguistic levels (see Bokamba 1982, Kachru 1969a, 1975a and 1982b and Zuengler 1982).

3.0. EARLIER LEXICOGRAPHICAL RESEARCH: A CASE STUDY

Let us now consider a specific lexicographical tradition of an institutionalized non-native variety of English. This will help to show the development of a tradition and its possible relevance to other varieties. In terms of theoretical framework and methodology, the earlier lexicographical research on Indian English is of no serious interest now, but it provides a substantial source of data. The earlier dictionaries (e.g., Brown 1852; Carnegy 1877; Robarts 1800; Stocqueler 1848; Wilson 1855; Yule and Burnell 1886) indicate the restricted uses of Indian English up to 1886.

In the early nineteenth century, Indian English was primarily used in certain restricted administrative registers. Mainly the language of the colonizers, it slowly assimilated a large number of native lexical items for different Indian contexts (see Kachru 1969a, 1975a). These dictionaries are basically lists of words of Indian origin, or of non-Indian origin (e.g., Arabic, Persian) but borrowed into Indian English via other Indian languages. Some of these lexical items found their way into native varieties of English (e.g., American or British English) and have not only survived but have also been assimilated. Consider, for example, *bhakti*, *cummerbund*, *curry*, *chutney*, *guru*, *juggernaut*, *karma*, *pundit*, *purdah*, *raj*, *satyagraha*. The reasons for this large-scale lexical borrowing in Indian English were primarily contextual.

In his preface to *The Oriental Interpreter* Stocqueler (1848 : iii) emphasizes the practical need of the 'Companion to "The Handbook of British India" 'in the following words:

> This is a compilation. It has been suggested by the compiler's daily experience of the almost universal ignorance of Oriental terms, phrases, expressions, places. Every fortnight brings a mail from India, and the intelligence which it imparts is fraught with words which perplex the speeches in Parliament, turning upon Eastern affairs—the Oriental novels, travels, and statistical works—likewise abound with terms 'caviare to the general.' The new arrival in India, ignorant of the language of the country, is puzzled, for sometime, to comprehend his countrymen, whose conversation 'wears strange suits,' and even he, who has been for years a sojourner in India is, to the last, unacquainted with the meaning of numerous words, which occur in his daily newspaper, the Courts of Law, and the communications of his Mofussil or upcountry correspondents.

Referring to his compilation, Stocqueler says:

> The following pages impart a knowledge of all the terms in question as far as they have occurred to the communicant during an examination of two or three years, diligently pursued, and an appeal to his recollection of the phrases in common use in India and Persia.

Wilson (1855 :i) observes:

> In many cases, no doubt, it might be difficult or impossible to discover exact equivalents for the native words in English, and the use of the original term most expressively conveys its meaning to those to whom the occasion of its employment is familiar. . . . .

The other reasons given by Wilson for the earlier use of Indian words in Indian English are : first, 'pedantic affectation of conversancy with the native languages' ; second, a non-linguistic reason, 'indolence to a reluctance to take the trouble of ascertaining the proper use of the word, and of seeking for a suitable equivalent'.

The titles of some of these lexical lists are both explanatory and purpose-specific. Here are a few:

Brown, C. P. *The Zillah Dictionary in the Roman character, explaining the Various Words used in Business in India*, 1852.

Carnegy, P. *Kachahri Technicalities, or A Glossary of Terms, Rural, Official, and General, in Daily use in the Courts of Law, and in Illustration of the Tenures, Customs, Arts, and Manufactures of Hindustan*, 1877.

Indian Vocabulary, to which is prefixed the Forms of Impeachment, 1788.

Robarts, T. T. *An Indian Glossary, consisting of some Thousand Words and forms commonly used in the East Indies . . . extremely serviceable in assisting Strangers to acquire with Ease and Quickness the Language of that Country*, 1800.

Stocqueler, J. H. *The Oriental Interpreter and Treasury of East India Knowledge*, 1848.

Wilson, H. H. *A Glossary of Judicial and Revenue Terms, and of useful words occurring in Official Documents, relating to the Administration of the Government of British India from the Arabic, Persian, Hindustáni, Sanskrit, Hindi, Bengáli, Uriyá, Maráthi, Guzaráthi, Telugu, Karnáta, Támil, Malayálam, and other languages*, 1855.

The above titles make it clear that these works are mainly lexical guides and handbooks for the administrators who came to India under what was then called the Indian Civil Service (I.C.S.), or as junior officers in mofussil (upcountry, rural) towns.

The first such word list was appended to the Fifth Report of the Select Committee of 1812 by Sir Charles Wilkins. There were various other register-restricted word lists of no special significance. In the above tradition, however, the best 'glossary' was compiled by Wilson in 1855. This was the outcome of a resolution passed by the Court of Directors of the East India Company in August 1842: 'It was resolved to adopt measures for forming a Glossary of words in current use in various parts of India, relating to the administration of public business in every department, the want of which had long been found a source of much inconvenience.'

Although the title of Wilson's glossary specifies that it is restricted to 'Judicial and Revenue Terms,' it covers a wider area. The resolution of the East India Company resulted in several glossaries, by Charles Phillip Brown, Henry Elliot, and Richard Clark, to mention just three.

In 1855 George Clifford Whitworth published a 350-page diction-

ary entitled *An Anglo-Indian Dictionary*, with a more illuminating subtitle, *A Glossary of Indian terms used in English, and of such English or other
non-Indian terms as have obtained special meanings in India.* This is the first
attempt toward including extended semantic features of 'pure English words'. It is insightful in the sense that it expressed the desirability of an 'Indian Supplement to the English Dictionary' (Whitworth,
1855: vii). In a serious sense this supplement 'to the English Dictionary' is yet to be provided; the recent attempt of Nihalani *et al.* (1978)
has only partly fulfilled the need. In Whitworth's opinion, his glossary was distinct from earlier ones in several respects; for example,
'It seems to have been the usual practice, in compiling a glossary upon
any Indian subject, to take and define every native word relating to
the subject. But it is no part of the object of this glossary to serve the
purpose' (Whitworth, 1885:viii). In his glossary he also 'endeavoured
to exclude words of minute technical or of very restricted use' (ix).

The majority of lexical items were from Indian languages and had
become part of Indian English registers. A few English words were also
included with their Indian semantic features. These words are of not
only linguistic, but also historical interest, since they reflect the beginning of the process of the Indianization of English approximately
one hundred years ago. Consider the following : *agent* (administrative
register), *banyan, bearer, bell music, betel, black-crop (-gram, -soil, -wood),
blisterfly, boy* (domestic servant), *brinjal, butler, carpet snake, cashew, classer*
(agricultural register), *collector* (administrative register), *compound, dan-
cing-girl, elephant-apple, evil-eye, fire-worshiper, flying-fox, king-crow, left-
hand* (caste system), *mango-bird (-fish), milk bush, non-regulation, rat-snake,
rest-house, right-hand* (caste system), *rock snake, sacred bull (-cord, -shirt,
-thread), snake-bird (-gourd, -stone), soap stone.*

It was not until 1886 that a monumental glossary entitled *Hobson-
Jobson* was first published. The first edition was compiled by Col. Henry
Yule and A. C. Burnell. The 'new edition,' edited by William Crooke,
was published in 1903.[3] In its methodology, though not in its attitude
toward Indian English, *Hobson-Jobson* is a healthy break from the tradition of earlier lexical research on this variety of English. It is the first
attempt at applying the then-current techniques of lexicographical research. In their introductory remarks the compilers are, therefore, correct in asserting that

Of modern Glossaries, such as have been the result of serious labour, all, or
nearly all, have been of a kind purely technical, intended to facilitate the
comprehension of official documents by the explanation of terms used in the

Revenue department, or in other branches of Indian administration. (1886: xv).

Referring to their own work and contrasting it with earlier glossaries, they emphasize:

> This kind is, however, not ours, as a momentary comparison of a page or two in each Glossary would suffice to show ... in its original conception it [*Hobson-Jobson*] was intended to deal with all that class of words which, not in general pertaining to the technicalities of administration, recur constantly in the daily intercourse of the English in India, either as expressing ideas really not provided for by our mother-tongue, or supposed by the speakers (often quite erroneously) to express something not capable of just denotation by any English term....

In their dictionary, Yule and Burnell proposed to

> ...deal with a *selection* of those administrative terms, which are in such familiar and quotidian use as to form part of the common Anglo-Indian stock, and to trace all (so far as possible) to their true origin—a matter on which, in regard to many of the words, those who hourly use them are profoundly ignorant— and to follow them down by quotation from their earliest occurrence in literature. (1886: xvi)

In this sense, then, *Hobson-Jobson* also has a historical and etymological dimension.

All the lexical work in this tradition had limitations of several types: first, in terms of goals and users; second, in terms of the source materials and the data presented; third, in terms of the attitude which the compilers reveal about the then developing Indian English; fourth, in terms of the native language sources listed for various lexical items, which are not always reliable. The goals were essentially pragmatic: namely, to provide lexical manuals for visiting Western administrators, travellers, and in some cases for specialists in various fields. As shown above, the source material was often register restricted.

In the early nineteenth century the English language had not yet become part of the mainstream of India's educational and cultural life. In the north, Persian still continued to play a dominant role in certain areas, especially as the court language. It is, therefore, not surprising to find a reluctance to include in these glossaries English words, with their typical Indian semantic features or Indian pronunciations. As late as 1886 this attitude toward Indian English continued, and in certain prominent circles it prevails even now (see, e.g., Prator 1968).

In *Hobson-Jobson* there is a list of what Yule and Burnell term 'corruptions, more or less violent, of Oriental words and phrases which have put on an English mask' (1886: xxi). The list includes *maund, fool's rack, bearer, cot, boy, belly-band, Penang-lawyer, buckshaw, compound, college-pheasant, chopper, summer-head, eagle-wood, jackass-copal*. In the same dictionary, other innovations are characterized as 'hybrids and corruptions of English fully accepted and adopted as Hindustani by the natives with whom we have to do, such as *simkin, port-shrāb, brandy-pānī, apīl, rasīd, tumlet* (a tumbler), *gilās* (for drinking vessels of sorts), *rail-ghārī, lumber-dār, jail-khānā, buggy-khānā*, etc.' (1886: xxi). We have already discussed their observation of the 'obsolete' words in Indian English in section 1.0.

The types of Indian lexical innovations and the features of the Indianization of the English language discussed in *Hobson-Jobson* may be categorized as:

a) HYBRIDIZATION: this is a very productive process in Indian English (e.g., the above *brandy pānī, bottle-khānā*; see also chapter 5, pp. 153–62).

b) PHONETIC CHANGE: this includes those English lexical items which have undergone a phonetic change due to the influence of a substratum (e.g., the above *apīl* 'appeal', *rasīd* 'receipt', *gilās* 'glass').

c) SEMANTIC SHIFT: this involves extension of semantic features of an English lexical item (e.g., the above *boy* for *bearer* or a *waiter*; see also Kachru 1965 and later).

In determining the range of the corpus for a dictionary of Indian English, or any other non-native variety of English, the first step is to determine the norm for a standard or educated English user. This problem is universal in lexicographical research, even in the varieties of English used as first languages (see Quirk 1960:70–87; Zgusta 1971: 164–96). However, in the case of the non-native varieties of English there are further complexities. In addition to English serving as a second language, one must also take into account area variation, social variation, and competence variation, as in any other living language. This aspect has not yet been fully studied. Above all, attitudes toward different forms of such varieties also vary (for a discussion of 'varieties within a variety', see chapter 8, pp. 224–33).

In the current literature on language surveys or methodology for lexicographical research, no absolute criteria have been provided for the range and type of corpus (see Hulbert 1955; Quirk 1960; Zgusta 1971). In the case of, for example, Africanisms, Indianisms, or Filipinoisms, one might use the following criteria for selecting a nativized or a native item used in a non-native variety of English. First, a formal innovation should be contextually and/or linguistically justifiable in terms of the local sociocultural and linguistic context. Second, the area-restricted regionalisms used within a non-native variety should be identified as such (e.g., in the case of Indian English the item *religious dewan* (*IN* 12 June 1969).[4] Third, the register range of a variety should be examined in order to mark the low frequency register-restricted or author-specific items.

It is important to decide what role the frequency of an item should play in the selection of a lexical entry. Creative Indian English literature contains innumerable lexical items which are author-specific or text-specific; their frequency is highly restricted, e.g., *salt-giver* (*K* 32), *sister-sleeper* (*VG* 130). It seems to me that a decision concerning their inclusion in a dictionary is a matter not of linguistic value judgment but of the dictionary's scope. A dictionary need not necessarily be prescriptive and or frequency oriented. In this context, the following observation of Trench (1857:4–5) is worth mentioning:

> ...It is no task of the maker of it [a dictionary] to select the good words of a language. If he fancies that it is so, and begins to pick and choose, to leave this and to take that, he will at once go astray. The business which he has undertaken is to collect and arrange all the words whether good or bad, whether they do or do not commend themselves to his judgment, which, with certain exceptions hereafter to be specified, those writing in the language have employed. He is a historian of it, not a critic. The *delectus verborum*, on which so much, on which nearly everything in style depends, is a matter with which *he* has no concern.

4.0. THE EXPONENTS OF *INDIANNESS*

In conventional dictionaries, the markers for a lexical entry are generally determined by the focus of the dictionary. The *OED*'s emphasis is on historical information; the same is the case with the *Dictionary of American English*. On the other hand, *A Dictionary of Americanisms* 'has taken great pains with pronunciation ' (Hulbert 1955: 53–57). Generally a lexical entry may have markers which provide information relevant to the following linguistic levels: orthographical, phonetic, grammatical, semantic, and etymological. In the more extensive dictionaries one might find the collocational 'spray' of items, and their contextualized uses in a chronological order.

In the earlier sections of this chapter I have shown that, in the existing dictionaries of Indian English, the information on the above levels is very sketchy; indeed, some levels—generally phonetic—are completely ignored. The recent 'handbook' on usage and pronunciation of Indian and British English has, however, not ignored the phonetic level (see Nihalani *et al*. 1978). The only existing dictionary which closely approximates a serious lexical work is Yule and Burnell (1886), but in certain areas even this monumental work is only partially complete.

The treatment of the lexical items *bangle, butler, chota hazry (haziri)* in Whitworth (1885) and Yule and Burnell (1886) gives some idea of the scope of these two dictionaries. The difference between the lexical notes in the two is significant, but both are inadequate.

1. Whitworth (1885):

Bangle: (A corruption of Hindustani *bangri*) a bracelet (30).
Butler: This is presumably the English word, but is used in the Bombay Presidency to denote the head servant in a household; he is not specially connected with the wine cellar, but perhaps with all the duties of the Bengal khansaman and the sardar-bearer (55).
Chota: (Hindustani *chhota*) little, small. The word is often used in English with an Indian noun; as *chota haziri,* a light early breakfast; *chota saheb,* the younger gentleman; *chota barsat,* the little rain, a fall that usually precedes the heavy fall of the monsoon (69).

2. Yule and Burnell (1886):

Bangle, s. H. *bangri* or *bangrī.* The original word properly means a ring of colored glass worn on the wrist by women; [the *churī* of N. India]; but *bangle* is applied to any native ring-bracelet, and also to an *anklet* or ring of any kind worn on the ankle or leg. Indian silver bangles on the wrist have recently come into common use among English girls... (60).
Butler, s. In the Madras and Bombay Presidencies this is the title usually applied to the head-servant of any English or quasi-English household. He generally makes the daily market, has charge of domestic stores, and superintends the table. As his profession is one which affords a large scope for feathering a nest at the expense of a foreign master, it is often followed at Madras by men of comparatively good caste... [The citations listed are from 1616 to 1789. There is also a note. See also *Consuman* in Yule and Burnell, 1886: 133.]
Chota-hazry, s. H. *Chhotī hāzīrī,* vulg. *hāzri,* 'little breakfast'; refreshment taken in the early morning, before or after the morning exercise. The term... was originally peculiar to the Bengal Presidency. In Madras the meal is called 'early tea'. Among the Dutch in Java, this meal consists (or did consist in 1860) of a large cup of tea, and a large piece of cheese, presented by the servant who calls one in the morning... (210).

It is evident that the above illustrative entries are incomplete and that the work of Yule and Burnell is essentially ethnographically oriented, as are some other works, such as Stocqueler (1848). The following 'definition' of the item *ayah* in Stocqueler is illustrative of the ethnographic bias of the earlier lexicons, whose 'definitions' are often subjective.

Ayah: a lady's maid in India. The Ayah has no innate taste for dressing, but can usually plait hair well, and contrives to fasten a hook, and to stick in a pin so that it shall soon come out again. She is often the wife of one of the Khedmutgars (q.v.), and then the double wages make the service valuable to the worthy couple. Frequently she is an Indo-Portuguese woman, and though a sad and ugly drab, is in most respects superior to the Musalman woman (Stocqueler 1848: 19),

In the same work (p. 68) the definition of *kurtā* reads: 'Coortah: The close-fitting jacket worn by the native women of India.' In this, too, the definition leaves much to be desired. It is perhaps this feature of ethnographic information and focus on the exotic which makes such lexicons of special interest to non-Indians. In these works there is no phonetic information, and stress markers that are sometimes shown on the South Asian lexical items are not always reliable.

5.0. LEXICAL STOCK AND INDIAN MARKERS

Let us consider the type of lexical stock which will provide the source material for an Indian English dictionary. The lexical items are mainly of two types: first, those South Asian items which have traditionally formed the corpus of Indian English glossaries, representative dictionaries of this type being Stocqueler (1848), Wilson (1855), Whitworth (1885), and Yule and Burnell (1886); second, those English lexical items which need assignment of typical Indian English features. In the earlier dictionaries the second type of corpus has generally been ignored, though a sprinkling of such items may be found in Whitworth (1885) and Yule and Burnell (1886). (For a detailed discussion, see chapter 5 and Rao 1954.) I shall present below some features of the English language in India, with illustrations to demonstrate the desirability of Indian markers at the various levels in the dictionary.

5.1. *Grammatical*. In order to incorporate grammatical information in a dictionary, we presuppose that a syntactic description of Indian English is already available. Unfortunately, such is not the case. In certain studies, fragments of Indian English syntax have been discussed (see Aggarwal 1982, Fox 1968; for further references, see Kachru 1969a and 1982a). All these studies put together do not result in even a tentative description. The paucity of such descriptions is mainly the result of the prevalent attitude in India—and elsewhere—that acceptance of any syntactic deviations from the traditional prescriptivism of British and American (pedagogical) grammars means accepting Indian English as substandard. In order not to mark Indian English as a separate variety, the tendency is to overlook deviations, or to regard them simply as 'mistakes.' Certain Western scholars writing on Indian English mark even certain productive processes—such as the typical Indian English compounding—with pejorative labels (see e.g., Goffin 1934; Whitworth 1907. Also see Kachru 1965 and later).

It is obvious that before embarking on a dictionary project—or side by side with such a project—the primary need is to prepare a grammatical description. On the basis of currently available studies, one can make only tentative claims about the types of (Indian) grammatical markers the dictionaries may include. First are those markers that indicate the class assignment of an item (e.g., noun, verb, adjective). Although this information is crucial for the assimilated (or unassimilated) South Asian lexical items in Indian English, the earlier dictionaries do not always incorporate it. For example, in Stocqueler (1848) this information is totally absent. On the other hand, Yule and Burnell (1886) do an admirable job so far as the entries of this type are concerned (*bandicoot, charpoy, dawk, devadasi, ghee*).

The second type of information is pertinent to English lexical items in various ways. I shall recapitulate here some such grammatical features to illustrate the point. A large number of Indianisms may be so termed because of *category change* or *category extension*. Consider, for example, the subset of verbs with *be + ing* in English. The members of this subset do not coincide with those in the native varieties of English; for example, *hearing, seeing, knowing*. On the other hand, in Indian English we have *I am hearing, I am seeing, you must be knowing* (see Kachru 1976b and 1982b). There is also a tendency toward deletion of the reflexive pronouns with reflexive verbs (e.g., *enjoy, exert*; see Kindersley, 1938). In Kindersley (1938) there is an interesting list of items which display category change, in the sense that intransitive verbs are used as transitive verbs or vice versa. One can also find grammatical explanations for what Goffin (1934) terms *phrase-mongering* (see chapter 4, pp. 135–37). Here I will not discuss the statistical variation of grammatical units (see Kachru 1969a : 644–647). I do not know how the dictionary can present the system of the category of article in the deictic system in Indian English, which is significantly deviant from the native varieties of English. In short, the description of Indian English grammar is yet far from satisfactory, and improvement of it is a crucial undertaking, from both lexicographical and pedagogical points of view. In lexicographical research on Indian English, word formation will also deserve attention. Among other things, consider the process of suffixation, as in *cooliedom* (*C* 44), *goondaism* (*H* 2 March 1964), *piceworth*, *policewala* (*SHA* 61 *U* 59), *Upanishadic* (*SR* 25).

5.2. *Phonetic*. As mentioned earlier, the phonetic level (or the pronunciation aspect) has generally been ignored in dictionaries of Indian English; Nihalani *et al.* (1978) and Hawkins (1976) are an exception. The primary reason for this treatment is that, traditionally, Indian English has been considered a substandard variety of British English. Earlier literature on this topic has used a variety of terms to refer to it in a derogatory sense, the term 'Indian English' being one such label (see chapter 1, pp. 42–43). British educators and lexicographers and British-trained Indian educators consider British English—precisely the Received Pronunciation—the desirable norm for Indian users of English. Traditionally, pronunciation was not represented, since (in the compiler's view) standard dictionaries of English already included that information. Both pedagogically and socially, the acceptable norm was always the (unattainable) Received Pronunciation (generally abbreviated RP). There was thus a difference between actual linguistic behaviour and a hypothetical norm.

This language attitude grew over the years, along with the peculiar relationship between colonizer and colonized. During the earlier period of English bilingualism in India, this position on Received Pronunciation was not altogether indefensible. Furthermore, in various geographical and language areas of India the pronunciation of English (even 'standard' Indian English) varies, due primarily to the influence of a substratum. Since most (if not all) earlier lexicographical compilation was done by administration-oriented scholars, they naturally showed no interest in Indian English as a distinct entity. For them, Indian English was merely a communication tool that was convenient for the administration of the raj; but when the process of Indianization set in—perhaps slowly, but definitely—the linguistic puritanism of members of the raj was hurt. This attitude toward Indian innovations in English is clearly demonstrated in Goffin (1934) and Whitworth (1907), to name just two. There was hesitation in granting 'status' (or recognition) to colonial varieties of English. One notices this attitude among the educated Indians who communicate in *Indian* English and prefer to label it 'Oxford English'. It is a unique case of linguistic schizophrenia, and is particularly marked in the Indian attitude toward pronunciation. The puristic attitude of the British scholars toward spoken Indian English was partly determined by the goals of their work; in fairness to them, that aspect should not be underestimated. The lexicographical research by these scholars was not done for any academic or pedagogical ends, but to provide glossaries for members of the administration—obviously a very pragmatic motivation.

It has, however, repeatedly been noted in the literature, with detailed descriptive statements, that at the phonetic level Indian English has distinct Indian characteristics. (For a detailed discussion see Bansal 1969; Kachru 1969a: 639ff; Masica 1966.) The differences in Indian English pronunciation are the result both of the substratum and of the spelling pronunciation, spoken English being seldom taught in Indian schools. The structural 'equivalence' between English and the native languages has the following possibilities, among others: (a) 'identical' structural equivalence may not be possible; (b) the structures may have 'identical' constituents (e.g., $CVCV$), yet the members of the system may not be identical. This point has been elaborated elsewhere with bibliographical references (see chapter 1), and tentative descriptions have been presented in Bansal (1969: 120–49) and Masica (1966).

Earlier studies have shown, both quantitatively (see Bansal 1969) and impressionistically (see Kachru 1982a), that the main features affecting the intelligibility of Indian English are stress and rhythm (for a recent discussion, see Nelson 1982). The variation in stress has resulted in a 'transparent' Indian rhythm of English. The reasons for this feature may again be traced back to the substratum: Indian languages are essentially syllable-timed, and in most of them the rhythm is determined by arrangement of long and short syllables. English, a stress-timed language, has its rhythm based on the arrangement of the stressed and unstressed vowels. In the currently available literature on spoken Indian English, no serious attempts have been made to structure Indian English stress and determine its predictability. An Indian English dictionary must then incorporate the pronunciation of those items which do not deviate in Indian English, as well as the characteristic Indian pronunciation of those entries which are deviant from the native models.

5.3. *Semantic.* In the case of Indian English, the typical Indian semantic features are relevant for two distinct types of lexical items: South Asian lexical items (see chapter 5) and English lexical items.

Many items belonging to these classes have undergone two types of semantic changes, which may be termed *semantic restriction* and *semantic extension*. A number of examples are available to illustrate this type of semantic shift (see Kachru 1970: 130–31). In order to account for these, the dictionary must assign [+] or [–] Indian (semantic) features to such entries. We also need features to indicate the register restriction of an item. Note, however, that register restriction itself may be a manifestation of semantic restriction. Consider, for example, lexical items such as *ahimsa, mulki, satyagraha,* and *sarvodaya*. These items (except, perhaps, *mulki*) are restricted to the political register in Indian English, while in the Indian languages from which these items are borrowed they have no such registral and collocational restrictions (see also chapter 5; sec. 4.3.2).

One may take other lexical items to demonstrate the same process which operates in the above examples. In listing such items there is no special problem, though a useful criterion has yet to be devised for determining an acceptable cut-off point. This procedural decision depends partly on the scope of the proposed dictionary.

A number of sociocultural, political, and linguistic reasons may be given for adding typically non-native semantic features to a number of English lexical items. The first may be termed *sociocultural and semantic*. This does not necessarily entail addition of an entry in the dictionary, but involves an extended (and nativized) definition of a lexical entry. The following from Indian English are illustrative: *communal, interdine, intermarriage, fissiparous tendencies* (*L* 23 November 1965). We find such examples plentiful in varieties of African English, too:

(a) Ghanaian English (Sey 1973: 75–91): *chewing-sponge* or *chewing-stick* ('twig used for cleaning teeth') ; *cover-shoulder* ('a blouse') ; *to destool* or *enstool* ('to depose or install a chief'); *hot drinks* ('alcoholic drinks') ; *knocking-fee* ('fee paid by a man to a woman's family for initiating negotiations about marriage') ; *small room* ('toilet') ; *tight friend* ('close friend').

(b) Kenyan English (Zuengler 1982): The verbs *task, get* and *cut* may be used in the sense of 'eat,' 'give birth to,' and 'stab,' respectively. The nouns and adjective *man, brat,* and *big* may be used in the sense of 'husband,' 'illegitimate child,' and 'adult' or 'mature,' respectively.

(c) Nigerian English (Bamgboṣe 1971, 1982): *barb,* ('to cut hair ,' from *barber*) ; *head-tie* ('woman's head-dress') ; *to travel* in the sense of 'to be away' (*my father has travelled* for 'my father is away').

In the case of Caribbean English, we have sufficient supporting data in Allsopp (1971, 1972, 1978) and in Craig (1982).

The list may be extended by including low-frequency author-specific items, or what Quirk terms 'minority forms' (see Quirk 1960:80), from creative literature written in African English, South Asian English, or Caribbean English. (For examples from South Asian English, see Kachru 1965, 1970, and 1982a.)

The second type includes those lexical items which have undergone a *register shift*. By register shift is meant the use of English lexical items in typically nativized registers of English. The lexical items under this category and those in the first category are not mutually exclusive; indeed, the list of such items is large (see, e.g., chapters 3 and 4), and enough data are present in various non-native registers of politics, the caste system, and administration, among others. (For African English, see Bokamba 1982; Bamgboṣe 1982; for Filipino English see Llamzon 1969 and 1981).

The third category may be called *archaisms*, for lack of a better term. An item may be considered an archaism with reference to its use in the native varieties of English (see Kachru 1970: 130). The fourth category, *non-native innovations*, is not well defined and partly overlaps with the above three categories. This may include loan shifts or loan blends (see chapter 4: 133–35), for example, the following kinship terms: *cousin-brother* (*FF* 131), *cousin-sister* (*RH* 29), and *co-son-inlaw* (see Kindersley 1938). In Indian English the kinship terms *cousin-brother* and *cousin-sister* are examples of lexicalization of a semantic area by two terms; i.e., a male-denoting term and a female-denoting term. In the native varieties of English (see Kachru 1970: 130). The fourth cate-This is one example among many in which a 'close set' of terms in Indian English has more members than in, say, American English.

6.0. LEXICAL STRUCTURE AND DICTIONARY ENTRIES

The entries in a dictionary may be single- or multi-component items (see Zgusta 1967). The single-component items have been subgrouped in two classes (see section 5). The multicomponent items are mainly of three types. First are those which comprise more than one constituent item, of which at least one component belongs to a native language and the other to English. This very productive innovation in Indian English has been termed *hybridization* (see e.g., chapter 5, pp. 153-62), and includes lexical items such as *deepavali* purchases (*H* 18

October 1971). Second are those consisting only of English lexical items, but which may be termed contextually (and formally) *Indianisms*; e.g., *bride-price, dining leaf (WM* 84), *forehead-marking MS* 206; see also discussion in chapter 4, pp. 131–33). Third are those which are traditionally termed 'fixed collocations' or idioms, e.g., *fissiparous tendencies* (*L* 23 November 1965), *nation building, dumb millions, pin drop silence.*

In arranging the lexical entries initially, two types of procedural decisions must be made: first, about the appropriate place for listing the multi-component items; second, about the listing of hybridized items. For example, do *police jamadar, police thana*, and *policewala* come under *police*? Or under *jamadar, thana*, and *-wala*? Many of these formations should present no problems. Consider the item *dining-leaf (WM* 84). This item will come under the entry *dining* and will retain the semantic features of the native varieties, but its phonetic representation will be [ḍainiŋ li:ph] or [ḍainiŋ li:ph], as opposed to ['dainiŋ li:f] in Daniel Jones. This formation will have a completely Indian English contextual definition, which might read something like '*-leaf, n*, improvised by combining plantain or other leaves for eating food; common in S. India and serving as an eating plate (Hind. *pattal*).' Thus, nativized contextual definitions will be essential for a large number of lexical items.

This characteristic, again, is not restricted to Indian English. Consider the following from African English: *bone-to-flesh dance* ('denotes a man dancing with a girl in contrast to the bone-to-bone-style') ; *long-legs* ('for using influence in high places to secure a service') ; *to take in* ('to become pregnant') ; *outdooring* ('first appearance of a baby in public'). Units such as *hard-ears* ('stubborn') and *to cut your eye* ('to make a contemptuous gesture with the eye [at somebody]') also belong to this category.

7.0. LEXICAL SETS AND CONTEXT

In the lexicography of the non-native varieties of English, the concept *lexical sets* may provide a step toward structuring the semantics of contextually determined lexical items. 'A contextual unit is set up in an attempt to demarcate the textually relevant features of a "situation" in terms of the *contextual parameters*' (see chapter 3, p. 104). Consider, for example, the entry *communal* with a typically Indian semantic feature. Dictionaries of English (British and/or American) either have

ignored the Indian uses of this entry, or have casually mentioned it
without listing the (Indian) collocational range of the item. In *OED*
under *communal* the following definitions are given: 1. of or belonging
to a commune; 2. of or pertaining to a (or the) community; 3. of or
pertaining to the commonalty or body of citizens. *Webster's Third New
International Dictionary* (1961) refers to the Indian use of *communal* as
'of or relating to rival communities, especially the communities of
India.' Then it lists two uses, *-division* and *-problem*. On the other hand,
in the *Random House Dictionary of the English Language*—one of the latest
in the fast-increasing number of dictionaries of English—no such (non-
native) variety-specific statement is made. The *Random House Dictionary*
gives the following definitions of the item *communal*: 1. pertaining to a
commune or a community: *communal life*; 2. of, by, or belonging to
the people of a community: *communal ownership*; *communal land*; 3. used
or shared in common by everyone in a group: *a communal jug of wine*;
4. engaged in, by or involving two or more communities: *communal conflicts*. In the same dictionary the definition of *communalism* is given as
'strong allegiance to one's own ethnic group rather than to society as
a whole.' It is unfortunate that, while compiling contemporary dictionaries of English, either (non-native) variety-specific lexical research is not undertaken at all, or it becomes the first casualty of
budgetary constraints.

In Indian English the lexical item *communal* may occur with the following lexical items, among others, as members of the set: *-attitudes*,
-bodies, *-colouring*, *-consideration*, *-disturbance*, *-distinctions*, *-parties*, *-pas-
sion*, *-press*, *-riots*, *-trend*, *-unity*; also *communally named*, *inter-communal*, *communal leader* (see chapter 3, pp. 121–22). Many such lexical sets can be
abstracted from Indian English data. Such information is both formally and contextually relevant for this variety of English as shown
in chapter 3.

8.0. REGIONALISMS IN A NON-REGIONAL DICTIONARY

A *regionalism* may be defined as an area-bound feature which manifests itself at any linguistic level within a non-native variety of English.
Such features (especially in pronunciation) may be language-bound
and may show transfer from the speaker's first language. At the lexical
level, such features may result from the sociocultural context specific
to a geographic and/or language area. In lexicographical research
several decisions are possible concerning regionalisms. The regional

variation in pronunciation may be represented in the lexicon after the standard (educated) non-native pronunciation; this would be a step toward structuring the regional variation in a non-native variety of English. Thus a lexical item such as *stick* as used in Indian English could have a phonetic representation as follows:

stick, sṭik, isṭik (H. A.) ; sṭik (B.A.) ; etc. [5]

One can see several pedagogical uses for this method, but the compilation would create serious problems. Another method—perhaps with fewer complications—would involve concentrating on the standard educated variety. One can also use the statistical frequency of an item as a criterion for determining acceptance or nonacceptance in the dictionary.

In earlier dictionaries of Indian English, a large number of area-bound lexical items have been included; these are area-bound in the sense that they are restricted to regional Indian English newspapers, or are used in specialized registers relevant to a specific area. A few such lexical items are : *coconut paysam* (*M* 1 January 1959) ; *dadan money* (*HS* 11 June 1959); *jibba pocket* (*WM* 19); *jutka driver* (*BA* 101)(also *-carriage*) ; *kuruvai crop, -harvest, -paddy, -season, -yield* (all in *H* 18 October 1971) ; *mulki rules, -laws* (*DC* 22 October 1971). In Kindersley (1938) a limited attempt has been made to provide regional markers with certain typically Indian lexical and grammatical items. [6]

9.0. LEXICOGRAPHICAL SYNTAX

Almost a hundred years ago, in 1885, Sweet (1885:585) made a plea for what he termed 'lexicographical syntax'. Quirk (1960: 83) presents arguments in support of Sweet's view (see also Mathiot 1967 and Householder and Saporta 1962). In the earlier dictionaries or glossaries of Indian English, the lexical and grammatical levels have generally been treated as separate strata. This rigid separation may have occurred partly because of a pejorative attitude on the compiler's behalf toward the productive nativized grammatical innovations. In a dictionary one must determine (again, to take examples from South Asian English) how items such as *welcome-address, god-love, god-son*, and *B. A. pass* are to be treated. These items result from a productive grammatical process termed *rank reduction* (see chapter 4, pp. 136–37). In the native varieties of English these items would be equivalent to *an address of welcome, love of god, son of god,* and *one who has passed his B.A. examination* (or merely *B.A.*). Another set contains items which are not formally deviant but which show contextual constraints (see chapter 3, pp. 111–12). Only recently have some data become available on these aspects of non-native Englishes.

A distinction has also to be made between a mistake in language acquisition and a deviation as discussed earlier. For example, as Bokamba (1982) says, 'most African languages, including Ghanaian and Nigerian, do not have the equivalent of the English definite and indefinite article.' This is also true of South Asian languages (see, e.g., chapter 1, esp. section 3.4). This fact is reflected in these varieties of English, with the result that a 'deviant' system of article use is found in African and South Asian Englishes. The pluralization of uncountable nouns is another characteristic, certainly in African English (see Kirk-Greene 1971: 134; Bokamba 1982). Consider, for example, *aircrafts, apparels, equipments, deadwoods, furnitures, learnings*.

10.0. LEXICOGRAPHY AND NON-NATIVE ENGLISHES

At present, the lexicographical research on new Englishes is primarily restricted to the major dictionaries of English, which incorporate a sprinkling of African, Asian, or Caribbean lexical items. In these, preference is shown for 'encyclopaedic items'. Oxford University Press took a desirable and bold step by adding the supplement by R. E. Hawkins, referred to above, to *The Little Oxford Dictionary*. The 48-page supplement comprises about 1,900 items. The longest tradition of such research is on Indian English, much of which applies to South Asia as a whole. In this tradition the latest addition has been Nihalani *et al*. This work is

... by no means a comprehensive description of English as it is used in India but rather a selection of about one thousand items of the English language which are used in a distinctive manner by large numbers of educated Indian speakers of English. ...

The aim of this Lexicon is to provide teachers and learners of English in India with information about the way in which certain forms and patterns of English used in India differ from the contemporary version of the native speaker model to which Indian English is closest, namely British Standard English (1979:3–4).

As the subtitle indicates, *Indian and British English* is essentially a pedagogical handbook.

The credo for the Caribbean lexicon appeared in Allsopp (1972), entitled *Why a Dictionary of Caribbean English Usage?* This publication, termed 'Circular A,' was followed by 'Circular A2' and 'Circular A3' in June 1973. In this credo Allsopp made it clear that 'no simplified glossary of regionalisms will suffice' (1972:5). What is needed, he says,

... is an authoritative lexicographical account of English *usage* in the Caribbean which must do more than give 'meanings' in isolation, but refer words and phrases to their areas and contexts of occurrence; and which must do more than identify usage and occurrence, but offer some guidance as to the literate acceptability or otherwise of certain current word-forms; hence not a Dictionary of Caribbean English, but rather a *Dictionary of Caribbean English Usage* (1972: 5, his emphasis).

In a recent paper Allsopp (1978: 30) claims that 'the proposed *Dictionary of Caribbean English Usage* is still some way from completion.' But the recent paper provides 'the illustrative entries' (32–39), and 'methodology' (39–42). It also discusses the circumstances which 'seem to dictate certain features for *DCEU*' (31). This dictionary will 'differ importantly' from the earlier *Dictionary of Jamaican English*. Allsopp (1978) gives us some idea of the structure and organization of the forthcoming *DCEU*.

At present, nothing of the magnitude of *DCEU* has been projected for the African varieties of English. There are some fragmentary descriptions, primarily pedagogical and prescriptive, which consider 'deviations' as 'mistakes' (e.g., Hocking 1974). The title of Hocking's book is interesting: *All What I Was Taught and Other Mistakes, A Handbook of Common Errors in English.*

In South African English there are two projects, both initiated in 1969, namely the Dictionary of English Usage in South Africa and the Dictionary of South African English on Historical Principles. The former is overseen by the Department of English of the University of South Africa, and the latter by the Department of Linguistics and English Language of Rhodes University.

The Dictionary of English Usage is prescriptive and, as Prinsloo says (1978: 55), it 'aims, *inter alia*, at providing the following: a) a record of mistakes and problems current in the English of South Africa, and b) some guidance in overcoming mistakes and problems.

The Dictionary of South African English on Historical Principles includes the following information about the South African items in English: a) orthographic and phonetic forms, b) etymology, c) earliest recorded appearances and subsequent developments, d) grammatical patterning, e) lexical signification, f) 'status,' e.g., as colloquial, technical, obsolete or otherwise (see Prinsloo 1978; see also Branford 1978).

In 1975, the Oxford University Press published the *Dictionary of English Usage in Southern Africa*. The project continues and currently concentrates on army slang, schoolboy slang, and specialized terms in mining, industry, etc. This dictionary was followed by *A Dictionary of South African English*, also published by Oxford University Press in 1977 (see also Branford 1970).

There is no detailed lexicographical study of English in Southeast Asia (Singapore, Malaysia, and the Philippines). A number of recent studies provide illustrative data toward such studies; see, e.g., Crewe (1977); Llamzon (1969); Platt (1977); Platt and Weber (1980) Richards and Tay (1981); Tongue (1974).

11.0. CONCLUSION

The questions discussed in this chapter involve some formal and functional aspects of non-native Englishes, which have generally been neglected by both native and non-native users of English. Lexicographical research on some non-native varieties has already been initiated, but such attempts are marginal and restricted to only a few varieties. One cannot say that research in this area has been neglected purely for lack of interest; other reasons, including the magnitude of the undertaking and its time factors and financial implications, naturally discourage scholars. Furthermore, there is the general attitude toward these varieties which has by and large not been conducive to scholarly work in this area. But now the change in attitude is slowly becoming evident both among some native and non-native users of English.

The data presented here have been primarily from South Asian English, but the theoretical and methodological questions raised seem to apply to all the non-native Englishes. The formal and functional characteristics of a non-native variety of English are the result of the nativization of the language. One important aspect of the nativization is the acculturation of English in *new* (un-English) contexts, whether in Africa, Asia, or the West Indies (see Kachru 1981a). The variety-oriented dictionaries of English are therefore important in order to study the linguistic manifestation of English in these new contexts. Such dictionaries should also provide us with better insights about the interplay of language and culture in diverse sociocultural and linguistic contexts in various English-using parts of the world.[7]

NOTES

This chapter is adapted from 'Toward a Lexicon of Indian English' (Kachru *et al.*, eds., 1973:352 76), and 'The New Englishes and Old Dictionaries: Directions in Lexicographical Research on Non-native Varieties of English' (Zgusta, ed., 1980: 71–101).

1. In this chapter the term *non-native varieties* of English has been specifically used for the varieties which are primarily used as second languages; for example, in West Africa, South Africa, South Asia, and the Philippines. These *new* Englishes have developed as distinct varieties in varied sociocultural and linguistic contexts. (For a detailed discussion see Kachru, 1969a, and particularly Kachru 1981a and 1982a.) The case of Caribbean English is somewhat different. By and large English functions as first language in that region. However, a number of innovations termed 'Caribbeanisms' are motivated by the same formal and contextual reasons as are, for example, South Asianisms and Africanisms.

2. For a detailed list, see Yule and Burnell (1886) [1903].

3. In his preface to the second edition (xi), Crooke says: 'In this edition of the *Anglo-Indian Glossary* the original text has been reprinted, any additions made by the Editor being marked by square brackets. No attempt has been made to extend the vocabulary, the new articles being either such as were accidentally omitted in the first edition, or a few relating to words which seemed to correspond with the general scope of the work. Some new quotations have been added, and some of those included in the original edition have been verified and new reference given. An index to words occurring in the quotations has been prepared.'

4. By an *Indian semantic feature* is meant the lexical meaning of a word that relates to typical Indian *context of situation* via an Indian language—in this case, Hindi-Urdu.

5. H. A. refers to the Hindi area and B. A. refers to the Bengali area.

6. For example, as mentioned in chapter 5, the extent of South Asian lexical items varies from as few as 188 items to as many as 26,000. Fennell (1892:xi) lists 399 words which belong to the following sources: Hindoo (sic), 336; Sanskrit, 32; Dravidian, 31. The *Oxford English Dictionary* lists 900 words of South Asian origin. Wilson (1855) has included 26,000 words from South Asian sources and also English words appropriate to South Asian contexts. Serjeantsen (1961:220–60) lists 188 such lexical items. In the *Random House Dictionary of the English Language* over 200 such encyclopaedic words have been listed.

7. As an aside, one might add here that the 'residual forms' of several European languages in addition to English provide examples of such lexical and other innovations in various parts of the world. Consider, for example, Malkiel's observation (1981: 253): 'Quite apart from the special position of French, which also reflects the earlier holdings of Belgium, we have the laboratory case of five presently independent countries in continental or insular Africa which favour Standard Portuguese as their official language, partly in rivalry with a local Portuguese creole, as L.F. Lindley Cintra's recent investigations have made plain. At the periphery of this labyrinth remain the instances of former Danish, Dutch and pre-1918 German colonies—as well as at least certain facets of the former multi-layered Spanish colonial empire. (In the Philippines, Spanish and American English have, perhaps uniquely, been in competition.)'

IV ENGLISH AND NEW VERBAL STRATEGIES

7

On 'Mixing'

In recent years several insightful studies on code-mixing and code-switching have been published which attempt to find answers to questions such as the following, concerning the use of these two linguistic devices as communication strategies: What are the functional motivations for their use? What formal devices are used in 'mixing' languages or dialects? What are the attitudes toward various types of mixing? What constraints are there to mark code-mixing as distinct from what a user of such a language device would term 'odd-mixing'? And, finally, what are the implications of such mixing on language change in a diachronic sense?[1]

This chapter attempts to discuss some of these issues with specific reference to a multilingual dinosaur, India. I consider the linguistic devices of code-mixing and code-switching as two distinct manifestations of language dependency and language manipulation. We notice these manifestations in the way a multilingual or a multidialect user of a language assigns areas of function to each code, and in the development of new mixed codes of communication. We might then say that code-switching and code-mixing mark communicative strategies of two distinct types. In the literature it seems that these two terms are alternately used for one manifestation, generally that of code-switching. In discussing these two linguistic devices one makes two presuppositions: that there is language (or dialect) contact, and that there are functional or pragmatic reasons for the use of code-switching or code-mixing.

1.0. DISTINCTION BETWEEN CODE-SWITCHING AND CODE-MIXING

These two devices may be separated on the basis of the following distinction. *Code-switching* entails the ability to switch from code A to code B. The alternation of codes is determined by the function, the situation and the participants. In other words, it refers to categorization of one's verbal repertoire in terms of functions and roles. Consider, for example,

Gumperz's study of Khalapur (Gumperz 1964a: 137–53), where the
'linguistic bounds' or 'switches' mark the situation and the relationship with the participants. The variants constituting the total verbal
repertoire are local dialects on the one extreme, and standard Hindi on
the other extreme. The local dialects are further divided into *moṭī bolī*
('rough dialect') and *sāf bolī* ('refined dialect'). These are functionally
marked: *moṭī bolī* is used within the context of the family, and *sāf bolī*
outside the immediate family circle. In addition, the verbal repertoire of these villagers includes 'market' and 'oratorial' varieties of
Hindi. One can provide case studies of this from south India to Kashmir. It seems to be a common phenomenon in India, as in Africa (see
Parkin 1974; Whiteley 1974 and Kachru 1982c), but has been little
studied.

However, in written texts—for example, in creative writing—there
is a long tradition of the use of *bhāṣā sankar* ('language mixture') in
Indian poetry, and code-switching for various types of effects. As a
representative sample of such writing, I am going to consider some
examples from *Rāg Darbārī*, a Hindi novel published in 1968, and an
anthology of short stories. In these works, as in everyday life in that
part of India, code-switching from standard Hindi may be used to express extreme anger, disapproval, in-group membership, asides, or so-
lidarity. Code-switching in such contexts is a marker of an attitude,
intensity of emotions, or various types of identities. Consider, for example, the following, in which the switch is from Hindi to a dialect
called Awadhi.

(1) maĩ sab samajhtā hũ. tum bhī khannā kī tarah bahas karne lage ho. maĩ
     sātvẽ aur navẽ kā pharak samajhtā hũ. [Switch to Awadhi] hamkā ab
     prinspalī kare na sikhāv bhaiyā. Jonū hukum hai, tonū čuppe karī auṭ
     karo, samjhyo nāhī. (p. 31)

     I understand everything. You also have started arguing like Khanna. I
     understand the difference between seven and nine. [Switch to Awadhi]
     Don't teach me, dear, how to be a principal. Whatever is the order, you
     carry it out quietly. Do you understand or not?

The above example illustrates code-switching. *Code-mixing*, on the
other hand, entails transferring linguistic units from one code into another. Such a transfer (mixing) results in developing a new restricted
or not so restricted code of linguistic interaction. One may consider
code-switching a process which can result in code-mixed varieties. A
multilingual or multidialectal person is generally able to associate a
function and an effect with various types of language or dialect mixes.
The code-mixed varieties thus provide sociolinguistic indicators of

various types. Let us consider the following illustrations.

(2) tum nahī̃ jāntī, he is chairman Mr. Mehta's best friend yahā̃ do čār din
ko hī āye haĩ. mãine sočā, I should not miss the opportunity. (*HLSK* 172)

(3) bhej do. Another fifteen minutes and I am off to the station. lautne tak
kāphī rāt ho saktī hai. khāne ke liye weiṭ mat karnā. (*HLSK* 175)

(4) kisī ne driver kā driving licence čhīnā, kisī ne registration card, koī backview mirror khaṭ khaṭāne lagā, koī truck kā horn bajāne lagā, koī brake
dekhne lagā. unhõ ne footpath hilā kar dekhā. (*RD* 14)

(5) ṭum apne hī̃ mukdame kī jāč kāmyābī se nahī̃ karā sakā to dūsre ko kaise
bačāegā? andherā ṭhā to kyā huā? ṭum kisī ko pahčān nahī̃ pāyā, ṭo
ṭumko kisīpar šak karne se kaun rokne sakṭā! (*RD* 22)

In examples (2)–(5), we find three functional types of mixing. The
type of mixing in examples (2) and (3) is now a socially accepted marker
of education and what may be termed *westernization* in India. It also
identifies membership in a particular social class. The lexical spread
in example (4) is determined by the context. In order to talk about the
parts of a truck, one has to use a certain type of lexis such as *driver, driving licence, registration card, backview mirror, truck, horn, brake, footpath*. One
might term this register-specific mixing. In example (5), we have a
special type of mixing which phonetically and lexically marks a character type by using what is generally termed *Army Hindustānī*. During
the colonial days this variety was used by non-Indian army officers
and the Anglo-Indians to establish a special identity, to mark authority
and to create an effect of power. But later it continued to be used by
non-Hindi-speaking army personnel, and sometimes even by the Hindi
or Panjabi-speaking army officers. The attitudinal reasons are not different from the ones which motivated its use by the British army. Note
the substitution of dental stops for retroflex stops and use of constructions such as *rokne sakṭā* for *rok sakṭā*.

2.0. CODE-MIXING, BORROWING, AND PIDGINS

One might now ask two questions specifically about code-mixing:
First, in what sense is code-mixing distinct from what has traditionally
been termed *borrowing*? Second, in what sense, if any, are code-mixed
varieties different from pidgins?

It is possible to consider code-mixing as borrowing if the term is used
in an extended sense and not in its restricted sense. Code-mixing entails
extended borrowing, for three reasons: It is not used merely for sup-

plementing lexical sets for contexts in which the borrowing language has lexical gaps. The transfer of linguistic items is extended to units higher than single lexical items, e.g., groups, clauses, sentences, collocations, and idioms. Such mixing results in the extension of the register-range and style-range of a language. Also, it provides an extended choice for lexicalization; for example, in Hindi, Kashmiri, Panjabi, and Kannada we find that there are at least three sources for lexicalization, and these three result in three distinct types of code-mixing, namely, Sanskritization, Persianization, and Englishization. The following examples from the Sanskritized, Persianized, and Englishized verb formations in Hindi with the structure V + operator are illustrative.

Englishized	*Persianized*	*Sanskritized*	
anger karnā	gussā karnā	krodh karnā	'to be angry'
love karnā	pyār karnā	prem karnā	'to love'
marriage karnā	šādī karnā	vivāh karnā	'to get married'
pity karnā	raham karnā	dayā karnā	'to pity'
worry karnā	phikir karnā	činta karnā	'to worry'

This is a productive process and 'mixers' seem to extend it to all word classes, resulting in various types of hybridization (Kachru 1978a).

The type of code-mixing discussed here is not pidginization as we understand the term. It is generally claimed that pidgins have three characteristics, namely, structural simplicity, inability to express abstract concepts, and restricted functional range. In addition, pidgins are considered as codes of communication between speakers of two mutually unintelligible languages (see, for example, Todd 1974:1–2). These characteristics do not apply to the code-mixed varieties discussed here. However, in attitudinal terms, the code-mixed varieties form a hierarchy in India and each variety expresses a different type of attitude.

Another characteristic of the code-mixed varieties is that in most situations, if widely used, they may be identified with a special name which is generally indicative of their 'mixed' nature. The labels used to identify them may be attitudinally loaded or not so loaded. In the literature we find the use of the following labels among others: Hinglish (Kachru 1979), Singlish (Fernando 1977), Spanglish (Nash 1977), Englañol (Nash 1977), Tex Mex (Gumperz 1970), Ṭangi Phārsī and Bazār Hindi (Apte 1974). However, not all the mixed varieties are accepted by the users or others in the speech community as desirable mixing. In Texas, for example '. . . such language mixture tends to be disparaged and referred to by pejorative terms such as Tex-Mex. It is rarely reported in the literature and frequently dismissed as abnormal' (Gumperz 1970:187). In India, Bazār Hindi ranks lowest on the cline.

3.0. MOTIVATIONS FOR 'SWITCHING' AND 'MIXING'

These two devices are essentially used as communicative strategies with various motivations. Their areas of function are not necessarily mutually exclusive, though in certain contexts they can be separated.

In discourse, code-switching may be used as a device to mark, among other things, an identity, an aside, or a specific role. The identity function, for example, is served by a switch from Telugu to Dakhini in Andhra Pradesh, or Hindi to Panjabi in Haryana (see Pandit 1978). Code-switching may be used to reveal or to conceal region, class and religion. In conversation it is used to make an aside, or to indicate non-membership of a person in the inner group. Often both devices are used with a clear effect in mind: for example, in Kashmiri, a professional discussion may be marked by code-mixing with English, and a switch from that may indicate change of context. (see Kachru 1982c.)

One might mention four functions, among others, in which code-mixing is used as a communicative strategy. First, its use for register identification. The formal exponents of register types vary on the basis of the context in which they function. The registral characteristics are realized by various types of lexicalization. For example, in administrative, political, and technological registers, Englishization takes place. On the other hand, in the legal register, especially that of the lower courts, the main lexical source used is Persian. In literary criticism or philosophical writing in Hindi, Sanskritization usually takes place. Second, code-mixing provides formal clues for style identification. In India, there are three distinct styles which may be termed Sanskritized, Persianized, and Englishized. Third, it is used as a device for elucidation and interpretation. This is particularly true of languages in which registers or terminologies have not been stabilized or have not received general acceptance. A person uses two linguistic sources in defining a concept or a term so as to avoid vagueness or ambiguity. Consider the following, for example.

āpekshit ghanatva māne relative density (*RD* 26).
. . . yeh thos kārban dāyaksāid (carbon dioxide) arthāt sūkhī baraph (*D* 7.1.7).

In these constructions, *māne* and *arthāt* both mean 'meaning' and are from Persian and Sanskrit, respectively. The mixing with English has been used to redefine in English what has already been expressed in Hindi, or a term in Hindi is used as a gloss for a term in English. Fourth, there is code-mixing for neutralization, or what in the Prague School terminology may be *automatization*. The aim is to code-mix in a language in order to use lexical items which are attitudinally and contextually neutral. In other words, they do not provide contextual clues and thus language is used to conceal various types of identities. In the literature, this aspect has been briefly referred to in Annamalai (1978), Di Pietro (1977:146), Fernando (1977:354–355), and S.N. Sridhar (1978:116). Annamalai (1978:242) rightly observes that in Tamil code-mixing with English is used to conceal 'the social and regional identity'. In order not to give away caste identity, a person prefers the English kinship term *brother-in-law* to the Tamil *maccaan* or *attimbeer*. One might use *rice* instead of *saadam* (Sanskritist) or *soru* (purist). In many contexts, a neutral kinship term like *wife* is preferred to *manaivi* or *peṇḍātti*, the first being formal and the second being colloquial in Tamil. The English word *wife* has no such connotations. In Kashmiri, as discussed earlier, Sanskritization is generally associated with 'Hindu Kashmiri' and Persianization with 'Muslim Kashmiri'. The Englishization has no such religious connotations and cuts across religious boundaries.

One can then claim that in register identification and style identification, code-mixing has the function of *foregrounding*, and in neutralization it has the function of automatization. Therefore, as a marker of register and style, code-mixing is used to attract attention, while in neutralization it is used for the opposite effect. We might see code-mixing as a contextually determined device. There is, therefore, a mutual expectancy between the type of code-mixing and the contextual unit in which it functions.

One formal characteristic which marks code-mixed texts as being separate is their lexis, and lexical cohesion (see Halliday and Hasan 1976:6–19). By the term *cohesion* we mean integration of the units of another code into the system of the receiving code, and organizing the units from two codes in a semantic relationship. A user of a code-mixed variety intuitively applies the process of the first language to nativize the linguistic elements of the other code. In Hindi-English code-mixing, most of the productive grammatical processes of Hindi-Urdu are applied to English items. Consider, for example, the following.

Number:

agency	ejensiyā̃ (agencies)
company	kampaniyā̃ (companies)
tie	ṭāiyā̃ (ties)
car	kārẽ

Gender:

master	māsṭarin *(f.)*
inspector	inspekṭrin *(f.)*

Abstract nouns:

doctor	ḍākṭarī
governor	gavarnarī
officer	aphsarī

This also applies to inflection assignment and other grammatical categories (see Bhatia 1967).

There seems to be a type of cline in mixing which starts with lexical mixing and then progressively extends to higher units, the maximum being an alternate use of sentences from two codes. The mixing at the lexical level may show a lexical spread which is associated with a register. Consider, for example, the italicized Persian lexical items in the following illustration. This type of Persianized lexical spread is typical of legal register in Indian languages.

mukdame ke liye ise ek purāne *phaisle* kī *nakal* čāhiye. uske liye pahle *tahsīl* mẽ *darkhāst* dī thī. *darkhāst* mẽ kučh kamī rah gayī, isliye vah *khārij* ho gayī. ispar usne dūsrī *darkhāst* dī. kučh din hue yah *tahsīl* mẽ *nakal* lene gayā. *nakalnavīs* čiṛīmār niklā. (*RD* 47)

On the other hand, in the following illustration there is almost an alternate use of units of Hindi and English.

'We are very good friends, Sir, lekin, lekin you know . . . mãi official work ko dostī se zyādā mahtva detā hū̃ . . . agar āp mān lẽ, to maĩ Batra ko khud is point par agree kar lū̃gā'. Aur vah Batra se jā kar kahegā—'You were wrong my dear—boss mere point par agree karte haĩ'. (171)

4.0. ATTITUDES TO 'MIXING'

It would be wrong to claim that, in multilingual settings, all the code-mixed varieties evoke identical attitudinal responses. A multilingual person seems to choose code-mixing of various types, deliberately evaluating what it will accomplish for him, pragmatically and attitudinally. The pragmatic reasons for code-mixing have to be seen in the context of situation. Code-mixing seems to be used as a communicative strategy with a clear end in mind.

I briefly discuss here four types of code-mixed varieties used in India, with special reference to their use as communicative strategies. I shall label these Englishization, Sanskritization, Persianization and pidginization.

Code-mixing with English is pan-South Asian. In attitudinal and functional terms it ranks highest and cuts across language boundaries, religious boundaries and caste barriers. It is a marker of modernization, socioeconomic position, and membership in an élite group. In stylistic terms, it marks deliberate style. The widest register range is associated with code-mixing in English. It continues to be used in those contexts where one would like to demonstrate authority, power, and identity with the establishment. One finds evidence for this attitude in various social contexts, in parents' language preference for their children, and in choice of preferred language in the colleges. In the following two examples, we find two attitudes toward English. A person in authority switches to English and the immediate response is:

prinsipal ne sočā: pradhān ho jāne ke bād sālā angrezī čhãṭ rahā hai, 'case' kahtā hai. (*RD* 408)
'The principal thought: After becoming the head this brother-in-law [curse word] is showing off in English; he says "case". . . .

In the second example, it is important to understand the registral function of English. In the classroom a teacher finds it difficult to explain the concept of 'relative density' in Hindi and then says:

science sālā [curse word] angrezī ke binā kaise ā saktā hai. (*RD* 26)
'How can you understand science *sālā* [curse word] without English?'

The second type of code-mixing, which again is shared by all Indian languages, results in Sanskritization. In stylistic terms it may mark religion and caste, as we have seen in the case of Kashmiri. It also has developed registers for philosophy, literary criticism and religious discourse. In other contexts, Sanskrit lexicalization is considered *panḍitāu* and thus marks 'pedantic style'. In oratorial style, Sanskritization is associated with rightist, revivalist politics—for example, that of the Rāshtrīya Swayam Sevak Sangh (RSS) and Ārya Samāj. The opposite of this is true in the oratorial style of the Drāvida Kazhagam in Tamil

Nadu, in South India, who emphasize deSanskritization.

The third type of code-mixing marks Persianization. It spread to all those parts of India which came under the domain of the Muslims during the Muslim period of Indian history. In registral terms it is associated with the legal register, primarily that of the lower courts. In certain parts of India, it is also a marker of religion and occupation.

The attitude toward code-mixing varies from one part of India to another. Let us, for example, consider code-mixing with Persian. In Kashmiri, both the Kashmiri pandits and Muslims use it in their daily life, in various professions, and in the educational system. In fact, in recent years, this style has received patronage from the state government, and All India Radio, Jammu, Leh and Srinagar has adopted it for news broadcasts. In the *madhya deśa*, or the so-called Hindi area, code-mixing with Persian was used by the Kayasthas as a strategy to identify with the Muslim rulers, as was done by the pandits in Kashmir.

The story of code-mixing with Persian in south India, however, is different. In Karnataka, where Kannada, a Dravidian language, is spoken, S.N. Sridhar (1978) has shown that

... the more educated a person the more he tends to mix elements from English in his Kannada, and the more earthy and 'physical' a person the greater the mixture of Perso-Arabic elements in his Kannada (1978:113).

He continues:

... the speech of all the educated characters is marked by varying degrees of code-mixing with English, with the language of his Highness, the Heir Apparent, verging on code-switching. The connotation of 'éliteness' carried by the variety of Kannada mixed with English is, no doubt, a reflection of the status of English as an élite language... (1978:109).

The last type of code-mixing, low on the hierarchy, may be termed *pidginization*. It is an attempt toward simplification of language used in situations where the participants speak languages which are not mutually intelligible. The result is what is termed 'Bazar Hindi' (see Apte 1974), 'Butler English,' or 'Chi Chi English' (see Kachru 1981a).

5.0. EXPONENTS OF 'MIXING'

The formal exponents of 'mixing', as stated in Kachru (1978a), form a hierarchy. In this hierarchy, mixing of simple lexical items ranks lowest and the mixing of sentences ranks highest. The following are illustrations at each rank.

1. *NP insertion*
   urad and moong fall sharply in Delhi. (*TI* 23 July 1977)

2. *VP insertion*
   apne career ke liye boss ko impress karnā koī dhāndhlī nahī̃ . . . (*HLSK* 1975)

3. *Unit hybridization*
   āp admit hoiye, situation log khud samajh jāyẽge. (*HLSK* 75)

4. *Sentence insertion*
   maī̃ āp ko batātī hū̃, he is a very trusting person, people have exploited him. (*D* 3 July 1977)
   Mr Shinde se bhī kah denā, kuċh alag tarīke se . . . don't be a fool, Rashi! kah denā, simply. I don't want to make it public. (*HLSK* 178–79)
   purānī hai to kyā hua, phāin to hai, but I do not like Rajesh Khanna . . . (*D* 27 April 1973)

5. *Idiom and collocation insertion*
   aur maī̃ parivartan ghar se surū karū̃gā kyū̃ki charity begins at/home! (*D* 29 April 1973)

6. *Inflection attachment and reduplication*
   This refers to certain productive processes which are typical of South Asian languages but are now extended to borrowed items in the code-mixed varieties of languages, e.g., *vālā* as in *sakūlīḍigrīvālā* 'a person who possesses a school degree'. (*D* 12 August 1973)

This process includes the use of reduplication of English items. In some South Asian languages, reduplication has the function of marking indefinitization, e.g., *peṭrol veṭrol* (*D* 17 June 1973), *akṭing vekṭing* (*SH* 29 July 1973) (also *ṭāim vāim, kār vār*).

6.0. CODE-MIXING VS. ODD-MIXING

In some earlier studies—for example, Kachru (1978b; earlier version 1978a), Lipski (1977), Pfaff (1976), and Timm (1975)—it has been shown that code-mixing is both functionally and formally a rule-governed phenomenon. It is not an open-ended process, but has various collocational and grammatical constraints. There is a point both in grammar and lexis when a user distinguishes between code-mixing and odd-mixing. The responses to code-mixed items by the users of such varieties seem to vary from 'yes, acceptable' to 'no, unacceptable,' 'well, depends,' and 'I don't know.' The types of constraints on code-mixing have yet to be extensively investigated in particular code-mixed languages and across such languages used by various speech

communities. In analyzing such texts, one has to distinguish between
the types of code-mixing and their linguistic constraints in, for example,
(a) formal texts, (b) informal texts, (c) various types of registers and (d)
texts delimited with reference to the status, age, and sex of participants.
In other words, various types of parameters have to be used to contextualize a text. In the case of code-mixing in Hindi, Kachru provides
the following illustrations of constraints. (For a discussion, see Kachru
1978a : 39–41.)

(a) *Rank-shift constraint*
1. *voh kitāb which is on the table merī hai.
2. *merā voh amrīkī dost who lives in Chicago aȳ hamāre ghar
āyegā.

(b) *Conjunction constraint*
3. *NP and NP āye the.
4. *maī usko akhbār detā but diyā nahī̃.
5. bhāi, khānā khāo and let us go.
6. John abhī āvā nahī̃ but I must wait for him.
7. *John abhī āyā nahī̃ lekin I must wait for him.

(c) *Determiner constraint*
8. *vahā̃ five sundar laṛkiyā̃ paṛh rahī thī̃ (numeral).
9. *tum this sundar laṛkī kī bāt kar rahe the? (demonstrative).

(d) *Complementizer constraint*
10. *mujhe lagtā hai that rām kal āyegā.
11. mujhe lagtā hai ki rām will come tomorrow.

In sentence 10, we see that, given two sentences from one language,
in this case, Hindi, a complementizer from another language, in this
case, English, is not used. On the other hand, if sentences are from two
languages (e.g., Hindi and English), the tendency is to prefer a complementizer from the language used in the first sentence, as we have
seen in sentence 11.

7.0. LANGUAGE MIXING AND LANGUAGE CHANGE

In the literature on mixing and switching, the focus has been essentially on the synchronic formal and functional aspects of these communicative devices. The implications of code-mixing or code-switching on language change, especially that of syntactic change, have
yet to be undertaken.

We already have evidence to show how code-mixing may result in
linguistic divergence. The cumulative effect of mixing may eventually result in distinct varieties of a language. Consider, for example,

the religion-based varieties of Kashmiri termed 'Hindu Kashmiri' and 'Muslim Kashmiri' (Kachru 1973b:7–11), or those of Bengali (Dil 1972). The divergence may take a more extreme form, as in Hindi and Urdu or in Dakhini. In these varieties the divergence is the result of mixing in phonology, lexis, and grammar. In addition, we might also say that the divergence is the result of identifying with two distinct cultural and literary traditions—in the case of Urdu with Persian and Arabic traditions, and in the case of Hindi with the native Sanskrit tradition. There are already several studies which concentrate on the phonological and lexical aspects of Persianization and Englishization of Hindi. The study of the impact of 'mixing' and 'switching' on the syntax of Hindi and other South Asian languages has recently been initiated.

In Kachru (1978a) a summary of such research with reference to Hindi has been presented, and some of the main points are summarized here. First, there is the change in word order: The preferred word order of Hindi is SOV, as opposed to the SVO of English. In creative writing in Hindi, or in the newspaper register, we find examples of SVO, too. This may be due to the influence of an English substratum (Mishra 1963:175–77) and the practice of fast translation from primarily English texts in journalism and broadcasting. Second, there is the introduction of indirect speech. In Hindi discourse, traditionally no distinction is made between direct and indirect speech. But in modern prose we now have constructions such as 'NP said that he will read' (e.g., *rām ne kahā ki voh paṛhegā* as against 'NP said that I will read' (e.g., *rām ne kahā ki mãĩ paṛhũgā*). Third, there is the use of impersonal constructions. By the term 'impersonal constructions' is meant constructions which translate as 'it is said,' 'it has been learnt,' or 'it is claimed.' In Hindi newspaper writing, we come across the translation equivalents of such constructions, for example, *kahā jātā hai, sunā gayā hai*. Fourth, in Indo-Aryan languages in general there is a tendency to delete the agent in passive constructions. It is claimed that passive constructions with agent-marking items such as *dvārā* or *zariye* may be due to the influence of English, e.g., *yah kavitā milṭan dvārā likhī gayī hai* ('This poem was written by Milton'). Fifth, the use of post-head relative clause with *jo* is also attributed to the influence of English (Tiwari 1966:293), and by some to the influence of Persian (Guru 1962:530–31), for example: *vah laṛkā jo ṭebal par baiṭhā hai merā bhāī hai* ('That boy who is sitting on the table is my brother'). Finally, one should also mention here the use of parenthetical clauses in Hindi, though there are two views about their development. It has been claimed that parenthetical clauses are the result of English influence. On the other hand, some scholars consider these as typically Indo-Aryan constructions and provide evidence in the texts of the Hindi writer Lallūjī Lāl (1763–1835) (see Tiwari 1966:294–98).

8.0. CONCLUSION

The linguistic, sociolinguistic or psycholinguistic implications of code-mixing or code-switching have not yet been fully investigated in a specific speech community, nor across various speech communities. Therefore, any generalizations, whether language specific or comparative, toward developing typologies in code-mixing are as yet premature. There is, however, enough evidence to show that code-mixing is not a marker of what Haugen calls 'low grade intelligence.' In his classic work discussing this aspect and rejecting pejorative references to code-mixing, Haugen further says (1952:70):

The conclusion by some critics that 'mixing' is an expression of snobbish contempt for the native tongue does not agree well with the fact that the very speakers who borrow are the ones who have clung persistently to the Norwegian language and passed it on to their children.

The available studies seem to confirm that in India, and in other multilingual areas, the devices of code-mixing and code-switching are being used as essential communicative strategies with clear functional and stylistic goals in view. The programmatic studies done in India (e.g., Gumperz 1964b; Kachru 1978a, 1978b; S.N. Sridhar 1978; Verma 1976) or other parts of South Asia (e.g., Fernando 1977) confirm that the motivations and formal manifestations of code-mixing are the same in Western and non-Western multilingual speech communities.

The theoretical implications of these two communicative devices are now being explored and some recent studies have made attempts in this direction (see Annamalai 1971; Bennett and Nall 1977; Lawton 1977; Lipski 1977; and Pfaff 1976). The attitude toward code-mixed languages has not changed much since Haugen (1952; reprinted 1969: 70) pointed out in defence of code-mixing that

No native speaker of English feels any esthetic or emotional revulsion over the 'mixed' character of his language which far exceeds that of most immigrant Norwegian speech.

It is evident that we generally seem to accept code-mixing in its 'fossilized' forms. The classical cases are, among others, English, Hindi,

Urdu and Dakhini. We are, however, hesitant to accept code-mixing as a synchronic linguistic phenomenon, and at most tolerate it as a communicative device without seriously recognizing its functional value. This attitude is clearly indicated in the attitude to code-mixed varieties such as Tex Mex, as Gumperz has mentioned (Gumperz 1970: 187). This attitude is also reflected in the reaction of the purists in India toward 'mixing' of Perso-Arabic or English with Hindi. In the past, linguists have by and large neglected this area of research both in South Asia and elsewhere. One might say that Haugen (1952) and Weinreich (1953) have been exceptions. On the whole in linguistic literature, such phenomena have been treated as linguistic exotica. It is only now that the linguistic and educational ostriches are slowly raising their heads and facing these communicative devices as linguistic realities. After all, this phenomenon has existed in Europe since the Middle Ages, and in Africa and South Asia, to mention two non-Western areas, for centuries. It is, therefore, reassuring that now code-mixing and code-switching are being studied in a functional-context, both cross-linguistically and cross-culturally. The Indian subcontinent provides substantial data for the study of code-mixing both diachronically and synchronically. This chapter has merely touched on this aspect of the Indian multilingual dinosaur.

NOTES

This chapter is a slightly modified version of 'Code-mixing as a Communicative Strategy in India', in James E. Alatis, ed., *International Dimensions of Bilingual Education*, Georgetown Monograph on Languages and Linguistics. Washington, DC: Georgetown University Press, 1978, pp. 107–24. This is a report on a project on code-mixing and code-switching which was initiated at the University of Illinois, and parts of which have appeared in Bhatia (forthcoming), Kachru 1978a, S.N. Sridhar 1978, and Warie 1977. I am thankful to the participants in the seminar in sociolinguistics which was devoted to this topic in spring 1977. Their comments, criticisms, disagreements, and the wealth of code-mixed data, provided from a variety of languages, was valuable in looking at this topic from a cross-cultural and cross-linguistic perspective.

1.   This body of literature is fast increasing. The following studies may be noted, among others: Abdulaziz-Mkilifi 1972; Annamalai 1971 and 1978; Ansre 1971; Bautista 1977; Bennett and Nall 1977; Bhatia, forthcoming; Blom and Gumperz 1972; Clyne 1967 and 1969; Diebold 1968; Di Pietro 1977; Dozier 1967; Fallis 1976; Fernando 1977; Gingras 1974; Gumperz 1964a and 1964b; Gumperz and Hernan-

dez-Chavez 1972; Hasselmo 1961, 1970; Kachru 1978a and 1982c; Lance 1975; Lawton 1977; Lipski 1977; McClure 1977; McClure and Wentz 1975; Nash 1977; Pandharipande 1981; Parkin 1974; Plaff 1976; Pillai 1967 and 1974; Redlinger 1976; Scotton and Ury 1977; Southworth 1977; S.N. Sridhar 1978; Timm 1975 and 1977; Verma 1976; Wakefield *et al.* 1975; Warié 1977; Weil 1978; Wentz 1977; Whinnom 1971; Whiteley 1974.

2. One can present a large number of examples from Indian literary texts; for example, Amir Khusrau (12th century) in Hindi, and Parmānanda (1791–1879) in Kashmiri. For code-mixing in literary texts see, for example, Pillai 1974, Timm 1977.

V INDIAN ENGLISH AND OTHER NON-NATIVE ENGLISHES

8

The Pragmatics of Non-Native Englishes

1.0. The distinction proposed in this chapter between the *native* Englishes and *non-native* Englishes is not motivated by an urge to foster linguistic divisiveness in the English-using speech community, nor is the
aim to identify varieties of English on the spectrum of colours, with
black, brown, and yellow on one side, and white English on the other
side.

This chapter attempts to present an overview of the pragmatics of
the new Englishes which have developed in new contexts, and to initiate linguistic, attitudinal and functional realism about their uses. It
seems that such an approach has become important, since in the fast-
growing body of literature on the English language, and its expansion
as an international language, there still is a lack of studies which focus
on the pragmatic or functional aspects of these varieties and distinguish these varieties from those Englishes which are used primarily as
native languages in, for example, North America, Australia, Britain,
Canada and New Zealand.[1] The non-native Englishes are the legacy
of the colonial period, and have mainly developed in 'un-English' cultural and linguistic contexts in various parts of the world, wherever
the arm of the Western colonizers reached.

The native speakers of English have essentially studied these varieties from a pedagogical angle, sometimes demonstrating linguistic tolerance, at other times showing amusement, and often expressing irri-
tation at the 'linguistic flights . . . which jar upon the ear of the native
Englishman' (Whitworth 1907:6; see also, e.g., Prator 1968). There
are very few studies in which a distinction has been made between the
functions of the non-native Englishes and those of the native varieties
of English, a distinction which would take into consideration formally
and functionally relevant questions such as the following: (1) the factors which introduced English in new non-native roles in Asia and
Africa; (2) the reasons which contributed toward retention of English
after the independence of the colonies; (3) the functional and pragma-

tic contexts in which the new varieties are used; (4) the linguistic and contextual parameters which contributed to the nativization and development of 'interference' varieties; (5) the sociolinguistic context which contributed to the development of varieties within a variety; and (6) the current linguistic interaction between the users of the new Englishes and the native speakers of English.

It is with reference to these questions that one can study the pragmatics of the new Englishes. I do not claim that all these questions have been raised or answered in the following pages—far from it. But there is an awareness of these questions in the discussion that follows.

2.0. TYPES OF ENGLISHES

In the literature (Bell 1976:152–57; Richards 1974:64–91; Strevens 1977:119–28; Quirk *et al*. 1972:13–32), several dimensions have been used to distinguish various types of Englishes, but in this chapter we are primarily concerned with the distinction between native Englishes and non-native Englishes. It is obvious that this dichotomy is too broad, since it gives the impression of a homogeneity within these two types. That is not how language actually works. Among the non-native speakers one must make a distinction between those who use English as a *second language* and those who use it as a *foreign language*. In the use of English as a second or foreign language there is, of course, substantial variation in competence. I have earlier used the concept of cline of bilingualism to account for this variation.

In studies on the uses of English in new contexts, various euphemistic and metaphoric terms have been used to refer to their special characteristics, for example, *transplanted* English, *transported* English, and *twice-born* English. The underlying idea for the use of such metaphorical terms is to show that the context in which these Englishes function is not the same as that of Britain, though historically all these varieties are related to *Mother English*, which is generally termed *English English* or *British English*. These terms have been used not only to designate the non-native varieties, but also for all those Englishes which function in the non-native contexts, in the sense that the context of these Englishes is different from British English. Thus, Turner (1966) and Ramson (1970) have used the term 'transplanted English' for *Australasian* English, and Mukherjee (1971) has used the term 'twice-born' for the English in Indian fiction since it is '. . . the product of two parent traditions . . .' (11), Indian and British.

The largest English-using population is now using a transplanted, transported or twice-born variety of the language; it includes a substantial number who use it as their first language. Our concern is, however, with a smaller number, specifically those who are not its native users.

At this point, therefore, a minor digression into some statistical data might provide factual basis for this general discussion. The speakers of the transplanted native varieties of English are spread on two continents, the largest group being speakers of American English (182 million), followed by the speakers of Australian and Canadian varieties of English who are equal in number (13 million each), and the smallest group being the users of New Zealand English (3 million). We did not include in this list the speakers of Mother English (British English) who number 55 million.

The following twenty-one countries have the largest enrollments in English. (See Gage and Ohanessian 1974, and Fishman *et al.* 1977)

TABLE 8.1. *Enrollments in English, 1977*

Countries	Millions of students
India	17.6
Philippines	9.8
USSR	9.7
Japan	7.9
Nigeria	3.9
Bangladesh	3.8
Republic of South Africa	3.5
West Germany	2.5
Malaysia	2.4
France	2.4
Indonesia	1.9
Mexico	1.9
South Korea	1.8
Pakistan	1.8
Kenya	1.7
Ghana	1.6
Brazil	1.6
Egypt	1.5
Thailand	1.3
Taiwan	1.2
Sri Lanka	1.2

The uses of non-native varieties show a wide range of competence, varying from a pidginized variety to what may be called ambilingualism. The figures given above are, however, based on enrollments in classes for formal English instruction. This figure is very impressive, and divided in terms of geographical areas, it gives us the following distribution. Asia (excluding the USSR), sixty million; Africa, twenty million; western and central Europe, fifteen million; Soviet Union, ten million; Western Hemisphere, ten million.

Thus, in South Asia alone, 24.8 million people are users of English, followed by Africa, which has 20 million English-users. If we add up the users of English (excluding Britain) we have 211.2 million who speak transplanted native varieties of English, 58% of the total number of English speakers. According to these figures then the non-native users of English add up to 85.6 million.

The main non-native varieties of English have a history distinctly different from the transported varieties used in North America, Australia, or Canada. There was no significant population of English speakers who settled down in, for example, South Asia or West Africa and then used their language in those countries (for South Asia see chapters 1 and 2 and for Africa see Spencer 1971a and 1971b). The English language came to the vast areas of Asia and Africa with the expansion of the Empire, with the spread of Christianity by zealous missionaries, and with eventual 'imposition' of the language due to local linguistic and cultral pluralism. However, during almost three hundred years of contact with Africa and Asia, English has been completely embedded in the local contexts and has slowly gone through the process of nativization.

The manifestations of nativization and the development of sub-varieties within a non-native variety have resulted in two types of reactions. We find one type in, for example, Prator (1968), who claims that the process of nativization should be curtailed, since it reduces intelligibility with the native speakers of English. Therefore, a non-native learner's model should be a native variety of English. The other type of reaction is that these varieties should be viewed with respect to their typical functions in the context in which they are used. In addition, these Englishes are viewed as going through a normal historical development, as did Latin and Sanskrit in the past,[2] therefore, nativization and local models should be recognized as part of the total *variety repertoire* of the international Englishes (Kachru 1976a, 1977a; Perren 1965:39 and Strevens 1977). This approach emphasizes that in establishing the criteria for concepts such as *communicative competence* one must take into consideration the *context of situation* of each non-native English-speaking community.[3] What marks the members of the speech community is certain shared features in their use of a language. But it is equally important to emphasize the non-shared culture-bound features which each variety has developed, and which mark these varieties and subvarieties as distinct. It is these characteristics which make these varieties '. . . capable of expressing the socio-cultural reality of that country' (Richards 1974:87).

The range of *verbal repertoire*, which forms an essential part of communicative competence, is determined by culture-bound parameters, and the concept of *acceptability*, *appropriateness*, and *intelligibility* cannot be used independent of this context. Therefore, the appropriateness and congruence of *speech acts* has to be related to the specific variety, for example *Indian* English, *Nigerian* English, or *Caribbean* English.

Language is essentially a social activity and the contexts for the use of language are determined by various parameters in the context of situation. It is, therefore, important that the non-native varieties of English be studied in the context of situation which is appropriate to each variety, its uses and user.

We shall present some restricted data here about the uses of non-native Englishes in four broad functions. Following Bernstein, we shall term these the *instrumental* function, the *regulative* function, the *interpersonal* function, and the *imaginative/innovative* function, and we shall discuss some cultural and linguistic processes which have contributed towards nativization of English in these functions (see Bernstein 1971).

3.0. NATIVIZATION: TEXT IN CONTEXT

There are various ways of defining the above four functions. In culturally and linguistically pluralistic societies, *instrumental* function implies the status given to English in the educational system, in which it functions as an instrument of learning at various stages. *Regulative* function entails the use of English in, for example, the legal system and administration. *Interpersonal* function provides a clue to how a non-native language is used as a *link* language for effective communication between speakers of various languages, dialects, ethnic groups, and religions, thus providing a code of communication for diverse linguistic and cultural groups. In addition to providing a code, in the interpersonal function, English may also symbolize élitism, prestige, and modernity. The more functional benefits a language provides to a user, the more its uses are stabilized and expanded. At present in several countries where English is a non-native language, it provides various status-marking advantages for which one prefers to become part of this speech community. This reminds one of the status-providing advantages of Persian during Islamic rule in India, French in parts of Africa, and Sanskrit in parts of South Asia. The *imaginative/innovative* function of English has resulted in the development of a large body of writing in English in different genres in various parts of the world. It is the use of English in creative contexts that has now resulted in a fast growing body of, among others, Indian English literature, West African literature, and Caribbean literature.

Let me now elaborate on these four functions with some data from India to illustrate the point. As an instrument of higher education, English continues to hold a dominant position in 83 Indian universities which include specialized institutes, considered 'deemed' universities by the University Grants Commission. Of these, 12 universities in the Hindi region (*madhya deśa*) have introduced Hindi as a medium of instruction. In addition, four universities in Gujarat and one in Rajasthan use the regional language at the B.A. and M.A. levels for instruction. In all, 19 universities continue to use English exclusively as the medium of instruction.

Instructional materials for the humanities are locally produced, sometimes at the state level, and the majority of these focus on India as opposed to the West, which was the case during the colonial days. In post-independence textbooks, it is normal now to include text materials from Indian English writers such as R. K. Narayan and Mulk Raj Anand. Thus, English is used not only as a tool to impart education to linguistically and ethnically pluralistic groups, but it is also primarily through textbooks in English that attempts are being made towards imparting what Indians call *all-India awareness*, and consciousness of the underlying cultural unity of the country. The situation in West Africa is not much different from the Indian situation.

The *regulatory* function basically involves the legal system and the administrative network. The legal system, especially the high courts, have traditionally used two non-Indian languages: earlier, Persian and later, English. In 1965, when attempts were made to use regional languages in the high courts and lower courts, the Indian Bar Council opposed the resolution claiming that 'deep study and felicity in the use of one common language are vital to the existence of an all-India Bar, each of which is in turn indispensable to national integration' (Shah, ed., 1968:168). As in education, in the legal system the claim is made that for 'national integration', and 'all India' standards, English must continue as a regulatory language, tough there are very vocal groups who do not support this view.

In administration, different languages are used at various levels, but there is no national consensus on policy. The discussion in favour of Hindi and regional languages, or in favour of the continuation of English is an on-going debate which provides both entertainment for people and an issue for politicians. In the meantime, however, English has the upper hand. During the period 1974-78, the Central and State governments released 539 publications, of which 38% (205) were in English and 21.3% (115) in Hindi. There are other indications, too, which demonstrate the dominance of English in the regulatory function; for example, 37.46% of the total amount spent on various types of advertisements by the government during 1978–79 was used for English language newspapers.[4]

These figures are only indicative of the use of a language, and may not necessarily interest a linguist or a language teacher, but, thereby hangs a linguistic tale. More interesting is to see how this regulatory use of English in the Indian setting results in language change, namely, the development of typically Indian registers of English in the legal system, administration, education and advertising. And after all, *Babu English* is a manifestation of such uses.

There are only two languages which are used for interaction all over India: English and Hindi (in various varieties), but the symbolic and attitudinal implications of English are greater than those of Hindi. A variety of English which ranks low on the cline of bilingualism is still preferred to the use of Hindi in many roles. The result is code-mixed conversation where linguistically there is no need for the fusion of English and Hindi as has been shown in chapter 7. In national communication, book production has an important role. The comparison of the years 1974 through 1979 shows that, of the fourteen major Indian languages (English included), book production in English has not only been the highest but has been increasing every year. See Table 8.2 on the following page.

The same study reveals that India produced more books in English than, for example, Canada, New Zealand, Japan, South Africa, and the USSR. India is among the ten largest book-producing countries in the world, and ranks third, after the USA and Britain, in the production of books in English. During 1974–79, book production in English constituted 40%, followed by Hindi (14.4%). In Ghana, Kenya, Nigeria, Pakistan and Sri Lanka, to name a few of the countries using English

TABLE 8.2. *Books produced in India in various languages, 1974–79*

Languages	1974	1975	1976	1977	1978	1979
Assamese	169	95	154	105	108	159
Bengali	862	943	1,146	1,031	1,030	1,039
English	5,501	4,700	6,733	5,663	4,393	7,089
Gujarati	560	565	760	690	972	971
Hindi	1,368	1,697	2,235	1,858	2,179	2,966
Kannada	394	867	1,261	888	784	823
Malayalam	480	430	450	417	345	819
Marathi	682	1,180	1,290	1,098	1,117	1,345
Oriya	113	321	73	384	216	270
Punjabi	213	346	241	368	222	273
Sanskrit	40	52	93	61	45	110
Tamil	826	675	697	825	1,083	1,595
Telugu	183	255	355	259	303	414
Urdu	195	511	269	92	93	401
Other languages	61	71	45	34	42	176
Total	11,647	12,708	15,802	13,773	12,932	18,450
Percentage of books in English	47.23	36.98	42.61	41.12	33.97	38.42

Source: Ministry of Education and Social Welfare, Government of India.

as a non-native language, the number of books published in English is out of proportion to the percentage of the English-speaking population. But then one can easily understand the reason for it.

In the production of professional journals English is understandably far ahead. During 1978, 152 out of 196 scientific journals were published in English (78%). This is again true of journals in engineering and technology. In 1978, out of 275 journals, 239 (87%) were published in English.

The above figures refer mainly to specialized professional journals. If we compare the number of newspapers and news magazines in India, English is among the five major languages, along with Hindi-Urdu, Tamil, Malayalam and Marathi, according to figures for 1978. In terms of the reading public, English-language newspapers commanded the highest circulation (22.1%) after Hindi (23.8%).

TABLE 8.3. *Circulation of English newspapers, 1974–78*

(in thousands)

Year	Dailies	Weeklies	Others	Total
1974	2,276	1,547	3,941	7,764
1975	2,240	1,332	4,366	7,938
1976	2,259	1,261	4,308	7,828
1977	2,535	1,377	5,037	8,949
1978	2,555	1,532	4,943	9,030

Source: Press in India, Part 1, 1975–79. Ministry of Information and Broadcasting, Government of India.

English language newspapers are published in 28 of the 31 States or Union territories. (The three areas which have no newspapers in English are Sikkim, Arunachal Pradesh and Lakshadweep.)

TABLE 8.4. *Radio news (Central Home and Regional Services), 1981*

Language	Number of bulletins	Total time in minutes
Assamese	5	45
Bengali	15	99
Dogri	4	40
English	16	$123\frac{1}{2}$
Gujarati	7	60
Hindi	26	$209\frac{1}{2}$
Kannada	6	50
Kashmiri	5	45
Konkani	4	40
Marathi	9	85
Malayalam	9	90
Nepali	3	25
Oriya	5	45
Punjabi	4	40
Sanskrit	2	10
Sindhi	2	20
Tamil	7	65
Telugu	7	70
Urdu	9	100

Source: Akashvani, April-May 1981.

In broadcasting, English and Hindi are the only two pan-Indian languages used by the All India Radio (AIR). AIR does, however, broadcast in other languages and dialects as well. Table 8.4 shows the number of news broadcasts in various languages and the total duration. News broadcasts in English and Hindi took up 2h 03m 30s (9.75%) and 3h 29m 30s (16.56%) respectively of the total broadcasting time of 21 hours.

In a sense the creative use (in Bernstein's terms, the imaginative or innovative function) incorporates the earlier three functions. And I must introduce it with a minor digression. In the rich literary tradition of the English language it was usual to point to Joseph Conrad as the lone writer who excelled in his creativity in English as a second language. One aftereffect of the colonization has been that the list of such writers has not only swelled, but an array of non-native English literatures has developed all over the globe. This fast-growing body of writing provides impressive evidence for linguistic and contextual nativization of the English language. The result is the development of English literatures with areal modifiers such as *West African* English literature, *Indian* English literature, *Caribbean* English literature, and so on. These are not only modifiers conveying the geographical variations, but the cultural and sociolinguistic attitudes, too. These literatures are one manifestation of the national literatures in multilingual and multicultural non-Western English-using nations. In India, for example, one can claim that there are only three languages in which pan-Indian literature is produced with an *all-India* reading public: English, Sanskrit and Hindi. Therefore, Iyengar (1962:3) is right when he says that 'Indian writing in English is but one of the voices in which India speaks. It is a new voice, no doubt, but it is as much Indian as others.' The African situation is not different. 'If you take Nigeria as an example, the national literature, as I see it, is the literature written in English; and the ethnic literatures are in Hausa, Igbo, Yoruba, Effik, Edo, Ijaw, etc.' (Achebe 1965:217; for further discussion see Kachru 1969a and 1976b, Mazrui 1973, Ramchand 1973 and Bailey and Görlach 1982). It is therefore these four functions of English, in situations diametrically opposed to native varieties of English, which have resulted in the nativization of English.

One can also claim that distinctive uses of English in, for example, America, and resultant nativization in American sociocultural (and linguistic) contexts contributed to its Americanness and mark it in

some respects separate from British English. This claim is justified and
has been made both aggressively, for example, by Mencken (1919),
who claimed the status of an independent *American language* for it, and
moderately, for example, by Mathews (1931) and Marckwardt and
Quirk (1964). The Australianness of Australian English has formed
part of several studies (e.g., Baker 1945, Morris 1898, Ramson 1966
and 1973, Turner 1966). Their aim again was to demonstrate how the
new cultural and linguistic contexts have initiated linguistic changes
in Australian English which mark it as distinct from Mother English.

The nativization of phonology and lexis have earlier formed part of
several studies[5] and have briefly been discussed in earlier chapters. I
would therefore like to elaborate on one particular aspect, that of the
influence of multilingual and multicultural contexts on the non-native
Englishes. In order to illustrate this point I shall consider three types
of linguistic evidence, namely, hybridization, collocations, and larger
formations which are culture-determined.

In a hybridized item there is, at least, one lexical item of English and
another item from the native language. There are various structural
variations possible, but we shall not go into that discussion here.[6] The
hybridized lexical items are used in all the non-native varieties. Consider for example, *ahimsa soldier*, *policewala*, and *lathi charge* from Indian
English, and *dunno drums*, *bodom bead*, and *Awerba lamps* from Ghanaian
English (Sey 1973:63).

On the other hand, a specifically non-native English collocation has
no lexical item from a native language, but there are other reasons
which make it specifically non-native. It may be a transfer ('translation') from a native language of a non-native user of English, it may
show semantic restriction or extension, and it may be culture-specific
and therefore have to be defined with special reference to, say, the
African, Caribbean or Indian sociocultural context. In West African
English, the following examples have one or more of the above characteristics: *chewing-sponge*, or *chewing stick* ('twig used for cleaning teeth'),
cover-shoulder ('a blouse'), *to destool* or *enstool* ('to depose or install a chief'),
hot drinks ('alcoholic drinks'), *knocking fee* ('fee paid by a man to a woman's
family for initiating negotiations about marriage'), *outdooring* ('first
appearance of a baby in public'), *sleeping cloth* ('cloth on which one
sleeps at night'), *small room* ('toilet') and *tight friend* ('close friend') (see
Sey 1973:75–91). Bamgboṣe (1971:43ff) gives an interesting example
of semantic change, for example *branch* in the sense of *call* ('I am going

to branch at my uncle's house') or *globe* used for *electric light* ('We had
no light because she broke the globe'), and *cup* used for a drinking
glass ('He drank a cup of water'). A large number of collocations from
Indian English have been discussed in chapters 3 and 4. Consider,
e.g., *forehead marking, nine-stranded thread,* and *dining leaf.* The transfer of
non-native English speaker's native linguistic and cultural elements
are not restricted to lexical items—hybrid or non-hybrid. It shows in
sentences and clauses, too, and in several cases results in unintelligibility with the native speakers, particularly in those formations which
are used in the interpersonal and creative contexts, for example, in
creative writing. Let us consider the following:

1. *May we live to see ourselves tomorrow.*
2. *He has no chest.*
3. *He has no shadow.*
4. *Where does your wealth reside?*
5. *What honourable noun does your honour bear?*

It is obvious that, from a native speaker's point of view, these five examples are not only contextually deviant, but the lexical selection also
is odd and unintelligible. On the other hand, from the point of view of
the non-native speakers of English—in this case, African and Indian—
the native speaker's point of view is not necessarily relevant because
these formations do form part of the *communicative repertoire* of specific
non-native varieties. It is easy to show the contextual equivalence of
these formations with the formations which a native speaker might use.
An African user of English, whose native language is Ijaw, might say
that *May we live to see ourselves tomorrow* is the equivalent of *Goodnight* in
Western societies. And sentences 2 and 3 are equivalent of *He is timid.*
Okara (1963:15) further comments on these formations:

Now a person without a chest in the physical sense can only mean a human that
does not exist. The idea becomes clearer in the second translation. A person
who does not cast a shadow of course does not exist.

The other two sentences (4 and 5) are used by the Indian English
writer Khushwant Singh in his *Train to Pakistan.* It is not necessary
that Indian English users will use these in their daily speech; they are
in fact author-bound and used by Singh for developing a typical Panjabi character in a Panjabi context. The contextualization of language,
through the device of translation, is one process of language nativization (as shown in chapters 3 and 4). At first these formations are unacceptable, as are any other linguistic innovations. Those of us interested

in lexicography should be familiar with the lexicographer's dilemma: whether or not to include formations of low frequency in a lexicon. But, as such formations gain currency, they become more acceptable, as have, for example in West Africa, the formations such as *bone-to-flesh-dance* ('denotes a man dancing with a girl, in contrast to the 'bone-to-bone' style'); *long legs* ('for using influence in high places to secure a service'), and *been-to* ('been to overseas') (Kirk-Greene 1971:138; see also Bokamba 1982 and Kachru 1982b).

The above mentioned examples of linguistic units are only a part of what results in a distinct style. Let us now consider how one's idea about what constitutes impressive *(grand)* style in English is also determined by the literary traditions and culture-bound notions about style. South Asian and West African (see Sey 1973) perception of good style is diametrically opposite to the view of (at least some) native speakers of English. In Ghana (Sey 1973:7)

... flamboyance of English prose style is generally admired ... and the speaker or writer who possesses this style is referred to in the vernaculars in such terms as 'the learned scholar who, from his deep mine of linguistic excellence, digs up on suitable occasions English expressions of grandeur, depth and sweetness'.

In Fante, for example, there is an expression 'brɔfo yɛ dur' meaning 'English is weighty, powerful'. I have earlier quoted (in chapter 1, section 4), the forceful words of the Indian English writer Raja Rao (1938:10) about the Indianized style of English. He says:

After language the next problem is that of style. The tempo of Indian life must be infused into our English expression, even as the tempo of American or Irish life has gone into the making of theirs. We, in India, think quickly, we talk quickly, and when we move we move quickly. There must be something in the sun of India that makes us rush and tumble and run on.

Achebe (1965:222) asks the question: 'Can an African ever learn English well enough to be able to use it effectively in creative writing?' And his answer is; 'Certainly yes'. But then, he qualifies it:

if on the other hand you ask: 'Can he [an African] ever learn to use it like a native speaker?' I should say, 'I hope not.' It is neither necessary, nor desirable for him to be able to do so.

And as a linguistic realist he adds:

... I feel that the English language will be able to carry the weight of my African experience. But it will have to be a new English, still in communion with its ancestral home but altered to suit its new African surroundings.

But to a native speaker such style may appear full of 'verbosity' and 'preciosity' (Sey 1973:124ff). According to Goffin (1934) the attributes of Indian style of English are 'Latinity' (e.g., preference for *demise* to *death, pain in one's bosom* to *pain in one's chest*), 'polite diction', 'phrase mongering' (e.g., *Himalayan blunder, dumb millions*) and a 'moralistic tone' (in the sense that Indians cannot keep God out of it). In Kindersley's study (1938:26) the use of 'clichés' is one of the stylistic features of Indian English (e.g., *do the needful, better imagined than described*). (For a detailed discussion and more examples, see Kachru 1982b).

4.0. THE CLINE OF VARIETIES: VARIETY WITHIN VARIETY

It would be misleading to say that the non-native varieties of English are homogeneous and that the users of these varieties are intelligible to all the users of each variety, and across the various sub-varieties. As we know, linguistic homogeneity is the dream of an analyst, and a myth created by language pedagogues. In reality, linguistic variation is the fact which realists have accepted, though slowly, and with rewarding results.

The variation within a non-native variety of English is perhaps much more exasperating and bewildering than it is in a native variety. There are reasons for it, one reason being, as Quirk *et al.* (1972:26) appropriately say, that the English language has developed several *interference varieties*

that are so widespread in a community and of such long standing that they may be thought stable and adequate enough to be institutionalized and regarded as varieties of English in their own right rather than stages on the way to a more native-like English.

Quirk *et al.* refer to 'India, Pakistan and several African countries, where efficient and fairly stable varieties of English are prominent in educated use at the highest political and professional level'. The interference is not only linguistic, but sociocultural as well.

The primary varieties of each non-native variety are again to be distinguished on the basis of the *users* and the participants in a speech act. We have varieties of English which are essentially used for local needs and consumption; say, for example, Indian English, which is used primarily in the *Indian* contexts, with *Indian* participants for typically *Indian* situations. All these uses may be incorporated under the term national uses. The appropriateness and role of an American or English native speaker is not necessarily relevant to such contexts. In fact, if it were culturally, linguistically, and politically expedient, India would have opted to use a language of *Indian* origin in such contexts. Note that I purposely mentioned a language of Indian origin and not an Indian language since in the Indian linguistic context it is now appropriate to consider English as an Indian language though not of Indian origin.

There is, however, a small group of Indians who use English for international communication. It is in this context that the participants entail the need for what may be termed *international* English. The Indians who function in these contexts will then use educated Indian English which may provide approximations to various degrees of, for example, British English or American English. But the Indians who function in international contexts form only a small number out of the total English-using population of India. Statistics can be deceptive, and in this case are misleading. If one accepts the present language statistics of India, there are almost 3% of the Indian population who are English-using bilinguals. But in numerical terms these account for almost eighteen million people. In other words, this number is equal to 8.4% of the population of the United States, 139% of the Australian population, and 32.4% of the population of Great Britain. If we add the figures of the whole Indian subcontinent to these figures, the picture changes substantially: there are 3.8 million users of English in Bangladesh, 1.8 million in Pakistan, and 1.2 million in Sri Lanka. And this adds up to 24.8 million.

The distinction between *national* and *international* Englishes has a crucial importance in our understanding the concept of English as an international auxiliary language (EIAL). I shall return to this point later.

The varieties within the national varieties of non-native Englishes also provide a spectrum. Let us consider a specific variety, namely Indian English, from this point. One can intuitively say that there is significant deviation among the users of Indian English, as there is among the users of native Englishes. This intuitive impression is verified by empirical evidence presented by Schuchardt as early as 1891, when English was used in India as a highly restricted *foreign* (not *second*) language.[7] In later studies more evidence has been presented.

Schuchardt develops a cline of 'Indo-Englishes' (see Schuchardt 1891 [1980]) and attempts to provide the formal exponents for each type. The isoglosses with reference to areas which he sets up for each

226 *Indianization of English*

sub-variety are no more applicable, but these do provide some insight into the uses of English in India almost a century ago. The varieties he lists are *Indo-English; Butler English* (Madras); *Pidgin English* (Bombay); *Boxwala English* (itinerant peddlers, upper India); *Cheechee English* (or *chi-chi*), spoken by Eurasians, and *Baboo* (*Babu*) *English* (Bengal and other places).

Thus we find here an attempt toward explaining the varieties in terms of the speaker, and in terms of the user. This then is perhaps the first attempt toward structuring the variation in Indian English. Schuchardt's study, as Gilbert says in his introduction to his work, shows (see Schuchardt 1891 [1980]:38)

... great interest in problems associated with languages in contact, the nature of borrowing, the process of language 'mixture', and the linguistic structures produced by imperfect, socially stabilized second language acquisition. He points out the premature nature of many of the claims being made by linguists of his day (cf. his running feud with the neo-grammarians) and urges that the study of language be put on a more experimental basis, in the sense of field observation in a social context.

I shall briefly discuss these sub-varieties: The term *Indo-English* is roughly equivalent to the use of the term *educated* Indian English. In order to explain what we mean by an *educated* Indian we must of necessity use a circular definition, for example, an Indian who has a degree say at the bachelor's level and has English as one of the subjects. This is the type of approach Quirk *et al.* followed in their description of *educated* British English, and Sey (1973) adopted for defining *educated* Ghanaian English (EGE). It may sound circular, but in reality it is not so confusing, since description of such a corpus eventually resulted in a monumental description of English entitled *A Grammar of Contemporary English* (1972) by Quirk *et al.*

The best example of *Butler English* provided by Yule and Burnell (1886: 133–34) has been given in chapter 2 (see section 3.0).

... the broken English spoken by native servants in the Madras Presidency which is not very much better than the Pigeon-English of China: It is a singular dialect; the present participle (e.g.) being used for the future indicative, and the preterite indicative being formed by *done*; thus I telling = 'I will tell'; *I done tell* = 'I have told'; *done come* = 'actually arrived.

In Schuchardt (1891 [1980:47]) we have additional examples:

Butler's yevery day taking one ollock for own-self, and giving servants all half half ollock; when I am telling that shame for him, he is telling, Master's strictly

order all servants for the little milk give it—what can I say mam, I poor ayah woman? (*The Times* 11 April 1882, p. 8)
....an Englishman wishing to assure himself that an order has been duly executed, asks, *Is that done gone finished, Appoo?* and Appoo replies, in the same elegant phraseology, *Yes, sare all done gone finished whole*. (quoted in Schuchardt 1891 [1980:47])

The term *Chee-Chee English* is used both by Yule and Burnell (1886) and Schuchardt (1891) with reference to the speech of Eurasians or Anglo-Indians and applies both to the group and 'also to their manner of speech. The word is said to be taken from *chi* (Fie!), a common (S. Indian) interjection of remonstrance or reproof . . .' A citation of 26 August 1881 from *St. James's Gazette* says,

There is no doubt that the 'chee chee twang,' which becomes so objectionable to every Englishman before he has been long in the East, was originally learned in the convent and the Brothers' school, and will be clung to as firmly as the queer turns of speech learned in the same place. (Quoted in Schuchardt 1891 [1980:49–50]).

This sub-variety is marked in its 'mincing accent' and 'hybrid minced English', and specifically noticeable in pronunciation. But certain formations have been marked as peculiar to this sub-variety by Schuchardt (1891 [1980:50]). The following are illustrative.

CCE	English
to blow one's self	*to hit one's ownself*
to get tossed	*to be thrown from a horse*
to cover	*to sleep under a sheet or a blanket*
to roll a bird	*to hit a bird with a stone or pellet*

There are also alternate lexical items used, e.g., *hall-room* for British English *parlour*. The use of this term is also attitudinally marked since it refers to both an ethnic group and their variety of English.

The most talked about variety, however, is *Babu (Baboo) English*. The word *babu* has several uses in Indian languages: It is, however, primarily used for a clerk who could use various Indian registers of English. Since originally Calcutta was the main centre of business and administration it was, as Yule and Burnell suggest, used for a Bengali, who was 'often effeminate'. The main characteristic of Babu English is its extreme stylistic ornamentation and '. . .in Bengal and elsewhere, among Anglo-Indians, it is often used with a slight savour of disparagement, as characterizing a superficially cultivated, but too often effeminate, Bengali.' One can provide illustrations of this sub-variety from officialese and administrative registers. Note, for example, the following from Schuchardt (1891 [1980:51]):

The extreme stimulus of professional and friendly solicitation has led me to the journey of accomplished advantages to proceed with these elucidatory and critical comments; wherein no brisking has been thrown apart to introduce *prima facie* and useful matters to facilitate the literary pursuits of lily-like capacities. If the aimed point be embraced favourably by the public, all in all grateful acknowledgements will ride on the jumping border from the very bottom of my heart.

Babu (Baboo) English has provided inexhaustible resource for linguistic entertainment and has resulted in several volumes, for example, *Baboo Jabbarjee* (1898), *Honoured Sir from Babujee* (1931), and *Babuji Writes Home* (1935).

On the analogy of *brown Sahibs* ('brown Englishmen', used for Westernized Indians) we have the term *White Babus* used for 'English officers who have become de-Europeanized from long residence among undomesticated natives. . .' (see Yule and Burnell 1886:44) In due course the *White Babus* developed certain features in their English which separated them from those Englishmen who had not 'gone native'.

In the Indian context, as in the West African context, there developed what may be called *Pidgin English*. In a sense the pidginization of English was initiated with the first contact of Indians and Englishmen during the earliest phase of the activities of the East India Company, especially in the eastern parts of India. It has continued ever since in various degrees and forms. One might use the term *pidginization* as a cover term for the sub-varieties such as *Butler English* and *Box-wallah English* (see below) too, these then being two functional varieties in the range of pidginization.

The last sub-variety is termed *Box-wallah English*. In 1891, when Schuchardt collected his data, perhaps *Box-wallah English* was restricted to what he calls upper India. This variety is used by itinerant peddlers, who habitually carry a box containing their wares to the houses of foreigners and affluent Indians, or to hotels frequented by such people. The wares vary from antiques to *papier-mâché*, wood carving and silk and jewellry. Their command of English is restricted to what may be termed a type of trade language. In addition to *Box- wallah* English, there has also developed a *Box-wallah* Hindi, which such peddlers—for example, Kashmiri traders—use in selling their wares in the plains during the winter months, when the tourist trade in the highlands comes to a standstill.

On another non-native English-using continent, Africa, the picture is not different. In Ghana, Sey (1973) distinguishes primarily between three distinct types. The first type is *Educated Ghanaian English.* This includes 'any Ghanaian who has at least completed a course of formal instruction in the primary and middle schools in Ghana' (p.1). This does not entail competence in speaking RP since 'the type that strives too obviously to approximate to RP is frowned upon as distasteful and pedantic.' In educated Ghanaian English there are various degrees of competence varying from 'sub-Basic type' to ambilingualism, which is 'rare in the Ghanaian context.' The second sub-variety is *Broken English* , which is closer to what in the South Asian context has been called Butler English or Box-wallah English, e.g.,

I come go : I am going away, but I'll be back.
One man no chop : Eating is not the privilege of only one person.
This good, fresh sixpence : This is good and fresh, it's only sixpence.
He thief me : He robs, robbed, etc.,me.

Broken English has several characteristics of child language. Given the context, and the participants in the context, it is not only intelligible but also functional.

The third type is *Pidgin English*, which is associated with labourers who come from other parts of Africa, namely, Northern Ghana, Nigeria, Sierra Leone, and Liberia (Sey 1973:3).

In another part of West Africa, Nigeria, we find again the South Asian and Ghanaian situation repeated; the variation ranges from '. . . the home-grown pidgins and creoles at one end of the spectrum to the universally accepted formal written registers of standard English' (Spencer 1971:5). As in Ghana or in India, in Nigeria, too, it is 'agreed that the aim is not to produce speakers of British Received Pronunciation: even if this were feasible! ... Many Nigerians will consider as affected or even snobbish any Nigerian who speaks like a native speaker of English' (Bamgbose 1971:41); so will many Indians, and Ghanaians. Even in pidgins there exists considerable variety in terms of area and functions. (For details, see Schneider 1966 and Mafeni 1971.)

The Caribbean variety of English has its well-defined sub-varieties; Allsopp uses the following terms for them, *free vernacular, vernaculars of subculture, elevated vernacular, creolized English,* and *formal Caribbean English.*

In our discussion of the varieties within varieties, we cannot ignore the development of code-mixed varieties in South Asia (Kachru 1978a), Africa (Ansre 1971), the Philippines (Bautista 1977), and

Thailand (Warie 1977). Code-mixing as shown in chapter 7, is a result
of language contact and code-switching, and has to be distinguished
from just lexical borrowing. By code-mixing we mean

... the use of one or more languages for consistent transfer of linguistic units
from one language into another, and by such a mixture developing a new restricted—or not so restricted—code of linguistic interaction. (Kachru 1978a)

The implications of code-mixing are important from the point of view
of language attitude, élitism and language change. I have discussed
this in detail in chapter 7 with reference to the code-mixing of Hindi
and English. I shall present here a few examples from various studies to
show that the code-mixed varieties of English are part of the verbal repertoire of the non-native users of English, and that, functionally and
formally, code-mixing plays an important role in various contexts.

The process of mixing is not restricted to one unit, say lexical items,
but ranges from lexical items to full sentences and embedding of idioms
from English. In the previous chapter we have provided a large number
of examples from code-mixing in Hindi and English. But this situation
is not restricted to India. There are other such examples from all over
the English-speaking world. We shall consider some illustrations below.

1. ṭank va reḍār prāpt karne kī bhī yojnā
   tank and radar procure do of also scheme
2. sarkas aur numāyiś yahā̃ phél haĩ
   circus and exhibition here fail are
3. purānī hai to kyā huā, phāin to hai. *But I do not like Rajesh Khanna.*
   old is what happened fine however is
4. aur maĩ parivartan ghar se śurū karū̃gā kyū̃ki charity begins at home.
   and I change home from begin will do because charity begins at home.
5. akṭing vekṭing maĩ kyā jānū̃ re
   acting and the like I what should know hey
6. mujhe is bāt mẽ bilkul *doubt* nahī̃ hai, *rather I am sure* ki *this year B.Sc.examina-
   tion* ke *results* bahut kharāb haĩ. kuch to *examiners* ne *strictness* kī aur kuch
   papers bhī aisé *out of way* āyē ki *students* to *unexpected questions* ko *paper* mẽ *set*
   dekh kar *hall* kī *ceiling* hī *watch* karte rah gaye. itnā *failure* to *last three or four
   years* mẽ kabhī huā hī na thā abkī *admission* mẽ bhī *difficulty* uṭhānī paregī.
   Last year bhī *in spite of all attempts* kuch *applicants* ke *admission almost impossible*
   ho gaye the. *After a great stir registrar* ko *move* kiyā jā sakā, jisse kuch *seats* kā
   extra arrangement kiyā gayā (Bhatia 1967:55).

In the first five illustrations we find examples of the insertion of a
noun phrase (in 1), a hybrid noun phrase (in 2), a sentence (in 3), an
idiom (in 4) and reduplication (in 5). In 6 we have an extreme case of
code-mixing. The text contains 113 lexical items, out of which 44%
are from English.

Ansre (1971) has discussed code-mixing with special reference to West African languages. The following are illustrative.

1. Mele very sorry, gake mena every conceivable opportunity-i hafi wò let-m down (Ewe). *I am very sorry, but I gave him every conceivable opportunity and yet he let me down.*
2. Se wɔbɛ-report wo ma me bio a mebe- dismiss wo without further warning. (Twi)
   If you are reported to me again I shall dismiss you without further warning.
3. Ne phoneme nye minimal phonological unit eye morpheme nye minimal grammatical unit, la ɛkema lexeme anye minimal lexical unit. (Ewe).
   If the phoneme is the minimal phonological unit and the morpheme is the minimal grammatical unit, then lexeme will be the minimal lexical unit.

Bautista (1977) gives 'instances of language 1 NPs [Tagalog] appearing as subjects and complements in language 2 [English] units.' Consider the following illustrations:

1. Dito po sa atin . . . ang intensyon po talaga ng tinatawag na *national parks is to set aside an original area* na tinatawag po natig *may* magandang tanawin
2. Ang *family planning component* po dito *is really the most crucial at the moment.*
3. *They are given* ivong tinatawag na *academic appointments*

Warie (1977) considers the case of contact of Thai and English from this point and presents several examples:

. . . khɔɔ khuan cam kìaw kàp *income effect* kɔ̀ɔkhii wâa man pen bùak sàmɔ̀əpay čên nay kɔɔ-ra-nii kìaw kap khɔ̌ɔŋleew *inferior goods* nán *income effect* àat pen lóp dây.

Things to remember about income effect is that it is not always positive, for example, in case of inferior goods, the income effect can be negative.

Nash (1977) has discussed 'language mixture' in Puerto Rico and gives the following examples of what she terms 'mid-stream code switching' (p. 214):

1. *Buy your home in Levittown Lakes*, donde la buena vida comienza.
2. Yo y mi *Winston*-porque *Winstons taste good like a cigarette should.*
3. *If the boss calls*, dìgale que no estoy.

There are various motivations for code-mixing, some of these are *role-identification*, *register-identification* and *elucidation* as explained, for example, in Kachru (1978a) for code-mixing of English with Hindi and Kashmiri, Warie (1977) for Thai, S. N. Sridhar (1978) for Kannada, and Nash (1977) for Spanish.

The range of varieties, and varieties within varieties, discussed above should not give us the mistaken impression that there are no common shared features in the educated varieties of these Englishes. In spite of the range of variation there are many shared and transparent features. That is why we find that cover terms such as Caribbean English (Allsopp 1971), South Asian English (Kachru 1969a), and West African English (Spencer 1971:7) have been used in the literature. But such labels have to be used with caution, since if we look for homogeneous speech communities, or identical functions of varieties of English with differing cultural contexts, we will be disappointed. As we have seen, even more specific modifiers, such as *Ghanaian*, *Indian* and *Nigerian* with English do not imply non-variability. As Quirk *et al.* (1972: 13) appropriately warn us:

> The properties of dog-ness can be seen in both terrier and alsatian (and, we must presume, equally) yet no single variety of dog embodies all the features present in all varieties of dog. In a somewhat similar way, we need to see a common or nucleus that we call 'English' being realized only in the different actual varieties of the language that we hear or read.

The concept of dog-ness is an abstract concept, and so is the concept of speech community. The beholder is not only the judge, but he also has preconceived notions which are reflected in his language attitudes. From a native speaker's point of view, perhaps the range and variation in non-native varieties is alarming. A native speaker tends to have a protective attitude toward his language, and the more educated he is, the more ways he finds to show it. There are already several studies which express this alarming sort of attitude toward the other Englishes. We might find it therefore more useful to recognize the distinction which Firth (1959:208) suggested between 'a close *speech fellowship* and a wider *speech community* in what may be called the language community comprising both written and spoken forms of the general language'. This distinction is useful to show the pluralism of social roles and functions of each sub-variety, and the varying degrees of polydialectism which non-native varieties have developed, in the same way as have the native varieties of English.

These varieties within varieties, marked with reference to various speech fellowships, are not actually competing with each other. In West Africa, for example, 'in the life of the individual they usually have complementary roles' (Spencer 1971:5). That is also true of South Asia or the West Indies. This point has been well illustrated by Strevens (1977:140) with reference to Indian English. He argues that the term *Indian English* has several functional uses,

...since it refers not to a single variety but to a set of many varieties across the whole spectrum. The Indian (or Pakistani) doctor who communicates easily in English with professional colleagues at an international medical conference is using a type of 'Indian English'... the Indian clerk who uses English constantly in his daily life for communicating with other Indians, by correspondence or telephone, may employ an 'Indian English' in which the dialect is not standard English and the accent is regional or local. The lorry-driver who uses English occasionally, as a lingua franca, may be using an 'Indian English' which is for all practical purposes a pidgin.

And then asks whether the criticism of the teaching profession (e.g., that of Prator 1968) is justified concerning the above-mentioned second type of Indian English. Strevens rightly answers: 'The ultimate test of effectiveness of a variety of a language is whether it meets the communication needs of those who use it' (p. 140). Indian English seems to pass that test.

5.0. NON-NATIVE ENGLISHES AND NATIVE LANGUAGES

The nativization of English presents only one aspect of the Janus-like faces of the non-native varieties of English. The other face, which is equally important, is that of the process of *Englishization* of the native languages and literatures in those parts where there is a long tradition of contact with and use of English, especially in parts of Asia and Africa.

The two-way process has further embedded the English language into the cultural and linguistic traditions of these areas, and become a part of the linguistic and literary context. In West Africa (Ansre 1971: 149),

The languages of the former colonial masters continue to play important roles, not only as independent languages but in the way in which elements from them continue to find their way into the indigenous languages; and there is no reason to believe that this process will terminate in the near future.

In earlier studies it has been demonstrated that this contact has deeply influenced the phonology and lexicons of these languages (see, e.g., for Hindi, Bhatia 1967). The influence is much deeper and of vital structural importance. A casual look, as Ansre says (1971:160)

...at any given piece of a West African language that has been influenced by English leaves one with the impression that it contains many English lexical items but hardly any influences relatable to the grammatical categories of structure, system or class. Closer examination however shows that the grammar is also more deeply affected than is realized.

In Kachru (1979) it has been shown that contact with English has initiated several syntactic changes and innovations in Hindi such as introduction of impersonal constructions, a tendency toward change of word order from SOV to SVO, use of indirect speech, use of passivization with agent, and also introduction of certain types of post-head modifiers.

This influence of English language and literature is also reflected in the native literatures of Asia and Africa. There are a large number of studies devoted to this aspect. In the South Asian context all the literary languages demonstrate the influence of English; among others, Latif (1920) discusses the impact of English on Urdu literature, Sen (1932), Das Gupta (1935) and Bhattacharyya (1964) on Bengali, Misra (1963) on Hindi. I have briefly discussed the South Asian situation in earlier chapters (see especially, 1 and 2). In the case of South Asia, Gokak (1964:3) has rightly claimed that, 'It is no exaggeration to say that it was in the English classroom that the Indian literary renaissance was born.' The African case is almost identical to the South Asian situation, if not stronger. The colonialism, says Achebe (1965:218), gave Africans 'a language with which to talk to one another. If it failed to give them a song, it at least gave them a tongue, for singing.'

6.0. NEW ENGLISHES AND THE BATTLE OF ATTITUDES: WHO IS TO JUDGE?

We have mentioned earlier various ways in which members of a speech community may be marked as different from one another. In the case of English, even though no academy was entrusted with the task of regularizing the language standardization, the battle of attitudes was waged when the transplanted varieties developed their distinct characteristics in North America or in Australia (see Heath 1977, Kachru 1981b, Kahane and Kahane 1977). In this case the opponents in argument were native speakers using English on two different continents.

But with respect to non-native varieties, the attitude of native English speakers has not necessarily been one of acceptance or recognition. It is a story of a long battle of attitudes which has yet to be fully studied. Often positions are taken which are not based on linguistic realism, or do not show understanding of the reason why a particular country chooses English as a preferred second language. As we know, such attitudes are not essentially based on linguistic value judgement, but various other factors play an important role, one being a native speaker's fear of seeing *their* language 'disintegrate' in the hands of (or shall we say, the lips of) non-native users.

In the literature (e.g., Prator 1968) claims have been made that there are two broad views among the native speakers of English toward the non-native varieties. The two attitudes are those of the users of American English and that of British English. I have elsewhere shown (Kachru 1976a) that, like all generalizations, this generalization is misleading; what is more important, it is based on wrong attitudes which result in the *seven attitudinal sins* which may be summarized as

1. the sin of ethnocentrism;
2. the sin of wrong perception of the language attitudes on the two sides of the Atlantic;
3. the sin of not recognizing the non-native varieties of English as culture-bound codes of communication;
4. the sin of ignoring the systemicness of non-native varieties of English;
5. the sin of ignoring linguistic interference and language dynamics;
6. the sin of overlooking 'the cline of Englishness' in language intelligibility; and
7. the sin of exhibiting language colonialism.

I do not propose to embark on a long discussion on how native users of English have reacted to each non-native variety of English. However, a brief digression may not be out of place here. I find that there are six attitude-types shown toward the Indian (or South Asian) variety of English. They are tentatively labelled as follows:

1. descriptivists (attitudinally *neutral*)
2. cynics (attitudinally *sceptical*)
3. purists (attitudinally *norm-obsessed*, *élitists*)
4. realists (attitudinally *positive*)
5. prescriptivists (attitudinally *pedagogical*)
6. functionalists (attitudinally *pragmatic*)

Since a detailed discussion of these six attitude types is the topic of another study, I shall not elaborate on them here.[8] The last one, however, is important since the functionalist or pragmatic view is the topic of this chapter. I shall discuss it in the following section.

7.0. PRAGMATIC PARAMETERS FOR NON-NATIVE ENGLISHES

A pragmatic view of language use implies that language must be considered an integral part of the meaning system in which it functions, and related to the contexts in which it is used. There is a relationship between a *speech event* and a parallel *social event* which takes place in English within the context of, for example, West Africa or South Asia. This brings us back to viewing language function within a theoretical framework such as the Firthian *context of situation* or Hymes' *ethnography of communication* (see Hymes 1964, 1972, 1974). In the Firthian view (see Firth 1952:13) meaning is more than 'sights and sounds'. It is 'intimately interlocked not only with an environment of particular sights and sounds, but deeply embedded in the living processes of persons maintaining themselves in society'. It is these 'living processes' which result in the *newness* or the *non-nativeness* in non-native Englishes. The *newness* is not only due to *interference* (or *transfer*) from the native language(s) of the user, but also due to the new cultural context in which English has been assigned various roles. There is thus a situation of an 'alien' language functioning in 'unEnglish' contexts. The result is development of new sub-varieties, new styles, and new registers. As English undergoes through acculturation in non-native contexts, it shows various degrees of culture-boundness. The more culture-bound it becomes, the more distance is created between it and the native varieties.

The formal manifestations of contextualization have been discussed in some earlier studies (see chapters 3 and 4). In understanding the functions of the new Englishes, and relating these to the pragmatics of each variety one has to consider at least three important parameters within the *context of situation* : These are :

(a) *Cline of participants in a speech event : Speech fellowships* within the larger *speech community* is a useful concept, and provides a framework for understanding the role of sub-varieties such as Babu English and Box-wallah English. We may also find a spectrum of pidgins each having its place on the continuum. On the other hand, for example, *educated* Indian English or South Asian English has its role in the national context. The code-mixed varieties too have their function, and so have the sub-varieties, since a speaker may 'switch' within sub-varieties according to the role and context.

(b) *Cline of intelligibility :* In intelligibility too there is a cline, and this concept cannot be used exclusively from a native speaker's point of view. A speaker of an educated non-native variety has a repertoire of sub-varieties which vary in their Englishness. Note, for example, how effectively the West African novelist Chinua Achebe uses code-switching, introducing a blend of pidgin and educated West African English in the following conversation :

'Good! See you later.' Joseph always put on an impressive manner when speaking on the telephone. He never spoke Igbo or Pidgin English at such mo-

ments. When he hung up he told his colleagues: 'That na my brother. Just
return from overseas. B.A. (Honours) Classics.' He always preferred the fiction
of Classics to the truth of English.
It sounded more impressive.
'What department he de work?'
'Secretary to the Scholarship Board.'
'E go make plenty money there. Every student who wan' go England go de see am
for house.'
'E no be like dat,' said Joseph. 'Him na gentleman.
No fit take bribe.'
'Na so,' said the other in disbelief.

(No Longer at Ease, 1960)

(c) *Cline of roles*: The use of sub-varieties is role-dependent, and each
sub-variety of English performs a specific role or roles in a given context.
A number of these roles are *unEnglish*, since they are not typically American or British. Thus, the factor of acculturation is an important one,
and results in what I have termed *culture-bound* linguistic innovations.

In several roles the English language is preferred to a native language
for attitudinal reasons. That explains why even semi-literate Indians
use a sprinkling of English lexical items to demonstrate that they are
in the 'in-group' or working toward attaining a certain status, for English signifies modernity, elitism and prestige. This factor cannot be
ignored, as it is part of sociolinguistic reality. The difficulty is that,
however long a native speaker's arm may be, he cannot standardize and
codify such functions. Therefore, the argument that native models be
presented to *all* non-native speakers, for *all* contexts, and for *all* sub-
varieties is a constraint which is pragmatically undesirable, since human languages do not work that way.

I have attempted to present an overview of the non-native Englishes,
focussing mainly on their uses. I have argued that nativization (and
deviations) are determined by these new uses of English in new contexts. This is a sign that English is used as a living language in living
human situations. The result is *new* Englishes in non-native contexts.
The *newness* is not, as Bell (1976:155) believes, because 'the motivation
for or possibility of further learning is removed from a group of learners'
and thus, as he claims, results in a 'xized variety'. In his view, 'Indianized
English' or 'Anglicized Hindi' are examples of 'xized' varieties.

In the preceding discussion, I have attempted to be descriptive rather than prescriptive. I have argued that a pragmatic or functional
view is essential in understanding the uses of English in unEnglish contexts. It is especially true now, since English has already attained the

status of a universal language whose functions vary from situation to situation, from one continent to another. This warning came to us more than two decades ago from Firth (1956:97).

> ... English is an international language in the Commonwealth, the Colonies and in America. International in the sense that English serves the American way of life and might be called American, it serves the Indian way of life and has recently been declared an Indian language within the framework of the federal constitution. In another sense, it is international not only in Europe but in Asia and Africa, and serves various African ways of life and is increasingly the all-Asian language of politics. Secondly, and I say 'secondly' advisedly, English is the key to what is described in a common cliché as 'the British way of life'.

If we view the issue in the Firthian perspective, we are close to a pragmatic approach to the understanding of the non-native varieties of English.

8.0. CONCLUSION

The intent of this chapter is to present a synthesis of some of the issues raised concerning the non-native varieties of English. I have argued in favour of what may be termed a 'pragmatic' or 'functional' view of the uses of these Englishes. These functions have to be seen at various levels and in various contexts to make each variety within a variety pragmatically 'meaningful.' Such an approach should give us a new perspective in understanding several crucial issues, the following being some of these.

It seems to me that communicative competence has to be viewed with reference to the local, intranational and international uses of various varieties of English (see Kachru 1982a). It is with reference to these uses that one can then see at what level or levels we have to consider the native speaker as a relevant participant in a communicative act. It might turn out that for certain communicative acts a native speaker may have to learn certain characteristic features of a national or a local variety of English. Thus, an Englishman may have to 'de-Englishize' himself, and an American may have to 'de-Americanize' himself in order to understand these national varieties. The second question is more pedagogically oriented: it relates to the concept of 'model'. In discussing English as an international and intranational language it is difficult to raise the question of choice of model. The local, national, and international uses of English discussed in this chapter raise questions about the validity of *didactic* models, those which emphasize a *monomodel* approach to the teaching of English. One has to be realistic about such questions and aim at a *dynamic* approach, based on a *polymodel* concept. The choice of a model cannot be separated from the functions of the language. And naturally *appropriateness, acceptance,* and *intelligibility* cannot be isolated from the total pragmatic context (see Kachru 1977 and 1982a).

While discussing English in the international context, one might also wonder whether we have buried Basic English too soon, before it has had a chance to demonstrate its relevance and usefulness. We might find that Basic English, or Quirk's concept of *Nuclear* English (see Quirk 1981), would form a core on which one could further build, at various linguistic levels, *English for Special Purposes* (ESP). In a sense, ESP is closely related to the concept of register. And these two cut across the boundaries of varieties (and sub-varieties). If we use the term 'English as an international and intranational language' (EIIL) we are in a sense focussing on the shared and not-so-shared (national) uses of Englishes (for a full discussion see Kachru and Quirk 1981 and Smith 1981). And, what is more important, by introducing such a concept we are not rejecting the cline of uses of a large number of Englishes, which range from local uses at one end to international uses at the other. At this point one can go back to Firth; In the following statement there is perhaps, typical Firthian exaggeration (1957a [Palmer 1968:132]), but it is very close to the actual situation:

English as an expression of English life is of little importance—what matters is English in relation to the national languages in the changing Asian ways of life.

But then he agrees that

Whatever the media of instruction, auxiliary English or plain contemporary English with a practical bias would be desirable in schools and other institutions at the pre-university stage and possibly also in the university. (ibid.:133).

It seems that he is making a case here for English as an international auxiliary language: After all, Firth was a pragmatist.

NOTES

This chapter is a revised version of 'The Pragmatics of Non-native Varieties of English', in Larry E. Smith, ed., *English for Cross-Cultural Communication* (London: Macmillan, 1981), pp. 15–39.

1. However, I am aware of some exceptions to this generalization, e.g., Richards (1972) reprinted in Richards (1974:82–87), Quirk *et al.* (1972:25–27), and Strevens (1977: 129–46).

2. There is a large body of literature on how Latin changed under the influence of local languages; much less has been written on the changes of Sanskrit. For Latin consider, for example, von Wartburg 1951; Tagliavini 1969. The above authors have taken an explicit position on the influence of the local linguistic context on Latin. Also see, Elcock 1960; Posner 1966. I am grateful to Ladislav Zgusta for suggesting these references.

3. See chapter 3, pp. 103–24 for a discussion and references. Also see Kachru 1981c.

4. *Report 1979–80*, Government of India, Ministry of Information and Broadcasting, 1980.

5. For phonology see, for example, Ansre 1971: 158–60; Bansal 1969; Kachru 1969a; Sey 1973: 143–53. For lexis see Allsopp 1972; Rao 1954; Wilson 1940 and Yule and Burnell 1886. A detailed treatment of lexis and other Indian features is presented in chapters 3 and 4.

6. See chapter 5.

7. This work of Hugo Schuchardt was brought to my attention by Glenn G. Gilbert of Southern Illinois University at Carbondale, who has translated it into English. I am grateful to him for making available to me the manuscript of his translation in 1978 before it was published. Schuchardt's paper was originally published in *Englische Studien*, 1891, 15.286–305, under the title 'Beiträge zur Kenntnis des englischen Kreolische III. Das Indo-Englische'. The English translation is entitled 'Indo-English'.

8. Kachru (forthcoming) 'Indian English: a History of Attitudes'. Paper presented to the Linguistics Club of the Central Institute of English and Foreign Languages, Hyderabad, India, 2 August 1977.

Bibliography

The bibliography includes two types of items: 1. those which have been mentioned in the text or notes of this study, and 2. those selected items which deal with the linguistic, literary or historical aspects of the English language in South Asia in general and India in particular.

Abdulaziz-Mkilifi, M.H. 1972. 'Triglossia and Swahili-English bilingualism in Tanzania'. *Language in Society* 1.1.197–213.

Abercrombie, David. 1956. *Problems and Principles.* London: Longman.

——. 1964. 'A phonetician's view of verse structure'. *Linguistics: An International Review* 6 (June). 5–13.

Abrahams, Roger D. and Rudolph C. Troike, eds. 1970 *Language and Cultural Diversity in American Education.* Engelwood Cliffs, NJ: Prentice-Hall.

Achebe, Chinua. 1965. 'English and the African Writer'. In Mazrui 1973 (Originally published in *Transition*, Kampala, 18 April 1965.)

Aggarwal, Narindra K. 1982. *English in South Asia: A Bibliographical Survey of Resources.* Gurgaon and New Delhi: Indian Documentation Service.

Ahmad, M. 1964. 'A contrastive phonological study of English and Urdu with special reference to some major problems of pronunciation'. Unpublished paper, University of North Wales, Bangor.

Ahmad, Zainul A. 1941 *National Language for India.* Allahabad: Kitabistan.

Alatis, James E., ed. 1979. *International Dimensions of Bilingual Education, Georgetown Monographs on Languages and Linguistics.* Washington, DC: Georgetown University Press.

Allsopp, Richard S.R. 1971. 'Some problems in the lexicography of Caribbean English'. *Caribbean Quarterly.* Jamaica: University of the West Indies. 17:2.

——. 1972. 'Why a dictionary of Caribbean English usage?' Circular 'A' of the Caribbean Lexicography Project. Bridgetown, Barbados.

——. 1978. 'Some methodological aspects in the preparation of the dictionary of Caribbean English' (DCEU). In *Studies in Lexicography as a Science and as an Art.* 2.1. New York: Bantam Books. 30–43.

Altbach, Philip G. 1975. *Publishing in India.* Delhi: Oxford University Press.

Amirthanayagam, Guy, ed. 1982. *Writers in East-West Encounter: New Cultural Bearings.* London: Macmillan.

Amur, G.S. 1973. *Manohar Malgonkar.* New Delhi: Arnold-Heinemann.

Anand, Mulk Raj. 1948. *The King-Emperor's English: Or the Role of the English Language in Free India.* Bombay: Hind Kitab.

Anantham, Sundur. 1959. 'A study of the pronunciation problems involved in the teaching of English to Telugu speakers'. Unpublished Ed. D. dissertation, University of Michigan.

Annamalai, E. 1971. 'Lexical insertion in a mixed language'. *Papers from the Seventh Regional Meeting.* Chicago: Chicago Linguistic Society, University of Chicago. 20–27.

——. 1978. 'The Anglicized Indian languages: A case of code-mixing'. *International Journal of Dravidian Linguistics* 7.2.239–47.

Ansre, Gilbert 1971. 'The influence of English on West African languages'. In Spencer, ed. 1971a.

Apte, Mahadev L. 1974. 'Pidginization of a lingua franca: A linguistic analysis of Hindi-Urdu spoken in Bombay'. *International Journal of Dravidian Linguistics* 3.1.21–41.

Asrani, U.A. 1964. *What shall we do about English?* Ahmedabad: Navajivan Publishing House.

Bailey, Richard W. and M. Gorlach, eds. 1982. *English as a World Language.* Ann Arbor, MI: University of Michigan Press.

——, and J.L. Robinson, eds. 1973. *Varieties of Present-day English.* New York: Macmillan.

Baker, Sidney J. 1945. *The Australian Language.* Sydney: Currawong Publishing. (Reprinted by Angus and Robertson.)

Bamgboṣe, Ayọ. 1971. 'The English language in Nigeria'. In Spencer, ed. 1971a.

——. 1982. 'Standard Nigerian English: Issues of identification'. In Kachru, ed. 1982.

Banerjee, Surendranath. 1878. *Lord Macaulay and Higher Education in India.* Calcutta: I. C. Bose.

Bansal, Ram Krishna. 1962. 'A study of the vowel system of Indian English as spoken by educated Hindi speakers of Delhi, East Punjab and U.P.' *Bulletin of the Central Institute of English and Foreign Languages* 2. 159–65.

——. 1969. *Intelligibility of Indian English.* Hyderabad: Central Institute of English and Foreign Languages.

Barnes, Sir Edward. 1932. *The History of Royal College* (Colombo). (It was earlier called Colombo Academy.)

Barron, A. W. J. 1961a. 'The English dental fricatives in India.' *Bulletin of the Central Institute of English and Foreign Languages* 1:84–86.

——. 1961b. 'English vowels for Indian learners'. *Bulletin of the Central Institute of English and Foreign Languages* 1:77–83.

Basham, A.L. 1954. *The Wonder that Was India.* London: Sidgwick and Jackson.

——, ed. 1975. *A Cultural History of India.* Oxford: Clarendon Press.

Basu, A.N., ed. 1941. *Adams's Reports* (1835–38). Calcutta: Bureau of Education, Government of India.

Bautista, Ma. Lourdes S. 1977. 'The noun phrase in Tagalog-English code-switching'. *Studies in Philippine Linguistics* 1.1.1–16.

Bayer, Jennifer. 1979. 'Anglo-Indians and their mother tongue.' *Indian Linguistics* 40 (2):78–84.

Bazell, C.E, J.C. Catford, M.A.K. Halliday and R.K. Robins, eds. 1966. *In Memory of J.R. Firth.* London: Longman.

Beeton, D.R. and Helen Dorner. 1975. *A Dictionary of English usage in Southern Africa.* Cape Town: Oxford University Press.

Bell, Roger T. 1973. 'The English of an Indian immigrant: an essay in error analysis'. *ITL: Review of Applied Linguistics.* 12.11–61.

——. 1976. *Sociolinguistics: Goals, approaches and problems.* London: Batsford.

Bennett, Michael E., and E. W. Nall. 1977. 'Relational network approaches to code-switching'. *The Fourth Lacus Forum*. Columbia, S.C.: Hornbeam Press. 250–62.

Bernstein, Basil. 1971. *Class, Code and Control I: Theoretical Studies Towards a Sociology of Language*. London: Routledge and Kegan Paul.

Bhargava, Prem Sagar. 1968. 'Linguistic interference from Hindi, Urdu and Punjabi and internal analogy in the grammar of Indian English'. Unpublished Ph.D. dissertation. Cornell University.

Bhatia, Kailash Chandra. 1967. *A Linguistic Study of English Loan Words in Hindi* (in Hindi). Allahabad: Hindustani Academy.

Bhatia, Tej K. 1974. 'The co-existing answering systems and the role of presuppositions, implications and expectations in Hindi simplex yes/no question. *Papers from the Tenth Regional Meeting*. Chicago: Chicago Linguistic Society, University of Chicago. 47–61.

——. Forthcoming. 'Aspects of code-mixing in Hindi'. Mimeographed.

Bhattacharyya, D. C. 1964. 'The impact of English borrowing on the Bengali language'. *Calcutta Review* 172.49–56 (July).

Bhushan, V.N., ed. 1945a. *The Moving Finger*. Bombay: Padma Publishers.

——, ed. 1945b. *The Peacock Lute*. Bombay: Padma Publishers.

Bills, Garland, ed. 1974. *Southwest Areal Linguistics*. San Diego: Institute for Cultural Pluralism, University of California.

Blom, Jan-Petter, and John J. Gumperz. 1972. 'Social meaning of linguistic structure: Code-switching in Norway'. In Gumperz and Hymes, eds. 1972.

Bloomfield, Leonard. 1938. *Language*. New York: Holt, Rinehart and Winston. (Reprinted 1951.)

Bokamba, Eyamba G. 1982. 'The Africanization of English'. In Kachru, ed. 1982.

Bose, Amalendu. 1968. 'Some Poets of the Writers Workshop'. In Naik, *et al.*, eds. 1968.

Bose, Buddhadeva. 1963. 'Indian Poetry in English'. In Spender and Hall, eds. 1963.

Branford, Jean. 1978. *A Dictionary of South African English*. Cape Town: Oxford University Press.

Branford, W. 1970. 'Reports 1 and 2 on the dictionary of South African English project'. Mimeographed. Grahamstown.

Brass, Paul R. 1974. *Language, Religion and Politics in North India*. London: Cambridge University Press.

Bright, William. 1960a. 'A study of caste and dialect in Mysore'. *Indian Linguistics* 21.45–50.

——1960b. 'Linguistic changes in some Indian caste dialects'. In Charles A. Ferguson, *et al.*, eds. 1960.

Brown, Charles Phillip. 1852. *The Zillah Dictionary in the Roman Character. Explaining the Various Words Used in Business in India*. Madras.: Printed by D.P.L.C. Connor Society's Press.

Brown, William N., ed. 1960. *India, Pakistan, Ceylon*. Philadelphia: University of Pennsylvania Press.

Buck, H.M. and G.E. Yocum, eds. 1974. *Structural Approach to South Indian Studies*. Chambersburg, PA: Wilson Books.

Bursill-Hall, G.L. 1961. 'Levels analysis: J.R. Firth's theories of meaning'. *The Canadian Journal of Linguistics* 2.3.124–35, 164–91.

Butter, P. H. 1960. *English in India.* Inaugural Lecture. The Queen's University, Belfast.

Carls, Uwe. 1979. 'Select bibliography of Indian English (up to 1978)'. *Zeitschrift für Anglistik und Amerikanistik.* 27.4.327–40.

Carnegy, P. 1877. *Kachahari Technicalities, or a Glossary of Terms, Rural, Official, and General, in Daily Use in the Courts of Law, and in Illustration of the Tenures, Customs, Arts, and Manufactures of Hindustan.* 2nd. ed. Allahabad: Allahabad Mission Press.

Catford, J.C. 1959. 'The teaching of English as a foreign language'. In R. Quirk and A.H. Smith, eds. 1959.

Cazden, Courtney B., Vera P. John, and Dell Hymes, eds. 1972. *Function of Language in the Classroom.* New York: Teachers College Press.

Census of India, 1961. 1964. Delhi: Manager of Publications, Government of India.

Ceylonese Vocabulary: List of Native Words Commonly Occurring in Official Correspondence and Other Documents. 1869. Colombo.

Chalapathi Rau, M. 1974. *The Press.* New Delhi: National Book Trust, India.

Chandola, Anoop C. 1963. 'Some linguistic influences of English on Hindi'. *Anthropological Linguistics* 5:2.9–13.

Chatterjee, Kalyan Kumar. 1976. *English Education in India: Issues and Opinions.* Delhi: Macmillan.

Chatterjee, Rama Krishna. 1973. *Mass Communication.* New Delhi: National Book Trust, India.

Chaudhuri, Nirad C. 1976. 'The English language in India—past, present and future'. In Niven, ed. 1976. 89–105.

Chomsky, Noam. 1965. *Aspects of the Theory of Syntax.* Cambridge, MA: MIT Press.

Clive, John, 1973. *Macaulay: The Shaping of the Historian.* New York: Knopf.

Clyne, Michael G. 1967. *Transference and Triggering.* The Hague: Martinus Nijhoff.

———. 1969. 'Switching between language systems'. *Actes due Xe congres internationale des linguistes,* Bucharest. Part 1. Bucharest: L'Academic de la Republique Socialiste de Roumanie. 343–49.

Craig, Dennis, R. 1982. 'Toward a description of Caribbean English'. In Kachru, ed. 1982.

Craigie, W.A. 1954. 'Introductory note'. In G. Subba Rao 1954.

Crewe, William, ed. 1977. *The English Language in Singapore.* Singapore: Eastern Universities Press.

Daruwalla, Keki N. 1980. *Two Decades of Indian Poetry 1960–1980.* Delhi: Vikas Publishing House.

Das Gupta, Harendra Mohan. 1935. *Studies in Western Influence on Nineteenth Century Bengali Poetry, 1857–1887.* Calcutta: Chuckervertty, Chatterjee and Co.

Das Gupta, Jyotirindra. 1970. *Language Conflict and National Development: Group Politics and National Language Policy in India.* Berkeley: University of California Press.

Datta, S. 1972–73. 'The pronunciation of English by Bengali speakers'. *Bulletin of the Central Institute of English and Foreign Languages* 9.35–40.

Deb, S.C. 1965. Presidential address delivered at the XVI session of the All-India English Teachers' Conference, Jadavpur. Allahabad : No publisher.

DeLanerolle, K. 1953. 'The intonation of Sinhalese and its relevance in the initial stages of the teaching of English as a second language to Sinhalese children'. Unpublished paper. Institute of Education, London.

Desai, Maganbhai P. 1964. *The Problem of English*. Ahmedabad: Navajivan.

Desai, Shantinath K., ed. 1974. *Experimentation with Language in Indian Writing in English (Fiction)*. Kolhapur: Department of English, Shivaji University.

Deshpande, Gauri, ed. 1974. *An Anthology of Indo-English Poetry*. Delhi: Hind Pocket Books.

Dhall, Golok Bihari. 1965. 'Observations on some common peculiarities in the English speech of the people of Orissa'. *Indian Linguistics* 16 :276–82.

Dhar, K.L. 1963. 'English loanwords in Hindi'. Unpublished paper. University of Leeds.

Diebold, Richard A., Jr. 1968. 'Code-switching in Greek-English bilingual speech'. In O'Brien, ed. 1968.

Dil, Afia. 1972. 'The Hindu and Muslim dialects of Bengali'. Unpublished Ph.D. dissertation. Stanford University.

Dil, Anwar S. 1966. 'The position of English in Pakistan'. In *Shahidullah Presentation Volume*, Special Issue of *Pakistani Linguistics* 185–242.

Di Pietro, Robert J. 1977. 'Code-switching as a verbal strategy among bilinguals'. In Eckman, ed. 1977.

Dozier, Edward P. 1967. 'Linguistic acculturation studies in the Southwest'. In Hymes and Bittle, eds. 1967.

Duff, Alexander. 1837. *New Era of the English Language and English Literature in India*. Edinburgh: J. Johnstone.

Duggal, K.S. 1980. *Book Publishing in India*. New Delhi: Marwah Publications.

Dustoor, Phiroze Edulji. 1950. 'An introduction to the study of English usage in India'. In *Longman's Miscellany*. Calcutta: Longman.

——1950. *The English Language in India Today*. Agra University Extension Lectures 1 and 2. Agra. No publisher.

——. 1954. 'Missing and intrusive articles in Indian English'. *Allahabad University Studies* 31.1–70.

——. 1955. 'Wrong, usurping and dispossessed articles in Indian English'. *Allahabad University Studies* 32. 1–17.

——. 1956. Presidential Address delivered at the VII Session of the All-India English Teachers' Conference, Dharwar. Reprinted in *Shiksha : The Journal of the Education Department*, Government of Uttar Pradesh. April 1957.61–71.

——. 1957. 'The future of English in India'. *Allahabad University Magazine* 35. 1–18.

——. 1968. *The World of Words*. Bombay: Asia Publishing House.

——. n.d. 'Dominion Status in Language'. (Talk from the All India Radio, Lucknow, and published in the *Allahabad University Magazine*).

Eckman, F.R., ed. 1977. *Current Themes in Linguistics, Bilingualism, Experimental Linguistics and Language Typologies*. New York: John Wiley.

Education in India: Index and Bibliography. 1966. Ann Arbor, MI: University of Michigan Press.

Edwards, Sir Parker. n.d. *Statement Showing the Statistics of the Publications for the Year 1928*. Bombay.

Elcock, W.D. 1960. [1971]. *The Romance Languages*. London: Faber and Faber.

Ellis, Jeffrey. 1961. 'Some problems in comparative linguistics'. *Proceedings of the University of Durham Philosophical Society* 7.56.

——. 1966. 'On contextual meaning'. In Bazell *et al.*, ed. 1966.

Emeneau, Murray B. 1955. 'India and linguistics'. *Journal of the American Oriental Society* 75.145–215.

——. 1956. 'India as a linguistic area'. *Language* 32. 3–16.

Fallis, Guadalupe V. 1976. 'Social interaction and code-switching patterns: A case study of Spanish/English alternation'. In Keller *et al.*, eds. 1976.

Fennell, C.A.M. 1892. *The Standard Dictionary of Anglicized Words and Phrases*. Cambridge: Cambridge University Press.

Ferguson, Charles A, and John J. Gumperz, eds. 1960. *Linguistic Diversity in South Asia*. Bloomington, IN: Indiana University Research Center in Anthropology, Folklore and Linguistics. (Publication 13).

——, and Shirley B. Heath, eds. 1981. *Language in the USA*. New York and London: Cambridge University Press.

Fernando, Chitra. 1977. 'English and Sinhala bilingualism in Sri Lanka'. *Language in Society* 6. 341–60.

Firth, John R. 1930. *Speech*. London: Benn's Sixpenny Library, No. 121. Reprinted. London: Oxford University Press, 1966.

——. 1934. 'Linguistics and the functional point of view'. *English Studies* 16. 2–8.

——. 1937. *The Tongues of Men*. London. Reprinted. London: Oxford University Press, 1964.

——. 1950. 'Personality and language in society'. *The Sociological Review*, 42.2. 37–52. Also in Firth 1957b.

——. 1951a. 'Modes of meaning'. *Essays and Studies of the English Association*, N.S. 4.118–49. (The English Association). In Firth 1957b.

——. 1951b. General linguistics and descriptive grammar'. *Transactions of the Philological Society* 1951, 69–87. In Firth 1957b.

——. 1952. 'Linguistic analysis as a study of meaning'. In Palmer, ed. 1968.

——. 1956. 'Descriptive Linguistics and the Study of English'. In Palmer, ed. 1968.

——. 1957a. 'Applications of general linguistics'. *Transactions of the Philological Society* 1957, 1–4. In Palmer, ed. 1968.

——. 1957b. *Papers in Linguistics 1934–51*. London: Oxford University Press.

——. 1957c. 'A synopsis of linguistic theory'. *Studies in Linguistic Analysis*. Oxford: Blackwell. 1–32. Also in Palmer, ed. 1968.

——. 1959. 'The Treatment of languages in general linguistics'. *The Medical Press*. 146–7. In Palmer, ed. 1968.

Fishman, Joshua, A., ed. 1978. *Advances in the Study of Societal Multilingualism*. The Hague: Mouton.

——, Charles A. Ferguson, and Jyotirindra Das Gupta, eds. 1968. *Language Problems of Developing Nations*. New York: Wiley.

——, R. L. Cooper, A. W. Conrad. 1977. *The Spread of English: The Sociology of English as an Additional Language.* Rowley, MA: Newbury House.

Fox, Melvin J., ed. 1975. *Language and Development: A Retrospective Survey of Ford Foundation Language Projects 1952–1974.* New York: Ford Foundation.

Fox, Robert P. 1968. 'A transformational treatment of Indian English syntax'. Unpublished Ph.D. dissertation. University of Illinois.

French, F.G. 1949. *Common Errors in English.* London: Oxford University Press.

Gage, William W. and Sirarpi Ohannessian. 1974. 'ESOL enrollments throughout the world'. *Linguistic Reporter*, November. Also in *English Teaching Forum*, July 1977. 19–21.

Gilbert, Glenn G., ed. 1970. *Texas Studies in Bilingualism.* Berlin: Walter de Gruyter.

Gingras, R.C. 1974. 'Problems in the description of Spanish English intra-sentential code-switching'. In Bills, ed. 1974.

Gleason, Henry A., Jr. 1961. *An Introduction to Descriptive Linguistics.* New York: Holt, Rinehart and Winston.

Goffin, R.C. 1934. *Some Notes on Indian English.* S.P.E. Tract No. 41. Oxford: Clarendon Press.

Gokak, Vinayak K. 1964. *English in India: Its Present and Future.* Bombay: Asia Publishing House.

——. ed. 1970. *The Golden Treasury of Indo-Anglian Poetry.* New Delhi: Sahitya Akademi.

Goodwin, Kenneth L., ed. 1970. *National Identity: Papers delivered at the Commonwealth Literature Conference, University of Queensland, Brisbane.* London: Heinemann.

Gopalkrishnan, G.S. 1960. 'Some observations on the South Indian pronunciation of English'. *Teaching English* 6.2.62–67, April. Bombay.

Grant, Charles. 1831–32. 'Observations on the state of society among the Asiatic subjects of Great Britain, particularly with respect to morals, and the means of improving it', in *General Appendix to Parliamentary Papers 1831–1832.* London.

Gumperz, John J. 1964a. 'Hindi-Punjabi code-switching in Delhi'. *Proceedings of the Ninth International Congress of Linguists.* The Hague: Mouton. 115–24.

——. 1964b. 'Linguistic and social interaction in two communities'. In Gumperz and Hymes, eds, 1964.

——. 1970. 'Verbal strategies in multilingual communication.' In R. D. Abrahams and R. C. Troike. eds. 1970.

——, and E. Hernandez-Chavez. 1972. 'Bilingualism, bidialectalism, classroom interaction'. In C. Cazden, *et al.*, eds. 1972.

——, and D. Hymes, eds. 1964. 'The ethnography of communication'. Special publication of *American Anthropologist.* Part 2. 66.6.

——, and D. Hymes, eds. 1972. *Directions in Sociolinguistics: The Ethnography of Communication.* New York: Holt, Rinehart and Winston.

Guru, Kamta Prasad. 1962. *Hindi Grammar* (in Hindi). Varanasi: Nagari Pracharini Sabha.

Hai, Mohamad A. and W.J. Ball. 1961. *The Sound Structures of English and Bengali.* Dacca: University of Dacca.

Hall, Robert, A. 1955. *Hands Off Pidgin English!* Sydney: Pacific Publication.

Halle, Morris, *et al.*, eds. 1956. *For Roman Jakobson.* The Hague: Mouton.

Halliday, M.A.K. 1959. *The Language of the Chinese. 'Secret History of the Mongols'.* (Publication of the Philological Society 17.) Oxford: Blackwell.

——. 1961. 'Categories of the Theory of Grammar'. *Word 17.* 3.241–302.

——. 1964. 'Syntax and the consumer'. In Stuart, ed., 1964. 11–24.

——. 1966. 'Lexis as a linguistic level'. In Bazell, *et al.*, eds. 1966.

——, Angus McIntosh, and Peter Strevens. 1964. *The Linguistic Sciences and Language Teaching.* London: Longman.

——and Ruqaiya Hasan. 1976. *Cohesion in English.* London: Longman.

Harry, Promila. 1962. 'A study of spoken Gujarati in its relation to the teaching of English to Gujarati learners'. Unpublished paper. School of Applied Linguistics, University of Edinburgh.

Hartford, Beverly S. and A. Valdman, eds. 1982. *Issues in International Bilingual Education: The Role of the Vernacular.* New York: Plenum Publishing Corporation.

Hasselmo, Nils. 1961. 'American Swedish: a study in bilingualism'. Unpublished Ph.D. dissertation. Harvard University.

——. 1970. 'Code-switching and modes of speaking.' In Glenn G. Gilbert, ed. 1970.

Haugen, Einar. 1952. *The Norwegian Language in America.* Bloomington, IN: Indiana University Press.

Hawkins, R. E. 1976. 'A Supplement of Indian Words' in *The Little Oxford Dictionary.* Delhi: Oxford University Press.

Heath, Shirley B. 1977. 'A national language academy? Debate in the nation'. *Linguistics: An International Review.* 189. 9–43.

Hennessey J. 1969. 'British education for an elite in India'. In Williams, ed. 1969.

Hernandes-Chavez, E., A. Cohen, and A. Beltramo, eds. 1975. *El lenguaje de los chicanos.* Arlington, VA: Center for Applied Linguistics.

Hill, Leslie A. 1959. 'The pronunciation difficulties of Hindi speakers learning English'. *Teaching English* 6.1 (August). 23–25. Bombay.

Hill, Trevor. 1958. 'Institutional linguistics'. *Orbis* 7.2. 441–55.

Hockett, Charles F. 1956. 'Idiom formation'. In Halle, *et al.*, eds. 1956. 222–29.

——1958. *A Course in Modern Linguistics.* New York: Macmillan.

Hocking, B.D.W. 1974. *All What I was Taught and Other Mistakes: A Handbook of Common Errors in English.* Nairobi: Oxford University Press.

Holmstrom, Lakshmi. 1973. *The Novels of R.K. Narayan.* Calcutta: Writers Workshop.

Householder, Fred W., Jr. and S. Saporta, eds. 1962. *Problems in Lexicography.* Bloomington, IN: Indiana University Press.

Hulbart, James R. 1955. *Dictionaries British and American.* London: Deutsch.

Hunt, Cecil. 1931. *Honoured Sir from Babujee.* London: P. Allen.

——1935. *Babujee Writes Home.* London: P. Allen.

Hymes, Dell. 1964. 'Introduction: toward ethnographies of communication'. In Gumperz and Hymes, eds. 1964: 1–34.

——. ed. 1971. *Pidginization and Creolization of Languages.* London: Cambridge University Press.

———. 1972. 'Models of the interaction of language and social life'. In Gumperz and Hymes, eds. 1972. 35–71.

———. 1974. *Foundations in Sociolinguistics : An Ethnographic Approach.* Philadelphia, PA.: University of Pennsylvania Press.

———, and W.E. Bittle, eds. 1967. *Studies in Southwestern Ethnolinguistics.* The Hague: Mouton.

Indian Vocabulary, to which is Prefixed the Form of Impeachment. 1788. Stockdale.

Iyengar, K. R. Srinivasa. 1943. *Indo-Anglian Literature.* Bombay: International Book House.

———. 1945. *The Indian Contribution to English.* Bombay: Asia Publishing House.

———. 1962. *Indian Writing in English.* Bombay: Asia Publishing House.

Jalil, M.A. 1963. 'Major difficulties experienced by Bengali learners of English with regard to grammar and sentence structure'. Unpublished paper. University of Leeds.

Jespersen, Otto. 1933. *Essentials of English Grammar.* Drawer, AL: University of Alabama Press.

Jha, Amarnath. 1940. Address at Conference of English Professors, Playwrights and Critics. Lucknow. No publisher.

John, V.V. 1969. *Education and Language Policy.* Bombay: Nachiketa Publications.

Joos, Martin. 1960. 'The isolation of styles'. In *The Report of the Tenth Annual Round Table Meeting of Linguistics and Language Studies.* Washington, D.C.: Georgetown University Press.

Kachru, Braj B. 1959. 'An instrumental phonetic analysis of some prosodic features of Indian English and Received Pronunciation'. Unpublished Paper. School of Applied Linguistics, University of Edinburgh.

———. 1961. 'An analysis of some features of Indian English: A study in linguistic method'. Unpublished Ph.D. dissertation. University of Edinburgh.

———. 1965. 'The *Indianness* in Indian English'. *Word.* 21. 391–410.

———. 1966. 'Indian English: A study in contextualization'. In Bazell *et al.*, eds. 1966.255–87.

———. 1969a. 'English in South Asia'. In Sebeok, 1969:627–78. Revised and updated version in Fishman, ed. 1978.

———. 1969b. *A Reference Grammar of Kashmiri.* Urbana, IL: Department of Linguistics, University of Illinois.

———. 1970. 'Some style features of South Asian English'. In Goodwin, ed. 1970.

———. 1971. 'English in India: a pan-Indian and international link'. *English Around the World.* (May). 1–7.

———. 1973a. 'Toward a lexicon of Indian English'. In Kachru *et al.*, eds. 1973. 352–76.

———. 1973b. *An Introduction to Spoken Kashmiri.* Urbana: Department of Linguistics, University of Illinois.

———. 1975a. 'Lexical innovations in South Asian English'. *International Journal of the Sociology of Language.* 4. 55–74.

———. 1975b. 'A retrospective study of the Central Institute of English and Foreign Languages and its relation to Indian universities'. In Fox, ed. 1975: 27–94.

——. 1976a. 'Models of English for the Third World, white man's linguistic burden or language pragmatics?' *TESOL Quarterly*, 10. 2.221–39.

——. 1976b. 'Indian English: A sociolinguistic profile of a transplanted language'. *Studies in Language Learning.* 1:2. Special issue on *Dimensions of Bilingualism: Theory and Case Studies.* Urbana, IL: Unit for Foreign Language Study and Research, University of Illinois. 139–89.

——. 1977. 'The New Englishes and old models'. *English Language Forum.* (July). 29–35.

——. 1978a. 'Toward structuring code-mixing: An Indian perspective'. In Kachru and Sridhar, eds. 1978. 27–46.

——. 1978b. 'Code-mixing as a verbal strategy in India'. In Alatis, ed. 1979. 107–24.

——. 1979 'The Englishization of Hindi: notes on language rivalry and language change'. In Rauch and Carr, eds. 1979. 199–211.

——. 1980a. 'The new Englishes and old dictionaries: directions in lexicograpical research on non-native varieties of English.' In Zgusta, ed. 1980. 71–101.

——. 1980b. Review of Nihalani *et al.* 1978. *English World-Wide: The Journal of Varieties of English.* 1.2. 274–78.

——. 1981a. 'The pragmatics of non-native varieties of English'. In Smith, ed. 1981.

——. 1981b. 'American English and other Englishes'. In Ferguson and Heath, eds. 1981.

——. 1981c. 'Socially realistic linguistics': The Firthian tradition.' *International Journal of the Sociology of Language.* 31.65–89. Special issue on *Sociolinguistic Theory,* ed. Haver C. Currie. (An earlier version in *Studies in the Linguistic Sciences.* 10.1.85–111.)

——. 1982a. 'Models for non-native Englishes.' In Kachru, ed. 1982.

——. 1982b. 'Meaning in deviation: toward understanding non-native English texts'. In Kachru, ed. 1982.

——. 1982c. 'The bilingual's linguistic repertoire.' In Hartford and Valdman, eds. 1982.

——. 1982d. 'Language policy in South Asia.' *Annual Review of Applied Linguistics, 1981.* 2. 60–85.

——. 1982e. 'South Asian English.' In Bailey and Görlach, eds. 1982.

——. ed. 1982. *The Other Tongue: English Across Cultures.* Urbana, IL: University of Illinois Press.

——, Robert B. Lees, Y. Malkiel, A. Pietrangeli, and Sol Saporta, eds. 1973. *Issues in Linguistics: Papers in Honour of Henry and Reneé Kahane.* Urbana, IL: University of Illinois Press.

——, and Randolph Quirk. 1981. 'Introduction'. In Smith, ed. 1981.

——, and S.N. Sridhar, eds. 1978. *Aspects of Sociolinguistics in South Asia.* Special issue of *International Journal of the Sociology of Language.* 16.

Kahane, Henry and Renée Kahane. 1977. 'Virtues and vices in the American language: A history of attitudes'. *TESOL Quarterly*, 2.1. 185–202.

Kandiah, Thiru. 1964. 'The Teaching of English as a second language in Ceylon'. *Journal of the National Education Society of Ceylon* 5.4 (November). 8–12.

——. 1971. 'New Ceylon English'. (Review Article). *New Ceylon Writing* 90–94.

——. 1981. 'Lankan English schizoglossia'. *English World-Wide: A Journal of Varieties of English* 2.1:63–81.

Kanungo, Gostha Behari. 1962. *The Language Controversy in Indian Education: Historical Study.* Chicago: Comparative Education Center, University of Chicago.

Katz, J.J. and J.A. Fodor. 1963. 'The structure of a semantic theory'. *Language* 39.2. 170–210.

Kelkar, Ashok R. 1957. 'Marathi English: A study in foreign accent'. *Word* 13:2.268–82.

Keller, Gary D., R.V. Teschner and S. Viera, eds. 1976. *Bilingualism in the Bicentennial and Beyond.* New York: Bilingual Press.

Khan, Hamid Ahmad. 1964. *Pakistani Linguistics* (1963). Lahore: Linguistic Research Group of Pakistan.

Kindersley, A.F. 1938. 'Notes on the Indian idioms of English: style, syntax and vocabulary'. *Transactions of the Philological Society* 25–34.

Kirk-Green, Anthony. 1971. 'The influence of West African languages on English'. In Spencer, ed. 1971a.

Krishnamurti, Bh. 1978. 'Spelling Pronunciation in Indian English'. In Mohan, ed. 1978.

Krušina, A. 1966–1967. 'Indian English: samostatná varianta angličtiny?' (Indian English: an independent variety of English?). *Ciz i Jazyky ve Škole.* Prague. 10.25 54.

——. 1970. 'Angličtina v Indii' (English in India). *Sbornik lingvistických praci.* Prague. 96–118.

Kumar, Vinod. 1980. *Book Industry in India: Problems and Prospects.* New Delhi: Federation of Publishers and Booksellers Associations in India.

Lahiri, K.C. 1956. 'Peculiarities in spoken English of Indians and the question of a standard for them'. *The Research Bulletin (Arts) of the University of Punjab* 19:3.

Lal, P. 1968. *The Concept of Indian Literature: Six Essays.* Calcutta: Writers Workshop.

——. 1969. *Modern Indian Poetry in English.* Calcutta: Writers Workshop.

Lance, Donald M. 1975. 'Spanish-English code-switching'. In Hernandez-Chavez et al. 1975. 138–53.

Langendeon, D.T. 1968. *The London school of linguistics: a study of the linguistic theories of B. Malinowski and J. R. Firth.* Cambridge, MA: MIT Press.

Lanham, L.W., and K.P. Prinsloo, 1978. *Language and Communication Studies in South Africa.* Capetown: Oxford University Press.

Latif, Sayed Abdul. 1920. 'The influence of English literature on Urdu literature'. Unpublished Ph.D. dissertation. University of London.

Law, Narendra Nath. 1915. *Promotion of Learning in India by Early European Settlers.* London: Longman.

Lawton, David L. 1977. 'Bilingual strategies of communication: evidence from the text'. *The Fourth Lacus Forum.* Columbia, SC: Hornbeam Press. 218–25.

Lees, Robert B. 1960. *The Grammar of English Nominalizations.* International

Journal of American Linguistics Supplement. 26.3. The Hague: Mouton.

Lentzner, Karl A. 1891. *Colonial English. A Glossary of Australian, Anglo-Indian, Pidgin English, West Indian and South African Words.* London: Kegan Paul.

LePage, Robert B. 1964. *The National Language Question.* London: Oxford University Press.

Limaye, M.R. 1965. ' "H" for Marathi Speakers of English'. *English Language Teaching* 20:1.72–76.

Lipski, John M. 1977. 'Code-switching and the problem of bilingual competence'. *The Fourth Lacus Forum.* Columbia, SC: Hornbeam Press. 263–77.

Llamzon, Teodoro A. 1969. *Standard Filipino English.* Manila: Ateneo University Press.

——. 1981. 'Essential features of new varieties of English'. Paper presented at the sixteenth regional seminar on varieties of English at SEAMEO Regional Language Centre, Singapore, 20–24 April 1981.

Mafeni, Bernard. 1971. 'Nigerian Pidgin'. In Spencer 1971b.

Majumdar, Asoke Kumar. 1965. *Problem of Hindi.* Bombay: Bharatiya Vidya Bhavan.

Makkai, Adam, Valerie Becker Makkai and Luigi Heilmann, eds. 1977. *Linguistics at the Crossroads.* Padova: Liviana Editrice and Lake Bluff, IL.: Jupiter Press.

Malhotra, D.N. and N. Kumar. 1980. *Indian Publishing since Independence.* Delhi. The Bookman's Club. Distributed by Stirling Publishers, New Delhi.

Malkiel, Yakov. 1981. Review of Zgusta, ed. 1980. *Language* 57.1. March 1981. 251–53.

Manuel, M. and K. Ayyappa Paniker, eds. 1978. *English and India.* Delhi: Macmillan.

Marckwardt, Albert H. and Randolph Quirk. 1964. *A Common Language: British and American English.* London: British Broadcasting Corporation.

Masica, Colin P. 1966. *The Sound System of General Indian English.* Hyderabad: Central Institute of English and Foreign Languages.

——. 1976. *Defining a Linguistic Area: South Asia.* Chicago and London: University of Chicago Press.

Mathai, Isaac, ed. 1960. *India Demands the English Language.* Bombay: Mathai's Publications.

Mathai, Samuel. 1951. 'The Position of English in India'. In Partridge and Clark. 1951.

Mathews, M.M. 1931. *The Beginnings of American English: Essays and Comments.* Chicago: University of Chicago Press.

Mathiot, Madeleine. 1967. 'The place of the dictionary in linguistic description'. *Language* 43: 703–24.

Mazrui, Ali A. 1973. *The Political Sociology of the English Language: An African Perspective.* The Hague: Mouton.

McClure, Erica. 1977. 'Aspects of code-switching in the discourse of bilingual Mexican-American children'. In Saville-Troike, ed. 1977. 93–115.

——, and James Wentz. 1975. 'Functions of code-switching among Mexican-American children'. *Papers from the Parasession on Functionalism.* Chicago: Chicago Linguistic Society, University of Chicago.

McCully, Bruce T. 1940. *English Education and the Origins of Indian Nationalism.* New York: Columbia University Press.

McCutchion, David. 1968. *Indian Writing in English: Critical Essays.* Calcutta: Writers Workshop.

McDavid, Raven I. 1980. *Varieties of American English.* Stanford: Stanford University Press.

McIntosh, Angus. 1961. 'Patterns and range'. *Language* 37.325–37.

Mehrotra, Raja Ram. 1977. 'English in India: The current scene'. *English Language Teaching* 21.2. 163–170.

——. Forthcoming. *Indian English: Texts and Contexts.*

Mencken, H. L. 1919. *The American Language.* New York: Knopf. (British edition 1941. London. Routledge and Kegan Paul).

Metzger, D. and G.E. Williams. 1963. 'A formal ethnographic analysis of Tenejapa Ladino weddings'. *American Anthropologist* 65.5.

Mishra, Vishwanath. 1963. *The influence of English on Hindi language and literature 1870–1920* (in Hindi). Dehradun: Sahitya Sadan.

Mitchell, T.F. 1957. 'The language of buying and selling in Cyrenaica: A situational statement'. *Hespéris.* 44.1 and 2.31–71.

——. 1958. Syntagmatic relations in linguistic analysis. *Transactions of the Philological Society.* 101–18.

——. 1975. *Principles of Firthian Linguistics.* London: Longman.

——. 1978. 'Meaning is what you do—and how he and I interpret it: A Firthian view of pragmatics.' *Die Neueren Sprachen.* Heft 3/4: Frankfurt and Main: Verlag Moritz Diesterweg. 224–53.

Mohan, Ramesh., ed. 1978. *Indian Writing in English.* Madras: Orient Longman.

Morris, E.E. 1898. *Austral English.* London: Macmillan.

Morris, Henry. 1904. *The Life of Charles Grant.* London: J. Murray.

Mukherjee, Meenakshi. 1971. *The Twice-born Fiction: Themes and Techniques of the Indian Novel in English.* New Delhi: Arnold-Heinemann.

Naik, Madhukar Krishna. 1972. *Raja Rao.* New York. Twayne.

——, S.K. Desai and G.S. Amur, eds. 1968. *Critical Essays on Indian Writing in English.* Presented to Armando Menezes. Dharwar: Karnatak University.

Narasimhaiah,C.D. 1964. 'The English language in India'. *Hemisphere* 8:26–30 (April).

——. 1973. *Raja Rao.* New Delhi: Arnold-Heinemann.

——. ed. 1976. *Commonwealth Literature: A Handbook of Select Reading Lists.* Madras: Oxford University Press.

——. ed. 1978. *Awakened Conscience: Studies in Commonwealth Literature.* New Delhi:Sterling Publishers.

Nash, Rose. 1977. 'Aspects of Spanish-English bilingualism and language mixture in Puerto Rico'. In Makkai *et al.*, eds. 1977. 205–25.

Nehru, Jawaharlal. 1963. 'The language problem in India'. *Bulletin of the Central Institute of English and Foreign Languages* 3.1–6.

Nelson, Cecil N. 1982. 'Intelligibility and non-native varieties of English'. In Kachru, ed. 1982.

Nihalani, Paroo, Ray K. Tongue and Priya Hosali. 1978. *Indian and British English: A Handbook of Usage and Pronunciation*. Delhi: Oxford University Press.

Niven, Alastair, ed. 1976. *The Commonwealth Writer Overseas: Themes of Exile and Expatriation*. Bruxelles: Librairie Marcel Didier S.A.

Nurullah, Syed and J. P. Naik. 1951. *A History of Education in India, during the British Period*. 2nd ed. Bombay: Macmillan.

Oaten, Edward Farley. 1908. *A Sketch of Anglo-Indian Literature*. The La Bas prize essay for 1907. London: Paul, Trench, Trubner.

O'Brien, Richard J., ed. 1968. *Georgetown University Round Table Selected Papers on Linguistics* 1961–65. Washington, D. C.: Georgetown University Press.

Okara, Gabriel. 1963. 'African speech . . . English words'. *Transition*. 10.3. 13–18.

Palmer, Frank R., ed. 1968. *Selected Papers of J. R. Firth, 1952–59*. Bloomington, IN: Indiana University Press.

Pande, N.R.W. 1964. 'English in India'. *Triveni* 33. 68–75 (October).

Pandharipande, Rajeshwari. 1981. 'On the nativization of lexicon: The case of Marathi'. *Linguistics: An International Review* 19. 987–1011.

Pandit, Prabodh B. 1964. 'Indian readjustments in the English consonant system', *Indian Linguistics* 25.202–5.

——. 1978. 'Language and identity: The Panjabi language in Delhi'. In Kachru and Sridhar, eds. 1978. 93–108.

Parasher, S.V. 1979. 'Certain Aspects of the Functions and Form of Indian English: A Sociolinguistic Study'. Unpublished Ph.D. dissertation. Central Institute of English and Foreign Languages, Hyderabad.

Parkin, D. J. 1974. 'Language switching in Nairobi'. In Whiteley, ed. 1974. 189–215.

Parthasarathy, R., ed. 1976. *Ten Twentieth-Century Indian Poets*. Delhi: Oxford University Press.

——. 1981. 'Tradition and Freedom'. *The Indian Journal of English Studies*. 21.2.47–59.

——. 1982. 'Whoring After English Gods'. In Amirthanayagam, ed. 1982.

Partridge, Eric and J. W. Clark. 1951. *British and American English since 1900*. New York: Philosophical Library.

Passé, H.A. 1947. 'The English language in Ceylon'. Unpublished Ph.D. dissertation. University of London.

——. 1955. *The Use and Abuse of English*. London: Oxford University Press.

Patel, M.S. 1959. *The Representation of English Sounds in the Gujarati Script*. Baroda: M.S. University of Baroda.

Pattanayak, Debi Prasanna. 1981. *Multilingualism and Mother-Tongue Education*. Delhi: Oxford University Press.

Peeradina, Saleem, ed. 1972. *Contemporary Indian Poetry in English: An Assessment and Selection*. Bombay: Macmillan.

Perren, G.E. and M.F. Holloway. 1965. *Language and Communication in the Commonwealth*. London: C.E.L.C./H.M.S.O. 88.5354.

Pfaff, Carol W. 1976. 'Functional and structural constraints on syntactic variation in code-switching. In *Papers from the Parasession on Diachronic Syntax*. Chicago: Chicago Linguistic Society, University of Chicago.

Pietrzyk, A. 1964. 'Problems in language planning: the case of Hindi'. In Varma, ed. 1964. 249–70.

Pillai, Shanmugan. 1967. 'English borrowings in educated Tamil'. *Studies in Indian Linguistics. Volume Presented to Murray B. Emeneau on His Sixtieth Birthday.* Poona: Deccan College, 297–306.

———. 1974. 'Code-switching in the Tamil novel'. In Buck and Yocum, eds. 1974.

Platt, John T. 1977. 'The sub-varieties of Singapore English: their sociolectal and functional status'. In Crewe, ed. 1977.

———, and Heidi Weber. 1980. *English in Singapore and Malaysia—Status, Features, Functions.* Kuala Lumpur: Oxford University Press.

Plechko, Z. P. 1971. 'Nekotorye foneticheskie osobennosti angliiskogo yazyka v Indii'. (Some phonetic peculiarities of Indian English). *Inostrannye yazyki v vysshei shkole*, Moscow, 6.

Posner, Rebecca R. 1966. *The Romance Languages: A Linguistic Introduction.* New York: Anchor Books.

Prabhakar Babu, B. A. 1971. 'Prosodic features in Indian English: Stress, Rhythm and Intonation'. Unpublished diploma dissertation. Central Institute of English and Foreign Languages, Hyderabad.

Prator, Clifford H. 1968. 'The British heresy in TESOL'. In Fishman *et al.*, eds. 1968. 459–76.

Press in India 1974, *18th Annual Report of the Registrar of Newspapers for India*, Part 1. New Delhi: Ministry of Information and Broadcasting, Government of India.

Prinsloo, K.P. 1978. 'Institutions presently conducting research and inquiry in the field of language in South Africa'. In Lanham and Prinsloo, 1978.

Quirk, Randolph. 1960. 'The survey of English usage'. *Transactions of the Philological Society.* 40–61.

———. 1972. 'Linguistic bonds across the Atlantic'. *The English Language and Images of Matter.* London: Oxford University Press.

———. 1981. 'International communication and the concept of nuclear English'. In Smith, ed. 1981.

———and A.H. Smith, eds. 1959. *The Teaching of English.* Studies in Communication 3. London: Secker and Warburg.

———, Sidney Greenbaum, Geoffrey Leech, Jan Svartvik. 1972. *A Grammar of Contemporary English.* London: Longman.

Rajagopalachari, Chakravarti. 1962. *The Question of English.* Madras: Bharathan Publications.

Rajan, Balachandra. 1965. 'The Indian virtue'. *The Journal of Commonwealth Literature* 1:80–81 (September).

Ramakrishna, D., ed. 1980. *Indian English Prose: An Anthology.* New Delhi: Arnold-Heinemann.

Ramchand, Kenneth. 1973. 'The language of the master?' In Bailey and Robinson, eds. 1973.

Ramson, W.S. 1966. *Australian English: An Historical Study of the Vocabulary 1788–1898.* Canberra: Australian National University Press.

———. ed. 1970. *English Transported: Essays on Australian English.* Canberra: Australian National University Press.

Rao, G. Subba. 1954. *Indian Words in English: A Study in Indo-British Cultural and Linguistic Relations.* Oxford: Clarendon Press.

Rao, K.S.N. 1961. 'A footnote to the Indian pronunciation of the initial/k t p/ and /v/ and /w/ in English'. *Indian Linguistics* 22:160.

Rao, Raja. 1938. *Kanthapura.* London: Allen and Unwin. 2nd edition, 1974 with an introduction by C. D. Narasimhaiah. Madras: Oxford University Press.

——. 1978a. 'The caste of English'. In Narasimhaiah, ed. 1978.

——. 1978b. *The Policeman and the Rose.* Delhi: Oxford University Press.

Rauch, Irmengard and Gerald F. Carr., ed. 1979. *Linguistic Method: Papers in Honor of Herbert Penzl.* The Hague: Mouton.

Ray, Punya Sloka. 1969. 'The economics for and against English in India'. *Language and Society in India.* Simla: Indian Institute of Advanced Study, 8. 118–21.

Read, Allen Walker. 1962. 'The labelling of national and regional variation in popular dictionaries'. In Householder and Saporta 1962, eds. 217–27.

Redlinger, Wendy E. 1976. 'A description of transference and code-switching in Mexican-American English and Spanish'. In Keller *et al.*, eds. 1976. 41–52.

Reid, T.B.W. 1956. 'Linguistics, structuralism and philology'. *Archivum Linguisticum.* 8.1.28–27.

Report of the English Review Committee. 1965. New Delhi. University Grants Commission.

Report of the Official Language Commission. 1956. New Delhi (1957): Government of India Press.

Richards, Jack C., ed. 1974. *Error Analysis: Perspectives on Second Language Acquisition.* London: Longman.

—— and M.W.J. Tay, 1981. 'Norm and variability in language use'. In Smith, ed. 1981.

Richter, Julius. 1908. *A History of Missions in India.* Trs. by Sydney H. Moore. New York: F.H. Revell.

Rizvi, S.N.A., ed. Forthcoming. *The Twofold Voice: Essays in Honour of Ramesh Mohan.* Salzburg: Universität Salzburg.

Roberts, T.T. 1800. *An Indian glossary, consisting of some thousand words and forms commonly used in the East Indies ... extremely serviceable in assisting strangers to acquire with ease and quickness the language of that country.* London: Murray and Highley.

Roy, Rammohun. 1823. 'Letter to Lord Amherst, 11 December'. In *Selections from Educational Records, Part I (1781–1838)* 99–101. Calcutta: Bureau of Education, Government of India.

Rubdy, Rani. 1981. 'A Study of Some Written Varieties of Indian English'. Unpublished Ph.D. dissertation. Central Institute of English and Foreign Languages, Hyderabad.

Ruberu, Ranjit, 1962. *Education in Colonial Ceylon.* Kandy: Kandy Printers.

Sagert, H. 1951. 'Indisches Wortgut im Englischen' (Indian words in English). Unpublished Ph.D. Thesis, Berlin.

Samarajiva, C. 1967. 'From Sinhala Raban Pada to English Rhythm. (Some suggestions for teaching English rhythm to Sinhalese children)'. *English for Our Schools*, Sri Lanka, 1.1.215–40.

—— and R.M. Abeysekera. 1964. 'Some pronunciation difficulties of Sinhalese learners of English as a foreign language'. *Language Learning* 19.1.45–54.

Sarma, Gobinda Prasad. 1978. *Nationalism in Indo-Anglian Fiction*. New Delhi: Sterling Publishers.

Saville-Troike, Muriel, ed. 1977. *Georgetown University Round Table on Languages and Linguistics*. Washington, D.C.: Georgetown University Press.

Schneider, Gilbert D. 1966. *West African English*. Unpublished Ph.D. dissertation. Hartford Seminary Foundation, Hartford, CT.

Schuchardt, Hugo. 1891a. 'Beiträge zur Kenntnis des englischen Kreolisch III. Das Indo-Englishche'. *Englische Studien* 15. 286–305.

——. 1891b. 'Indo-English'. Translation of Schuchardt 1891a into English. In *Pidgin and Creole Languages: Selected Essays* by Hugo Schuchardt. Edited and translated by Glenn G. Gilbert. 1980. London and New York: Cambridge University Press.

Scotton, Carol Myers, and William Ury. 1977. 'Bilingual strategies: the social functions of code-switching'. *International Journal of the Sociology of Language* 13.5–20.

Sebeok, Thomas A., ed. 1969. *Current Trends in Linguistics: Vol.5, South Asia*. The Hague: Mouton.

——, ed. 1971. *Current Trends in Linguistics: Vol.7. Linguistics in Sub-Sahara Africa*. The Hague: Mouton.

Sen, Priyaranjan. 1932. *Western Influence in Bengali Literature*. Calcutta: University of Calcutta.

Serjeantsen, M.S. 1961. *A History of Foreign Words in English*, (especially chapter X). New York: Barnes and Noble.

Seshadri, C. K. 1965. 'British English and Indian English. A linguistic comparison'. *Journal of the University of Baroda* 14.1. 17–27.

——. 1978. 'Second language planning for a multilingual country: English language instruction in India'. Unpublished Ph.D. dissertation, University of Toronto.

Sey, K.A. 1973. *Ghanaian English: An Exploratory Survey*. London: Macmillan.

Shah, Amritlal B. 1968. *The Great Debate: Language Controversy and Higher Education*. Bombay: Lalvani.

Shahane, Vasant A. 1972. *Khushwant Singh*. New York:Twayne.

—— and M. Sivaramkrishna, eds. 1980. *Indian Poetry in English: A Critical Assessment*. Delhi: Macmillan.

Sharma, P. Gopal, and Suresh Kumar, eds. 1977. *Indian Bilingualism*. Agra: Kendriya Hindi Sansthan (Central Institute of Hindi).

Sharp, Sri Henry, ed. 1920. *Selections from Educational Records*. Calcutta: Bureau of Education, Government of India.

Sherring, Matthew A. 1884. *The History of Protestant Missions in India from their Commencement in 1706 to 1871*. London and Edinburgh: Religious Tract Society.

·Sidhanta, N. K. 1961. 'English studies today'. *Bulletin of the Central Institute of English and Foreign Languages* 3–6.

Singh, Amrik and Philip G. Altbach. 1974. *The Higher Learning in India.* Delhi: Vikas Publishing House.

Singh, Bhupal. 1934. *A Survey of Anglo-Indian Fiction.* London: Oxford University Press.

Singh, Rajendra Pal. 1964. 'The language issue and Macaulay's infamous minutes', *Program of Education* 39.52–5 (September).

Sinha, Krishna Nandan. 1972. *Mulk Raj Anand.* New York: Twayne.

Sinha, Surendra Prasad. 1978. *English in India: A Historical Study with Particular Reference to English Education in India.* Patna: Janaki Prakashan.

Sisson, R. R. 1971. 'The description and comparison of stress in Southern British English and Hindi'. *Linguistics: An International Review* 17.35–60.

Sledd, James, and Ebbitt, Wilma R. 1962. *Dictionaries and THAT Dictionary.* Chicago: Scott, Foresman.

Smith, Larry. 1976. 'English as an international auxiliary language'. *RELC Journal* 7.2:38–42.

——, ed. 1981. *English for Cross-Cultural Communication.* London: Macmillan.

Smith-Pearse, T. L. N. 1934. *English Errors in Indian Schools.* Bombay: Oxford University Press.

Southworth, Franklin C. 1977. 'Functional aspects of linguistic heterogeneity'. In Sharma and Kumar, eds. 1977.

Spencer, John. 1957. 'Notes on the pronunciation problem'. *Shiksha: The Journal of the Education Department,* Government of Uttar Pradesh, April, 91–7.

——. 1966. 'The Anglo-Indians and their speech: a sociolinguistic essay'. *Lingua* 16: 57–70.

——. 1971a. 'Colonial language policies and their legacies'. In Sebeok, ed. 1971: 537–47.

——, ed. 1971b. *The English Language in Africa.* London: Longman.

Spender, Stephen and Donald Hall, eds. 1963. *The Concise Encyclopaedia of English and American Poets and Poetry.* London: Hutchinson.

Sreekantaiya, T. N. 1940. 'English as the Kannadiga speaks it'. *The Bulletin of Phonetic Studies* 1, October. Mysore: University Phonetic Association. 11–19.

Sridhar, Kamal K. 1977. 'The development of English as an elite language in the multilingual context of India: its educational implications.' Unpublished Ph.D. dissertation. University of Illinois, Urbana.

——. 1979. 'English in the sociocultural context of India'. *Studies in Language Learning* 2:1. Urbana, IL: Unit for Foreign Language Study and Research, University of Illinois. 63–79.

——. 1982. 'English in South Indian urban context'. In Kachru, ed. 1982.

Sridhar, S. N. 1978. 'On the functions of code-mixing in Kannada'. In Kachru and Sridhar, eds. 1978. 109–17.

——. 1982. 'Non-native English literatures: Context and relevance'. In Kachru, ed. 1982.

The Statesman's Yearbook 1979/80. New York: St Martin's Press.

Stocqueler, J. H. (Siddons, Joachim Heyward). 1848. *The Oriental Interpreter and Treasury of East India Knowledge: A Companion to 'The Handbook of British India'.* London: C. Cox.

Strevens, Peter. 1977. *New Orientations in the Teaching of English*. London: Oxford University Press.
——. 1980. *Teaching English as an International Language*. Oxford: Pergamon Press.
Stuart, C. I. J. M., ed. 1964. *Report of the Fifteenth Annual (First International) Round Table Meeting on Linguistics and Language Study*. Washington, D.C.: Georgetown University Press.
Sundaram, P.S. 1973. *R. K. Narayan*. New Delhi: Arnold-Heinemann.
Sweet, Henry. 1885. 'The practical study of language'. *Transactions of the Philological Society* 577–600.
Swift, Jonathan. 1712. 'A proposal for correcting, improving and ascertaining the English tongue'. In *The Works of Jonathan Swift*, with notes by Walter Scott, Vol.IX. London, 1883. Printed for B. Tooke.
Tagliavini, C. 1969. *Le origini delle lingue Neolatine*. Bologna: Patròn.
Taylor, Susan. 1969. 'Preliminary study of the stress system in Indian English'. Division of English as a second language, University of Illinois, Urbaba. Mimeographed.
Tickoo, Makhan Lal. 1963. 'English pronunciation in India: The choice of a model'. *Language Learning* 13:3–4. 171–75.
Theivananthampillai, K. 1968. 'Some structural differences between English and Tamil and their implications for teaching'. Part 1. *English for Our Schools*, Sri Lanka, 1.3.7–9.
——. 1970. 'A comparative study of the English and Tamil auxiliary verb systems and prediction of learning problems for Tamil students of English'. *IRAL: International Review of Applied Linguistics in Language Teaching* 8.1.21–47.
Timm, L.A. 1975. 'Spanish-English code-switching: El porque y by how- not-to'. *Romance Philology* 28.473–82.
——. 1977. 'Code-switching in war and peace'. *The Fourth Lacus Forum*. Columbia, SC: Hornbeam Press. 236–49.
Tiwari, Bholanath. 1966. *The Hindi Language* (in Hindi). Allahabad: Kitab Mahal.
Todd, Loreto. 1974. *Pidgins and Creoles*. London. Routledge and Kegan Paul.
Tongue, R. K. 1974. *The English of Singapore and Malaysia*. Singapore: Eastern University Press.
Trench, Richard Chenevix. 1857. 'On some deficiencies in our dictionaries'. *Transactions of the Philological Society*, Part 2. 1–70.
Turner, George W. 1966. *The English Language in Australia and New Zealand*. London: Longman.
Tyrner-Stastny, Alice G. 1969. 'Indo-Anglian Literature and the Colonial Indian Elite'. Unpublished Ph.D. dissertation. Cornell University.
UNESCO Statistical Yearbook 1980. Paris: United Nations Educational, Scientific and Cultural Organization.
Universities Handbook. 1979. New Delhi: Association of Indian Universities.
Usmani, Mufti A.H. 1965. 'A study of the teaching of English as a foreign language in the secondary schools of the Peshawar region'. Unpublished Ph.D. dissertation. Texas Technological College.
Valentine, Elias. 1978. 'Some non-segmental features of Anglo-Indian English'. In M. Manuel and K. A. Paniker, eds. 1978. 190–212.

Varma, B.N., ed. 1964. *Contemporary India*. Bombay: Asia Publishing House.

Varma, Siddheswar. 1957. 'The pronunciation of English in north-western India'. *Indian Linguistics* 18: 86–8.

Verma, Manindra K. 1971. *The Structure of the Noun Phrase in English and Hindi*. Delhi: Motilal Banarsidas.

——. 1974. 'English in Indian education.' In Singh and Altbach, eds. 1974. 251–77.

Verma, Shivendra K. 1964. 'A study in the systematic description of Hindi grammar and comparison of the Hindi and English verbal group'. Unpublished Ph.D. dissertation. University of Edinburgh.

——. 1973. 'The systemicness of Indian English'. *ITL: Review of Applied Linguistics* 22:1–9.

——. 1976. 'Code-switching: Hindi-English'. *Lingua* 38. 153–65.

——. 1978. 'Syntactic irregularities in Indian English'. In Mohan, ed. 1978. 207–220.

Vermeer, M. H. and H. J. Vermeer. 1963. 'Das Indo-Englische' (Indo-English). *Lebende Sprachen* 8. 135–38, 184.

Vest. E.B. 1948. 'Native words learned by American soldiers in India and Burma in World War II'. *American Speech* 23.224–31.

Viswanath, L. 1964. 'Kanarese and English: a comparison of their phonologies'. Unpublished study. Bangor: Department of Linguistics, University College of North Wales.

Von Wartburg, W. 1951. *Die Entstehung der Romanischen Völker*. 2nd ed. Tübingen: Max Niemeyer Verlag.

Wadia, A.R. 1954. *The Future of English in India*. Bombay: Asia Publishing House.

Wakefield, James A., P.E. Bradley, B. Yom, and E.B. Doughtie. 1975. 'Language-switching and constituent structure'. *Language and Speech* 18.1.14–19.

Walatara, D. 1960. 'The scope and limitations of bilingualism with a second language with specific reference to the case of Ceylon'. *Teaching English*. 6.3.3–9.

Walsh, William, ed. 1973. *Readings in Commonwealth Literature*. Oxford: Clarendon Press.

Warie, Pairat. 1977. 'Some aspects of code-mixing in Thai'. *Studies in the Linguistic Sciences* 7.1.21–40.

Weil, Shalva. 1978. 'Verbal interaction among the Bene Israel'. *International Journal of the Sociology of Language* 13.71–85.

Weinreich, Uriel. 1953. *Languages in contact: findings and problems*. New York: Publication of the Linguistic Circle of New York. No.1. Reprinted 1963. The Hague: Mouton.

Weir, Ann L. 1982. 'Style range in New English literatures'. In Kachru, ed. 1982.

Wentz, James P. 1977. 'Some considerations in the development of a syntactic description of code-switching'. Unpublished Ph.D. dissertation. University of Illinois, Urbana.

Whinnom, Keith. 1971. 'Linguistic hybridization and the "special case" of pidgins and creoles'. In Hymes, ed. 1971: 91–115.

Whitlev. W.H. 1974. *Language in Kenya*. Nairobi: Oxford University Press.

Whitworth, George C. 1885. *An Anglo-Indian dictionary: A glossary of Indian terms used in English, and of such English or other non-Indian terms as have obtained special meanings in India.* London: Kegan Paul.

———. 1907. *Indian English: An examination of the errors of idioms made by Indians in writing English.* Letchworth, Herts: Garden City Press.

Widdowson, H.G. 1979. 'Pidgin and babu'. *Explorations in Applied Linguistics.* Oxford: Oxford University Press.

Williams R., ed. 1969. *Governing Elites.* New York: Oxford University Press.

Wilson, H.H. 1855. *A Glossary of Judicial and Revenue Terms and of Useful Words Occurring in Official Documents, Relating to the Administration of the Government of British India.* London: W.H. Allen. Indian ed. Delhi: Munshiram Manoharlal. 1968. (Another edition 1940).

Yule, Henry, and A.C. Burnell. 1886. *Hobson-Jobson: A Glossary of Colloquial Anglo-Indian Words and Phrases, and of Kindred Terms, Etymological, Historical, Geographical and Discursive.* 2nd ed. by William Crooke. London: John Murray, 1903.

Zgusta, Ladislav. 1967. 'Multiword lexical units'. *Word* 23: 578–87.

———. 1971. *Manual of lexicography.* The Hague: Mouton.

———, ed. 1980. *Theory and Method in Lexicography: A Western and Non-Western Perspective.* Chapel Hill, NC: Hornbeam Press.

Zuengler, Jane, E. 1982. 'Kenyan English'. In Kachru, ed. 1982.

Index

The index includes selected names, subjects, and technical terms which occur in the text and the notes. The references are to pages. A number followed by 'n' indicates that the reference is to a footnote on that page.

264 *Index*

Arabic, 21–22, 29, 61n, 67–68, 139, 170
archaism, 83, 168, 182
Army Hindustani, 195
article, 12, 78; absence of a parallel
 category of, 32; definite, 186; indefi-
 nite, 186; missing and intrusive, 78;
 wrong, usurping and dispossessed, 78
Arunachal Pradesh, 72, 219
Ārya Samāj, 200
Asia, 166, 188, 211, 214, 233–34, 238
Asrani, U. A., 65n
Assamese, 55, 71–72
assimilated item, 82, 152
association of a collocation, 139. *See also*
 collocation.
Aurobindo, Sri, 88
Australasian English, 212
Australia, 67, 111, 124n, 143n, 211, 214,
 234
Australian English, 18, 142n, 147, 150,
 167, 213, 221
Australianism in English, 67, 143n
Australianization of English, 166
Australianness in English, 211
author-specific item(s), 10–11, 102, 113,
 175, 182
automatization, 198
Awadhi, 194
axes: paradigmatic, 103, 128;
 syntagmatic, 103, 128

Babu English (spelled also Baboo) 17,
 25, 59n, 70, 73, 217, 226–28, 236.
 See also Bearer English; Boxwalla
 English; Butler English; Cheechee
 English; Kitchen English
Bailey, Richard W., 85, 220
Baker, Sidney J., 167, 221
Ball, W. J., 27, 30, 62n
Bamgbose, Ayọ, 165, 181–82, 221, 229
Banerjee, G. C., 92
Banerjee, Surendranath, 61n, 69
Bangladesh, 9, 24, 26, 52, 56, 61n, 66,
 147, 168, 225; newspapers in different
 languages in, 56
Bansal, Ram Krishna, 62n, 84, 147, 166,
 180, 240n

Barnes, Sir Edward, 20
Barron, A. W. J., 27
Basham, A. L., 127
Basic English, 239
Bautista, Ma. Lourdes S., 206, 229, 231
Bayer, Jennifer, 61n, 70, 93
Bazār Hindi, 196–97, 201
Bazell, C. E., 124n
Bearer English, 25, 70. *See also* Babu
 English; Boxwalla English; Butler
 English; Cheechee English; Kitchen
 English
Bell, Roger T., 212, 237
Bengal, 20–21, 29, 35, 93, 113, 176,
 226–27; West, 156
Bengali, 7, 21, 29, 35, 47, 50, 52–53,
 55–57, 61n–62n, 64, 72–74, 131, 143n,
 204, 227, 234
Bennett, Michael E., 205–6
Bentinck, Lord William, 22, 68
Bernstein, Basil, 215
Bhatia, Kailash Chandra, 50, 199, 206,
 223
Bhattacharya, B., 108, 110, 131
Bhattacharyya, D. C., 50, 234
Bhushan, V. N., 43, 63n, 88
Bihar, 113, 141n
bilingualism, 18–19, 22–23, 58, 67–68,
 89; cline of, 10, 25, 32–33, 70–71, 74,
 99, 124–25n, 129, 134, 212, 217; dif-
 fusion of, 93; in English, 179; restricted,
 141n; unrestricted, 141n
bilingual (s), 129–30, 134, 141n; English-
 knowing, 99; English-using, 225;
 Indian, 141n; minimal, 129; scale
 of, 129; standard (educated) Indian
 English, 129
Black American English, 79
Black English, 12
Blom, Jan-Petter, 206n
Bloomfield, Leonard, 5, 134, 141n
Bokamba, Eyamba G., 12, 165, 169, 182,
 186, 223
Bombay, 20, 176; English-speaking groups
 in, 10; university established at, 22, 69
bookishness in Indian English, 41
borrowing, 195, 226; extended, 195; lexical, 9, 47, 50, 107–8, 118, 170, 230